Trade, Development, and Political Economy in East Asia

Essays in Honour of Hal Hill

The **Institute of Southeast Asian Studies (ISEAS)** was established as an autonomous organization in 1968. It is a regional centre dedicated to the study of socio-political, security and economic trends and developments in Southeast Asia and its wider geostrategic and economic environment. The Institute's research programmes are the Regional Economic Studies (RES, including ASEAN and APEC), Regional Strategic and Political Studies (RSPS), and Regional Social and Cultural Studies (RSCS).

ISEAS Publishing, an established academic press, has issued more than 2,000 books and journals. It is the largest scholarly publisher of research about Southeast Asia from within the region. ISEAS Publishing works with many other academic and trade publishers and distributors to disseminate important research and analyses from and about Southeast Asia to the rest of the world.

Hal Hill

Trade, Development, and Political Economy in East Asia

Essays in Honour of Hal Hill

EDITED BY
Prema-chandra Athukorala,
Arianto A. Patunru and
Budy P. Resosudarmo

ISEAS

INSTITUTE OF SOUTHEAST ASIAN STUDIES
Singapore

First published in Singapore in 2014 by
ISEAS Publishing
Institute of Southeast Asian Studies
30 Heng Mui Keng Terrace
Pasir Panjang
Singapore 119614

E-mail: publish@iseas.edu.sg
Website: http://bookshop.iseas.edu.sg

ISEAS Library Cataloguing-in-Publication Data

Trade, development, and political economy in East Asia : essays in honour of Hal Hill / edited by Prema-chandra Athukorala, Arianto A. Patunru, Budy P. Resosudarmo.
1.   East Asia — Economic policy.
2.   Southeast Asia — Economic policy.
3.   Indonesia — Economic policy.
4.   East Asia — Economic conditions.
5.   Southeast Asia — Economic conditions.
6.   Indonesia — Economic conditions.
7.   International trade.
I.   Athukorala, Premachandra.
II. Patunru, Arianto A.
III. Resosudarmo, Budy P.
HC460.5 T761   2014

ISBN 978-981-4620-04-8 (soft cover)
ISBN 978-981-4620-05-5 (hard cover)
ISBN 978-981-4620-06-2 (e-book, PDF)

Photo of Hal Hill by Ayu Srimoyo
Printed in Singapore by Mainland Press Pte Ltd

Contents

Tables

Figures

Contributors

Kym Anderson
George Gollin Professor of Economics, School of Economics, University of Adelaide; CEPR Fellow; and Professor of Economics, Arndt-Corden Department of Economics, Crawford School of Public Policy, Australian National University

Prema-chandra Athukorala
Professor of Economics, Arndt-Corden Department of Economics, Crawford School of Public Policy, Australian National University and Honorary Professorial Research Fellow, School of Environment and Development, Manchester University, UK

Anne Booth
Professor of Economics, School of Oriental and African Studies, University of London

Ian Coxhead
Professor of Economics, Department of Agricultural and Resource Economics, University of Wisconsin-Madison

Chris Manning
Adjunct Associate Professor, Arndt-Corden Department of Economics, Crawford School of Public Policy, Australian National University

Peter McCawley
Visiting Fellow, Arndt-Corden Department of Economics, Crawford School of Public Policy, Australian National University, and former Dean, Asian Development Bank Institute, Tokyo

Ross H. McLeod
Adjunct Associate Professor, Arndt-Corden Department of Economics, Crawford School of Public Policy, Australian National University

Jayant Menon
Lead Economist, Office of Regional Economic Integration, Asian
Development Bank

Mari Pangestu
Minister of Tourism and Creative Economy (since 2011), and formerly
Minister of Trade (2004–2011) and Senior Economist, Center for
Strategic and International Studies, Indonesia

Arianto A. Patunru
Fellow, Arndt-Corden Department of Economics, Crawford School of
Public Policy, Australian National University

Thi Thu Tra Pham
Lecturer in Economics, Royal Melbourne Institute of Technology —
Vietnam, Ho Chi Minh City, Vietnam

Eric D. Ramstetter
Professor of Economics, International Centre for the Study of East Asian
Development and Graduate School of Economics, Kyushu University

Budy P. Resosudarmo
Associate Professor and Head of Indonesia Project, Arndt-Corden
Department of Economics, Crawford School of Public Policy, Australian
National University

James Riedel
William L. Clayton Professor of International Economics, School of
Advanced International Studies, Johns Hopkins University

Kunal Sen
Professor of Development Economics and Policy, Institute for
Development Policy and Management, School of Environment and
Development, University of Manchester, UK

C. Peter Timmer
Non-resident fellow at the Center for Global Development; and
Thomas D. Cabot Professor of Development Studies, *emeritus*, Harvard
University

Foreword

Ross Garnaut

Over 8 percent of humanity resides in Southeast Asia — much more than in any of North or South America, or Europe. Located on the sea routes between the global giants of India and China, it sometimes recedes from the view of the international community. Southeast Asia rarely attracts the attention in the old centres of scholarship in North America and Europe that is warranted by its importance and interest.

Southeast Asians have enjoyed a particular experience of modern economic development. That experience is important simply because it embodies the lives of a major part of humanity. It is also important because it provides an opportunity for observation of unique characteristics of modern economic development — in the words of the Editors of this book, a 'laboratory' for observation of new perspectives on the reality of development (p. 1).

People all over the world who are interested in modern economic development and sufficiently well informed to know how much Southeast Asia matters are hugely indebted to the life's work of Hal Hill that is honoured in this book. Through the forty years I have known him, Hill has worked steadily, diligently, and productively to understand the political, social, and economic contexts of development in Southeast Asia.

Hill has consistently and reliably brought insights from mainstream modern economic analysis to account in seeking to understand his subject. Hence the consistent reaffirmation in Hill's work of such established verities in economics as the value of free multilateral trade and the dangers that arise from well-meaning variations on the theme; the importance of sound fiscal and monetary policy; the value of market exchange to human welfare wherever the conditions for markets to work effectively are present; and the importance to successful development of effective interventions by government to provide public goods that are essential for development and to allow markets to contribute positively to development.

Hill does much more than this. His work recognises the importance of complex institutional realities that vary across countries and regions and are themselves changed by the experience of economic development. The embedding of his work through his professional life in a Department and School of scholars interested in development in Southeast Asia in all of its social and political complexity enriched his work. This context led over time to analysis of the political economy of development—of the need to recognise that governments are influenced by private interests. Hill's work is highly relevant to economic policy, and recognises that good policy is built on realistic assessment of political economy and wider institutional constraints—that if something will only work in theory it does not work at all.

Hill's books on the Indonesian economy and on regional dimensions of Indonesian development are essential to understanding modern Indonesian development. His later books are similarly important in understanding modern Philippine and Malaysian development. His long editorship and many contributions to the *Bulletin of Indonesian Economic Studies* helped make it the most important locus of publications on the Indonesian economy and the most globally influential of economic journals produced in Asia and the Western Pacific.

Hill has played an essential role in maintaining and extending the network connecting economists in Australia and Southeast Asia. The ASEAN–Australia Joint Research Project that he managed from 1983 until its conclusion was the starting point for relationships that have expanded and deepened over the years. His Indonesian students and close colleagues have been crucial to the close and productive relationships among Indonesian and Australian economists that have enriched official as well as intellectual relations between the two countries over the past couple of decades.

This book is a fitting tribute to the life's work of a fine scholar. Its publication provides an opportunity to reflect upon the high social value of rigorous applied research on social science issues relating to developments in Australia's neighbourhood in Southeast Asia and the Southwest Pacific, and to the conditions that make that work possible. Hill's work has required immense investment of time, effort, and resources in mastering the Indonesian language and cross-cultural personal relationships as well as the historical and institutional contexts of developments in countries that are different from those in which modern economic development first emerged. These essential building blocks for successful scholarship take time and effort, and therefore explicit recognition in research and education funding. This was better understood by earlier generations of Australian leaders of allocation of research and education resources than it is today.

But for now, let us celebrate the contributions Hal Hill has made to global scholarship and the quality of Australia's relations with our region, and be glad of the quality of his continuing work.

Acknowledgments

First of all we are most grateful to the contributors to this volume, who responded swiftly to our request even though we had an unusually strict timeline. We thank Chris Manning, Peter McCawley, and Ross McLeod, who helped us design and implement the festschrift project, while keeping it a secret from Hal to the last minute. Finally, we gratefully acknowledge financial support received from the ANU Indonesia Project.

The views expressed in the individual chapters are the authors' own and do not necessarily represent the views of the organisations they belong to.

Prema-chandra Athukorala
Arianto A. Patunru
Budy P. Resosudarmo

Canberra, November 2014

Glossary

ACTA	Anti-Counterfeiting Trade Agreement
ACFTA	ASEAN–China Free Trade Agreement
ADB	Asian Development Bank
AEC	ASEAN Economic Community
AFTA	ASEAN Free Trade Area
AIPEG	Australian Indonesia Partnership for Economic Governance
ANU	Australian National University
APEC	Asia–Pacific Economic Cooperation
ASEAN	Association of Southeast Asian Nations
ASEAN-4	the four largest developing economies in the Association of Southeast Asian Nations (Indonesia, Malaysia, the Philippines, and Thailand)
ASEAN-6	Indonesia, Malaysia, Brunei, Thailand, Singapore, and the Philippines
ASEAN-10	ASEAN-6 plus Cambodia, Laos, Vietnam, and Myanmar
BI	Bank Indonesia
BERNAS	Padiberas Nasional Berhad
BPS	Biro Pusat Statistik (Central Bureau of Statistics)
CAG	comptroller and auditor general
CGE	computable general equilibrium
CEPR	Centre for Economic Policy Research
CMLV	Cambodia, Myanmar, Laos, Vietnam
CPI	consumer price index
CSO	civil society organisation
DDA	Doha Development Agenda
DOT	Direction of Trade
DOTS	Direction of Trade Statistics, published by the IMF
EGS	environmental goods and services
EIF	Enhanced Integrated Framework

EOI	export-oriented industrialisation
EU	European Union
FAO	Food and Agriculture Organization
FAPRI	Food and Agricultural Policy Research Institute
FCFS	first-come, first-served
FDI	foreign direct investment
FTA	free trade agreement
G20	Group of Twenty
GCI	Global Competitive Index
G/GDP	government expenditure as a share of GDP
GDP	gross domestic product
GDPPC	GDP per capita
GNP	gross national product
GPA	Government Procurement Agreement
GSO	General Statistics Office of Vietnam
HS	harmonised system
HSC	Higher School Certificate
ICRG	International Country Risk Guide
ICSEAD	International Centre for the Study of East Asian Development
IFI	international financial institution
IFLS	Indonesia Family Life Survey
IFPRI	International Food Policy Research Institute
IFS	International Financial Statistics, published by the IMF
IT	information technology
ILO	International Labour Organization
ILSSA	Institute of Labor Science and Social Affairs
IMF	International Monetary Fund
ISIC	International Standard Industrial Classification
ITA	Information Technology Agreement
KHL	Kebutuhan Hidup Layak (Decent Standard of Living Index)
MFA	Multi Fibre Arrangement
MFN	most-favoured nations
ML	million litres
MNE	multinational enterprises
MOMT	Ministry of Manpower and Transmigration
MOT	Ministry of Telecommunications
MRA	mutual recognition arrangement
MW	minimum wage
NAFTA	North American Free Trade Agreement
NAMA	non-agricultural market access
NGO	non-government organisation
NIE	newly industrialising economy

NTB	non-tariff barrier
NPV	net present value
OECD	Organisation for Economic Cooperation and Development
OLS	ordinary least squares
OREC	Organization of Rice Exporting Countries
PISA	Programme for International Student Assessment
PPA	percent per annum
PPP	purchasing power parity
R&D	research and development
RCEP	Regional Comprehensive Economic Partnership
RER	real exchange rate
ROO	rules of origin
ROW	rest of the world
RSPS	Research School of Pacific Studies
SAFTA	South Asia Free Trade Agreement
Sakernas	Survei Angkatan Kerja Nasional (National Labour Force Survey)
SBY	Susilo Bambang Yudhoyono
SOE	state-owned enterprise
SPS	sanitary and phytosanitary
TBT	technical barriers to trade
TPP	Trans–Pacific Partnership
TRAI	Telecom Regulatory Authority of India
TTIP	Transatlantic Trade and Investment Partnership
UMNO	United Malays National Organisation
UN	United Nations
UNCTAD	United Nations Conference on Trade and Development
US	United States (of America)
WCI	World Competitiveness Index
WDI	World Development Indicators
WDR	World Development Report
WTO	World Trade Organization

Currencies

$	US dollar
A$	Australian dollar
Rp	Indonesian rupiah
NTD	New Taiwan dollar
RMB	Chinese renminbi
VND	Vietnamese dong

1 Introduction

Prema-chandra Athukorala, Arianto A. Patunru,
and Budy P. Resosudarmo

This volume is a tribute to Hal Hill, one of the most distinguished and internationally renowned Australian development economists and a stimulating, considerate, and compassionate colleague and friend. Over a highly productive career spanning almost four decades, Hal has greatly advanced our understanding of the process of economic development and policy challenges, using Southeast Asia as his laboratory. The enthusiastic response to our invitation to contribute to this volume from such a distinguished group of scholars who are at the forefront of their own chosen subject areas is a reflection of the high regard and esteem in which Hal is held in our profession. The span of nationalities of the contributors testifies to the international dimension of his research interests. We feel privileged to have the opportunity to compile and introduce this volume in honour of Hal Hill, 'the economist and the man'.

Hal Hill was born in Melbourne in 1948. He grew up in three cities (Melbourne, Ballarat, and Bendigo) as his family moved with the postings of his father, a school headmaster in the Victorian public school system. Hal's original career ambition was to become a schoolteacher, following in the footsteps of his father.

After delaying sitting for the Higher School Certificate by one year to captain Bendigo High School's tennis team, Hal entered Monash University in 1967 under a Secondary Teachers Scholarship offered by the Victoria Department of Education. He graduated from Monash in 1970 and obtained a Diploma in Education from La Trobe University the following year.

Following a career experiment combining secondary school teaching with winemaking,[1] Hal returned to Monash in 1973 as a Master's student. During the final year of this program, he was captivated by a seminar on the Indonesian economy given at Monash by Professor Heinz Arndt, the then Head of the Division of Economics (later renamed the Arndt-Corden Department of Economics) in the Research School of Pacific Studies (RSPS) of the Australian National University (ANU). In 1976 Hal moved to the ANU under a Commonwealth Postgraduate Research Award to undertake doctoral research under the joint supervision of Heinz Arndt and Peter McCawley.

After completing his PhD in 1980, Hal spent two years as a visiting scholar in the School of Economics at the University of Philippines, one of Southeast Asia's leading universities, under the International Development Program of Australian Universities and Colleges. This was followed by a short stint as a Senior Project Officer at the Bureau of Industry Economics in Canberra. Hal then joined the Division of Economics of the RSPS as a Research Fellow in May 1983, a move that marked the beginning of his amazingly productive academic career. He was promoted to Senior Fellow in July 1986 and to Professor in July 1997. After his great mentor passed away in 2001, Hal's professorial position was renamed by the university as the 'HW Arndt Professor of Southeast Asian Economies'. Hal was the Head of the Indonesia Project in the RSPS Economics Department during 1986–1998, and the Convener (head) of the Department during 2004–2007.

Hal is a leading authority on Southeast Asian economies. He began his work in the region with his doctoral research. He undertook two years of fieldwork in Indonesia (Java) and developed competence in the Indonesian language—a capacity he has maintained and since developed. In his thesis, entitled 'Choice of techniques in the Indonesian weaving industry', he examined the technological dualism between the modern and the small-scale sectors of the Indonesian weaving industry and made recommendations for narrowing the divide with a view to achieving the objective of creating productive employment opportunities for a rapidly growing labour force (Hill 1979).[2] During his tenure as

---

1 In 1972 Hal and his wife Glenda embarked on a winegrowing venture in Avoca (in Victoria) together with Hal's brother Mike, Mike's first wife, Kate, and a family friend, Mike Roberts. The vineyard was on Mike Roberts' property (free land) and the five partners provided free labour. The venture did not survive (luckily for the Australian economics profession!) because the labour pool depleted dramatically following the birth of Hal and Glenda's son, Sam.

2 A paper based on this thesis, and Hal's first journal paper, was published with only minor revisions in the Chicago journal, *Economic Development and Cultural Change* (Hill 1983). This paper is widely considered an important early

a visiting lecturer at the University of Philippines, Hal developed close professional relationships with many academics at various institutions in the Philippines and these links have been extended in the subsequent years. During 1983–1988, he was the Research Director of the ASEAN–Australia Joint Research Project in the Division of Economics at RSPS. This project brought leading Southeast Asian economists and senior Australian researchers together in an ambitious and successful research program that produced (what is still) a high proportion of the reputed economic research and publications on Southeast Asian economies. This research project built a network of Southeast Asian and Australian economists that placed Australia in an unequalled position in the region's economics profession during the ensuing quarter of a century. During Hal's leadership (1986–1998), the Indonesia Project became the leading centre of Indonesian economic studies in the world (outside Indonesia). More recently he initiated and led two major research projects involving scholars from East Timor and Malaysia. Over the past four decades Hal has been the single most important Australian figure in the networks that bind the Australian and Southeast Asian economics professions.

Hal's publications on Southeast Asian economies in particular, and more generally on development economics, have been prodigious in volume and highly influential in the global economics profession. Hal is ranked as the most cited international author on the Indonesian economy. His magnum opus, *The Indonesian Economy since 1966* (first edition 1996, second edition 2000) published by the Cambridge University Press is the most widely used book in the world on the Indonesian economy. Excerpts from the book were reprinted as a chapter entitled 'Falling inequality in rural Indonesia' in Gerald M. Meier and James E. Rauch's *Leading Issues in Economic Development* (Oxford University Press, New York, 2005, pp 481–488). His research collaborations with scholars in the Philippines, Malaysia, and East Timor have resulted in three major, multi-author volumes on these economies (Hill and Saldanha 2001; Balisacan and Hill 2003; Hill, Yean, and Zin 2012). Hal's long list of publications includes 13 other books and edited volumes, and over 150 papers in scholarly journals and contributions to edited volumes. His scholarly articles have appeared in major field journals in development economics, including *Economic Development and Cultural Change*, *World Development*, *Journal of Development Studies* and *Oxford Development Studies*, most Asian economics journals, and general economic journals such as *Oxford Bulletin of Economics and Statistics*, *Economics Letters*, *Weltwirtschaftliches Archiv*, *World Economy*, and *Economic Record*.

---

contribution to the literature on choice of technology in developing country manufacturing.

Hal was the editor of the *Bulletin of Indonesian Economic Studies* for over 12 years (1986–1998). During this period, the *Bulletin of Indonesian Economic Studies* gained a worldwide reputation as the authoritative journal on the Indonesian economy. He currently sits on the editorial boards of 13 academic journals including *World Development*, *Oxford Development Studies*, *Asian Economic Journal*, *Asian–Pacific Economic Literature*, and *Asian Economic Policy Review*.

Hal has also made an influential contribution to the broader understanding of Southeast Asian politics and international relations in Australia, within Southeast Asia itself, and in the broader international community. He frequently advises governments, development agencies (including the World Bank, the Asian Development Bank, and various UN organisations), NGOs, and corporations on Southeast Asia. He is a frequent media commentator, and generally writes three or four op-ed pieces each year, mostly for the *Wall Street Journal* and the *Australian Financial Review*. He has contributed to the development of the Southeast Asian economics profession through actively participating in the governance and work of the region's professional organisations and journals. In addition to his own research output, Hal has nurtured the work of many PhD scholars and younger economists from the region. A number of his students have been members of recent Indonesian cabinets, occupying the main economic portfolios.

The twelve contributions in this volume are grouped thematically into three parts, to reflect Hal's wide-ranging research interests.[3] Part 1 contains three chapters dealing with trade policy issues central to the development policy debate. Chapter 2 by Mari Pangestu provides an insightful analysis of the current state of disarray in the world trading system, reform proposals, and their implications for Indonesia. A key theme running through the chapter is that safeguarding the integrity of the rules-based world trading system is vital for achieving sustained economic growth and other developmental goals of a country in this increasingly globalised world economy, regardless of the size of its domestic market. The chapter outlines some suggestions for Indonesian policymakers on how to respond to the now-fashionable bilateral and regional approaches to trade liberalisation without compromising the country's long-standing commitment to unilateral and multilateral reforms as an active member of the World Trade Organization (WTO).

---

3   The original Contents of this book contained a chapter on 'Indonesia–Japan economic relations' by Thee Kian Wie, a leading Indonesian economist, and Hal Hill's closest Indonesian friend for over four decades. It is with deep sadness that we mention his passing in February 2014. Kian Wie was the first of the prospective authors on our list to accept the invitation to write a paper.

Jayant Menon (Chapter 3) probes the disarray in the contemporary world trading system caused by the proliferation of bilateral and regional free trade agreement (FTAs), followed by a thought-provoking analysis of the viability of the recent initiative to form regional mega-trading agreements, in particular the Regional Comprehensive Economic Partnership (RCEP) proposed by the Association of Southeast Asian Nations (ASEAN) and the Trans-Pacific Partnership (TPP) proposed by the Obama administration, in redressing the disarray. The key message of the chapter is that, when the proposed mega-trading arrangements are imposed on the plethora of existing FTAs, the world trade system would appear more like a 'jigsaw puzzle', rather than a 'spaghetti bowl' as famously epitomised by Jagdish Bhagwati. There would be new puzzles, both regional and global, to be solved to clean up the world trade system: piecing together the blocs to form a coherent whole at a regional level, let alone globally, would be a herculean task. In this context, the only way forward, argues Menon, would be to return to the time-honoured modality of trade liberalisation, and unilateral actions, but this time involving the multilateralisation of preferences rather than unreciprocated reductions in tariff rates by individual FTAs.

The contribution by Kym Anderson (Chapter 4) is a particularly fitting tribute to Hal Hill, the wine man.[4] It provides a unique analysis of the agricultural trade consequences of Asia's economic growth using wine trade as a case study. After analysing the demand and supply trends and patterns of wine trade in Asia over the past two decades in the wider global context, the chapter comes up with supply and demand projections for the next five years under various scenarios of economic growth trends, demographic patterns, and macroeconomic policy regimes. The upshot of the analysis is that China has already become by far the most important wine-consuming country in Asia, and the above projections point to the enormous speed with which China may become an even more dominant market for super-premium wine. India potentially could be more important sooner, but trade restrictions and high taxes have, to date, confined the rapid growth in sales only to domestic winemakers.

The first chapter in Part 2 deals with selected themes of the on-going process of structural change and global economic integration in Asian economies. In Chapter 5, Anne Booth undertakes a comprehensive analysis of how economic links between the ASEAN countries and the two

---

4 Notwithstanding the failure of the wine-growing venture of his youth (see Footnote 1), Hal has remained an avid wine collector and connoisseur. The appreciation of a good 'drop' is one of his legacies to students, colleagues, and friends in Asia. When he travels to Asia, he always carries at least half-a-dozen bottles from his collection in his green Samsonite suitcase to give away to his friends.

Asian giants, China and India, have changed over the past two decades. The chapter begins with an analysis of the implications of the rise of China and India (particularly China) as world economic powerhouses for growth and structural adjustment in the ASEAN economies, focusing specifically on economic links between these countries within rapidly evolving global production networks. The second section examines patterns of ASEAN commodity trade, inter-regional investment, labour flows, and their role in economic transformation. The third section discusses the implications of the FTAs between ASEAN and China and ASEAN and India for patterns of trade and investment in the region. The main conclusion of the chapter is that, contrary to the 'crowding out fear' that pervades the policy circles in the region, the ASEAN countries have benefited from increased economic links with China, and also to a lesser extent with India. However, the growing intra-regional economic ties have not lessened the role of economic relations with the rest of the world, in particular the US and the European Union, due to the economic dynamism of these countries. It is the long-standing commitment to unilateral and multilateral trade and investment that has provided the setting for these countries to reap gains from economic globalisation. Trade patterns of the ASEAN countries are quite diversified by region and no single country or trading block dominates. There is no evidence to suggest that the FTAs between ASEAN and India and China would contribute to significant increases in bilateral trade or investment flows.

Kunal Sen (Chapter 6) undertakes a comparative analysis of growth acceleration episodes of Indonesia (1967–1996) and India (2002–2010), focusing on the issue of whether there have been common causes of the dissipation and end of each acceleration episode in both countries. The comparative analysis is undertaken in the context of the wider literature relating to 'boom and bust' growth in developing countries that has upheld the 'stylised fact' that massive, discrete changes in growth are common in developing countries and most, if not all, growth acceleration episodes are unique in terms of the factors that contributed to their dissipation and end. The previous studies on the growth trajectories of the Indonesian and Indian economies have commonly argued that the East Asian financial crisis acted as a catalyst for the end of rapid growth in Indonesia, and that the 'policy paralysis' of the ruling government, along with the global slowdown, was only the proximate cause of the growth slowdown in India. In a notable departure from this consensus view, the findings of this chapter lead to the interesting inference that broadly similar, deep institutional factors contributed to tapering of the rapid growth episodes in these two countries. The wider implication of the analysis in this chapter is that economic growth in developing contexts is episodic and prone to collapse because institutions do not evolve

over the growth process and rapid growth could even contribute to deterioration in the quality of institutions.

Eric D. Ramstetter (Chapter 7) examines wage differentials between
foreign-invested enterprises (FIEs) (affiliates of multinational enterprises (MNEs)) and locally owned firms using a new plant-level data-
set for Indonesian and Malaysian manufacturing. As an extension to the
existing literature that has led to the consensus view that FIEs often pay
higher wages than corresponding local firms, this chapter specifically
investigates whether FIE–local firm wage differentials depend on export
orientation. According to the findings based on plant-level data, wage
differentials were found to be somewhat smaller for exporting compared
to non-exporting firms in both countries, and the gap was particularly
large in Indonesia in some years. However, when the analysis is conducted at the industry level (plant-level data aggregated to the three-
digit level of the International Standard Industry Classification (ISIC)),
FIE–local firm wage differentials were not clearly related to export status.

Ian Coxhead (Chapter 8) examines the implications of the resource
boom in Indonesia in the 2000s for the structure of employment and
incentives for human capital investment in Indonesia. Based on a systematic analysis of data pieced together from scattered sources on
employment patterns, occupational composition, employment arrangements, and measures of inherent ability, as well as recorded education,
he finds that boom-related changes in the structure of labour demand for
lower-income workers reduced returns to investments in education for
low-wage workers and increased returns to cognitive and non-cognitive
abilities acquired in early childhood. These findings suggest that the
resource boom exerts downward pressure on the *demand* for schooling,
and reduces the impact of public investments aimed at increasing schooling *supply*. Through this channel, the resource boom could also have contributed to an increase in economic inequality in Indonesia. The findings
of the chapter are directly relevant for the policy debate in Indonesia and
other resource-rich developing countries on how to invest resource rent
in human capital development, a vital prerequisite for achieving sustained growth in the long term.

Chapter 9 by Chris Manning is an important contribution to the ongoing debate in Indonesia on labour market regulations and their implications for labour market efficiency and flexibility. In Indonesia, a large
proportion of the workforce — around two-thirds — is absorbed by low-
productivity agriculture and the informal sector. The process of these
workers moving into higher-productivity jobs in the modern sectors has
been rather slow, notwithstanding the reasonably rapid economic growth
over the past decade or so. After a stage-setting overview of economic
performance and labour market development during this period, the

remainder of the chapter provides an in-depth analysis of the impact of labour market regulations on employment, wages, and skill development training, focusing specifically on the implications of regulations relating to recruitment, firing, and minimum wages. The findings suggests that despite its ambitious employment targets, the Yudhoyono government made little progress towards a more flexible labour market, which is an effectual prerequisite if the government wants to make more progress towards creating better jobs and raising general living standards. The chapter ends on an optimistic note, 'Reforms in politically sensitive areas like labour are often more easily achieved by a more populist government that seems likely to hold sway in Jakarta for the next five years'.

In an influential paper published in 1993, James Riedel discussed the opportunities for Vietnam to follow 'the trail of the tigers' (Riedel 1993), to emulate the economic success of the high-performing East Asian economies, in particular Taiwan, in the process of economic transition from plan to market. In Chapter 10, Riedel revisits that paper, with his Vietnamese co-author Thi Thu Tra Pham, and examines why Vietnam, after a promising start, is now 'trapped on the trail of the East Asian tiger'. Following an overview of Vietnam's economic performance during the reform era until about 2006, when the country achieved impressive growth, the authors undertake a penetrating analysis of the causes of growth slowdown since then. The analysis leads to the inference that the momentum of export-oriented industrialisation dissipated and the economy entered a prolonged (and ongoing) period of declining growth and rising macroeconomic instability because of policy backsliding from the export-oriented development strategy, not due to inherent weaknesses of the strategy itself. Put differently, the now-fashionable concept of the 'middle-income trap', which implies an externally imposed constraint on growth, is a misnomer; Vietnam is now trapped on the trail of the tigers thanks to its own policy failures.

Part 3 of the book consists of three chapters on the political economy of development policy. In Chapter 11, Peter McCawley comes up with an insightful analysis of the capacity of the ASEAN states to meet the performance goals expected of them. The comparative analysis of public policy of the countries in the region suggests that limited fiscal capacity of governments is a key constraint on meeting performance goals, not only in the new ASEAN member countries, but also in Indonesia and the Philippines. The chapter makes a strong case for reconsidering the economic role of governments, including at provincial and subprovincial levels, to recognise the causes of limited fiscal capacities of governments in most ASEAN states.

Chapter 12 by Ross H. McLeod makes an interesting contribution to the literature on the political economy of exchange rate policy by examining the ill-fated currency board proposal made by S.H. Hanke for Indonesia in the aftermath of the East Asian financial crisis (1997–1998). The then president, Suharto, initially expressed interest in implementing this proposal, but soon abandoned it amidst vociferous domestic opposition. McLeod argues that this opposition, spearheaded largely by the urban intelligentsia to discredit the president, was ill-informed; there was no balanced, well-informed debate in the country at the time on the nature of the crisis as it played out in Indonesia and the underlying rationale of the currency board proposal in that context. McLeod argues that had Soeharto implemented the currency board proposal with a firm commitment, the rupiah would have strengthened, firms would have been in a better position to repay their borrowings from the banks, and the cost to the government of claims against deposit guarantees would have been much reduced. Swiftly restoring macroeconomic stability in these ways could have set the stage for speedy recovery, averting the massive constriction the Indonesian economy experienced during the two ensuing years.

The final chapter by C. Peter Timmer comes up with a generalised political economy framework for analysing the role of grain reserves in determining world food prices. Are the 'fundamentals' of supply and demand the basic factors in price volatility? Can national or international policies toward food grain reserves help to stabilise food prices? What are food stocks 'worth' if the levels of grain reserves, especially in large countries, affect food trade policies in these countries? This chapter systematically addresses these approaches in turn, leading to the inference that grain reserves are 'worth' little in a world where trade restrictions drive food price volatility.

As editors, we hope as readers you will join us in the view that this compendium of essays provides a fitting tribute to Hal Hill, who has been one of the most influential and lively contributors to our profession over the last four decades.

PART 1

Trade

2 Challenges of the world trading system and implications for Indonesia

*Mari Pangestu**

The world trading system has undergone a lot of flux and encountered great challenges in the last two decades. We have seen an increase in bilateral and regional free trade agreements (FTAs) as the multilateral trading system has faltered in its bid to reach agreement under the long-drawn-out Doha Development Agenda. Since the Asian financial crisis, the issue of a multipolar world and different speeds of development among developing countries is emerging. The way we do trade has also changed dramatically, moving from trading in goods produced from beginning to end in each country, to global production sharing,[1] trade in parts and components, and final assembly within global production networks. The global economic crisis in 2008 has also led to tensions and to challenges to the multilateral trading system and institutions.

The purpose of this chapter is to discuss challenges facing the world trading system, policy priorities for safeguarding the integrity of a global rules-based trading system, and their implications for Indonesia. It begins with an overview of the current state of the world trading system. This is followed by a discussion of policy changes. The penultimate section looks at the likely implications of the policy options under consideration for Indonesia and how the country should position itself in the ongoing policy dialogue.

---

* This chapter is partly based on Pangestu (2013) and reflects the personal views of the author.
1 In the recent international trade literature, an array of alternative terms has been used to describe this phenomenon, including international production fragmentation, intra-process trade, vertical specialisation, slicing the value chain, and offshoring.

2.1   THE CONTEXT

Despite the seeming chorus of anti-trade or anti-globalisation voices, trade continues to be an important engine of growth, job creation, and poverty reduction. Countries such as Indonesia, a large developing country, have seen their economies transformed by trade and the opening up of the economy. The imperative has not changed. Trade should remain an important engine of growth, especially given that sustainable recovery in the world economy continues to elude us.

During the global crisis of 2008–2009, world trade contracted by almost 20 percent (Almunia et al. 2010). However, the fear of protectionism and a 'second' great depression abated and most of the emerging economies rebounded in 2010–2011. The G20 leaders and others have seen the importance of ensuring trade continues to flow and called for a standstill or refraining from protectionism. Even though some protectionist measures were taken by some countries in the aftermath of the crisis, the existence of the rules-based framework and the peer-pressure review introduced by G20 helped minimise increased protectionism.[2] As a trade minister at the time from a G20 member country, I can attest that this peer pressure helped us to manage the types of measures we had to take in response to the crisis. However, we are not out of the woods yet. As unemployment continues to be a problem in all countries, including advanced countries, governments will continue to face pressure to grant assistance to individual companies and to preserve jobs. World trade growth slowed to 2.8 percent in 2012 and 3.0 percent in 2013, and is only expected to begin to recover in 2014 at 4.3 percent (IMF 2014). These growth rates can be compared with 5.4 percent average growth during the last 20 years and 6 percent in the five years right before the crisis.

---

2 In the *8th WTO, OECD and UNCTAD Reports on G20 Trade and Investment Measures* undertaken by G20 countries in October 2012, it was found that the increase in more restrictive measures slowed during the observed period of May to October 2012. Until October 2012, the total of such measures since 2008 is estimated to affect 3 percent of world merchandise trade. In terms of types of restrictive measures that increase, there was increased restrictiveness of customs procedures, while there have actually been tariff reductions. There was also increased use of trade remedies, especially anti-dumping initiatives, which increased by 43 percent in 2012 compared with 2011, and use of sanitary and phytosanitary (SPS) and technical barriers to trade (TBT) measures. Meanwhile, the most recent *WTO, OECD and UNCTAD Reports on G20 Trade and Investment Measures* in December 2013 shows that there was an upward trend of the imposition of restrictions during the six months observed period of May to November 2013. The total measures taken since October 2008 affect almost 5 percent of G20 merchandise trade. This trend again emphasises that we are not out of the woods yet.

Table 2.1   *Estimated gains from Doha Round liberalisation of agriculture and non-agricultural market access (US$ billion)*

Country/ region	Gains to GDP			Gains to exports	
	CEPII-CIREM	Peterson Institute	World Bank	CEPII-CIREM	Peterson Institute
United States	5.3	9.3	6.4	35.6	6.0
China	15.9	9.7	5.7	69.4	14.3
European Union	11.8	16.3	18.4	62.7	9.2
Japan	10.1	5.6	29.6	40.7	7.2
World	**69.6**	**55.5**	**93.5**	**334.6**	**54.4**

Source: Hufbauer and Schott (2012, Table 1).

In this context, it goes without saying that all countries have a shared interest in maintaining confidence in an open, rules-based, fair, and balanced trading system. The cure for increased protectionism would not just be to ensure that the rules-based framework of the World Trade Organization (WTO) works and that the peer-pressure review introduced by the G20 continues, but also to generate greater market access. This of course means the completion of the Doha Round negotiations, which would generate benefits for all. The estimated benefits vary depending on the assumptions and the elements of the package, but range from an estimated US$50–100 billion of additional GDP to US$55–300 billion of additional exports to the world economy (Table 2.1). Recent estimates have been higher if a comprehensive services and facilitation package is included. Besides completing the multilateral negotiations, market access will also come about from a robust trading system that can respond to other challenges facing the world trading system, such as a multipolar world, regional as well as plurilateral agreements, and the global value chain.

The world has changed since the Doha Round negotiations began in 2001. The spirit of the negotiations then was to redress imbalances and even injustices between developed and developing nations. However, twelve years down the road, a world economic crisis and the rise of emerging economies tell us that we live in a multipolar world. Emerging economies and regions have become the new poles of growth. Emerging economies such as China, India, Brazil, South Africa, Russia (a recently acceded WTO member), Turkey, and Indonesia are contributing a greater share of growth and trade flows. The slowdown in external demand by advanced countries in 2012 was partially offset by growth of demand in emerging economies. For instance, it is estimated that around two-thirds of French and German companies' export growth came from developing countries (World Bank 2013b). These shifts in development also impact on the balance of global governance and the need to account for the role of emerging economies.

The way we trade has also been changing and evolving rapidly because of the ongoing process of global production sharing. A decade or so ago, a country's engagement in global production sharing involved specification in a given task/slice of the value chain based on its relative cost advantage. Today the division of production is much more fragmented and it is not just about the production of goods. A recent study by the Organisation for Economic Cooperation and Development (OECD) and the World Trade Organization (WTO) shows clearly that the global value chain is more the norm in determining today's production location and trade flows (OECD and WTO 2013). It clearly shows the rapid growth of trade parts and components and services that go into the production of final goods. There has been a growing emphasis on reforming the trade data-recording and compilation system to account for the dramatic transformation in global trade patterns.

Global production sharing opens up opportunities for developing countries to participate in a finer international division of labour. The nature of factor intensity of the given segments and the relative prices of factor inputs in comparison with their productivity jointly determine which country produces what components. Small and developing countries can 'leapfrog' and choose to specialise in one or more of the value chains. Similarly, the global value chain also allows for small and medium-sized enterprises to specialise in any one part of the value chain and to be part of global trade. Developing countries like Indonesia should take into account these fundamental changes in the way international trade increasingly takes place in the form of trade in 'tasks' rather than in goods produced from the beginning to the end in a given country.

Trade based on global production sharing ('network trade' or 'value chain trade') will function more efficiently under a multilateral trading system with one set of rules, standards, and market access commitments (Lamy 2013). This can be contrasted with the more inefficient and higher cost of doing business, the alternative of multiple rules, standards, and schedules of tariff reductions under various bilateral and regional agreements. Rapid expansion of global production sharing also means that a country's success in reaping gains from the new international division of labour is related to attracting foreign direct investments and developments in the services sector to reduce the service-link costs involved in the operation of production networks. Multinational enterprises (MNEs) are the leading vehicle for developing countries to enter global production networks. This is because the production of final goods requires highly customised and specialised parts and components whose quality cannot be verified or assured by a third party (and it is not possible to write a contract between the final producer and the input supplier that fully specifies product quality). This is particularly the case when it comes to setting up production units in countries that are newcomers to global production networks.[3] A country is unlikely to be attractive as a production location for MNEs if the extra costs of service links associated with production sharing—costs involved in arrangements for connecting and coordinating activities into a smooth sequence resulting in the production of the final good—outweigh the gains from the lower costs of the activity abroad. These extra costs relate to transportation, communication, and other tasks involved in coordinating the activity in a given country with what is done in other countries within the production network (Jones and Kierzkowski 2004).

2.2 PRIORITIES FOR THE FUTURE OF THE WORLD TRADING SYSTEM

A recent survey of businesses by the WTO found that 95 percent believed that the WTO was vital for business and 72 percent believed the WTO had been successful in ensuring that governments complied with their commitments. These findings were echoed in the various meetings the author had with Chambers of Commerce in many countries during the first quarter of 2013. Thus, maintaining and strengthening the rules-based trading system and dispute settlement procedures, as well as monitoring the commitments to current agreements, is still very important proof of the importance of the WTO and the multilateral trading system. The current system is also deemed fair and equitable because it treats large and small, developed and developing, weak and strong countries the same. If there were no WTO, or no confidence in its rules and system, the rise in protectionism after the 2008 crisis would have been much worse and the world of bilateral and regional agreements could potentially have ended up as the feared, messy 'spaghetti bowl' (Bhagwati 1995). Therefore, we need to continue to strengthen the system, including updating the rules to keep up with the times (Pangestu 2013).

---

3 As the production unit becomes well established in the country and it forges business links with private- and public-sector agents, arm's length subcontracting arrangements for components procurement could develop, but this would depend on the domestic business climate.

The importance of trade in the structural transformation process of countries is well established. An open and rules-based multilateral trading system can facilitate the full integration of developing countries into global trade and support their structural economic transformation. However, in order to reap the full benefits of trade, a multilateral trading system has to be inclusive. That means bringing along the lesser- and least-developed countries so that they can benefit from greater market access.

For trade to support structural transformation, an appropriate national and international enabling framework must be in place to provide a level playing field and enable least-developed countries and developing countries to overcome their structural challenges. On the national front, opening up trade must be accompanied by complementary policies to ensure that the benefits are more equally shared and the downside risks for sectors or groups within the country are managed. On the international front, we need to ensure that market opening is accompanied by capacity-building initiatives to help those countries bring to market internationally competitive and tradable goods and services.

We need to reaffirm that special and differential treatment for developing countries and least-developed countries is an integral part of the WTO's agreements. However, we also have to recognise the growing role of emerging economies. Emerging countries still have underdeveloped regions and will need time to deal with transition and structural challenges. They can give more than the lesser and least-developed countries but they should not be expected to give as much as the advanced or developed countries. Least-developed countries should be exempt from some agreements and provided with institutional support and financial assistance for capacity building and infrastructure development. Developing countries with varying levels of development and needs will also continue to require well-targeted capacity building. At the same time, emerging economies, not just developed economies, should also now be in a position to provide this capacity building to lesser-developed and least-developed countries.[4]

Least-developed countries have concerns regarding the specific constraints they face in effectively implementing the commitments reached in negotiations. In the context of the WTO, this implies effective implementation of Aid for Trade and the Enhanced Integrated Framework (EIF) for Least Developed Countries. The Aid for Trade initiative provides a platform to help developing and least-developed countries to leverage fund-

---

4   This notion was mentioned also by the WTO's Director-General at that time, Pascal Lamy, in his speech at the IISS-Oberoi Discussion Forum, 'Putting geopolitics back at the trade table', in New Delhi on 29 January 2013.

ing to benefit from market openings. Least-developed countries need to be supported in mainstreaming trade into their national development plans and to address their trade capacity-building requirements.

The conclusion of the Doha Development Agenda launched in 2001 can play a transformative role in the development of least-developed countries. Elimination of trade-distorting policies in agriculture as well as improved product and market access for the products and services of all least-developed countries could be realised by concluding the Doha Round. Certainly business people feel this way, with 62 percent of businesses believing that the Doha Round can bring benefits to business and that the conclusion of the Doha Round will improve the current economic outlook (OECD and WTO 2013). There was a lot of momentum in the negotiations in the 2004–2008 period to define the framework and modalities of various components of the single undertaking, but negotiations have stalled since July 2008.

The progress made at the 9th Ministerial Conference in Bali in December 2013 in agreeing on the first 'early harvest' package has provided some momentum, but the core negotiations for market access are yet to be concluded. A more realistic strategy toward further progress seems to be to focus on implementing the agenda based on individual sectoral agreements rather than focusing on implementing the whole agenda (single undertaking approach), while respecting the principle of transparency and inclusiveness (Pangestu 2013). However, it is not an easy proposition to achieve these outcomes and the challenges are great.

The first issue is whether these agreements are applied to all WTO members on a most-favoured nation (MFN) basis, or applied on a preferential basis only among the parties to the agreement. This is a key point in considering consistency with WTO rules. The few examples of sectoral agreements have been based on a subset of members who make up a critical mass of trade in the sector and come under the first category of MFN application. The 1996 Information Technology Agreement (ITA) and the 2012 agreement on environmental goods and services (EGS) are also designed to be applied to all WTO members.[5] These were initally agreed at APEC meetings, and were then brought to the WTO for negotiation and made or intended to be applied on an MFN basis. The proposed second ITA is another critical-mass agreement that could initially be agreed upon at APEC and taken to the WTO for negotiation. These approaches

---

5   The ITA, which was agreed in Singapore in 1996, is an MFN agreement, with tariff eliminations applied by the parties to all WTO members. A second ITA is proposed on the same basis. APEC reached an agreement to eliminate tariffs and other barriers on environmental goods and services in 2012. The tariff reductions would be on an MFN basis for all imports on the agreed list.

are also good examples of complementarity between regional and multi-lateral processes. The first category of MFN application is consistent with the WTO.

In the second (non-MFN) category is the Government Procurement Agreement (GPA), which was approved by all members in Marrakesh, and the Anti-Counterfeiting Trade Agreement (ACTA) on counterfeit trade (not yet in force).[6] The plurilateral agreement on services has been negotiated among the parties that are interested in liberalising further trade in services, but its application to other members, and the terms on which that may be agreed, are not yet clear. In principle, these agreements are generally open to other parties to join at a later stage, although the conditions for joining (full acceptance, or on terms to be negotiated) vary from case to case. Such agreements can be regarded as 'open' even if applied on a discriminatory basis; but it may be misleading to describe them as inclusive.

Another category of variable geometry would be the increase in bilateral and regional agreements by WTO members, especially in the last fifteen years. Again, we have a subset of countries entering into various levels of comprehensive free trade or economic partnership agreements. They range from agreements on specific issues (such as trade in goods) to comprehensive agreements that include goods and services as well as investment, trade facilitation, competition policy, and intellectual property rights. Some agreements also cover the more sensitive areas such as government procurement, environment, and even labour.

One of the priority areas would be the environment because of its likely impact on trade policy measures to mitigate global warming. Many thought that if the post-Kyoto regime set firm targets for reducing carbon emissions, and if such targets were not uniformly enforced, there would be a rush to relocate carbon-heavy industries to areas that had less strict discipline. This would then be followed by tax or trade measures 'to re-establish a level playing field'. No such targets were in fact set and the danger has receded; but a lively debate about the rights and wrongs of applying WTO Article XX to such cases has not disappeared. Furthermore, to the extent that policies in the name of reducing

---

6   The GPA is applied only among the parties who negotiated the terms of the agreement with each other. It is therefore non-MFN, but this was approved by all WTO members in 1994 at Marrakesh as part of the results of the Uruguay Round and thus fulfils the transparency principle. The agreement is 'open' to other members, who can join the agreement by negotiation with the parties. ACTA is an agreement made between more than thirty WTO members in 2012, but not yet ratified and in force. It would be applied only by the parties to each other, but some measures would be applied to all imports. It would be open to third parties to join at a later stage.

CO_2 emissions, such as CO_2 emission threshold levels, are already being introduced unilaterally by countries and regions, adhering to the WTO principles of transparency, non-discrimination, and scientifically based criteria will be key.

Because of the continued uncertainties in the multilateral negotiations and also because of the concerns that the current multilateral negotiations leave out new issues, countries have begun to contemplate alternative approaches to facilitating economic integration. In the Asian region, the member countries of ASEAN started tariff elimination for intra-ASEAN trade, creating an ASEAN Free Trade Area (AFTA) in 2006, which soon evolved into an effort to create a comprehensive ASEAN Economic Community by 2015. This was followed by ASEAN signing free trade agreements with each of its main dialogue partners. These agreements all started as the classical form of trade agreement designed to establish free trade on a preferential basis among the parties, but evolved to become more comprehensive, embracing new issues such as the environment, and to become 'partnerships' by incorporating capacity building in recognising the different levels of development of members. Recently there have been new proposals for major regional agreements, such as the comprehensive and high-quality Trans-Pacific Partnership in the Asia–Pacific region, and the EU–US deal for free trans-Atlantic trade and investment, which will also be comprehensive in focusing on non-tariff barriers, regulations, and government procurement.

There have to be pathways for making these agreements comprehensive and multilateral at some point. Some basic principles to create such pathways could include open-architecture principles, such as open accession, transparency, and best standards and practices, which were adopted by the G20 leaders in consolidating the existing agreements into an East Asia Regional Comprehensive Economic Partnership Agreement. Also important is the trade and development principle of differentiated pathways of 'joining', combined with effective capacity building to account for different levels of development and ensure inclusiveness.

Comprehensive and high-quality regional or bilateral agreements such as the Transatlantic Trade and Investment Partnership (TTIP) betwen the US and the EU, if concluded, could also complement and act as a catalyst for completing multilateral negotiations. The existence of more comprehensive regional agreements and their progress can act as an impetus to the completion of negotiations, just as the negotiations for the North American Free Trade Agreement (NAFTA) and the creation of APEC led to the completion of the Uruguay Round. Furthermore, to the extent that these agreements address 'Doha plus' issues, they would also inform the ways of shaping future multilateral rounds.

2.3   FRAMING INDONESIAN TRADE POLICY

Given the above analysis of the challenges and dynamics of the trading system that developing countries will face, how should a country like Indonesia frame its trade policy moving forward? First and foremost, as already mentioned, trade will continue to be important for development and growth no matter how large the domestic market is. Thus, the post-global crisis debate of export-oriented growth versus domestic-oriented growth to reduce vulnerability to external shocks and to have greater sources of growth domestically is not a useful one. Nor will a strategy of limiting imports through an increased value-added strategy, or what used to be termed 'import substitution', lead to greater competitiveness. The main issue for Indonesia is more about how to be competitive in the production of goods and services to supply domestically, as well as to compete in the domestic and world markets. This implies that Indonesia should look at competitiveness in a comprehensive way.

What does this mean in terms of unilateral trade and investment policy? It means that an open-trade regime and one that can ensure fast and efficient movement of goods and people would ensure competitiveness, rather than one that tries to limit imports so that the increased trade deficit is addressed. This is because intermediate imports are still needed to ensure Indonesia's competitiveness. A recent study by the World Bank (2013b) based on sector-level and firm-level data indicates that firms that use imported intermediate inputs grow faster in terms of output, value-added and employment, have higher productivity, and pay higher wages. These firms have also contributed to improved quality of Indonesian products, as well as increased diversification. A related study has shown that increased quantities of imported intermediate inputs are needed both for exports and for domestic production. This increase in imported intermediate inputs is really about the global value chain approach – that is the way trade is being conducted today. Countries should no longer produce all of their own inputs, intermediate goods, and final goods domestically. It is firms that will decide which part of the value chain they will specialise in. This means that openness of trade so that firms can access internationally priced and quality inputs, as well as trade facilitation, investment in infrastructure, and efficient logistics services for goods to move in a timely and efficient way, are the keys to Indonesia's competitiveness domestically and internationally. It is well recognised that the cost of logistics is higher in Indonesia than in its competitors.

Another policy priority should be to have an efficient services sector that can be competitive on its own and contribute to the competitiveness of other sectors. The World Bank (2013b) showed that the services content of Indonesian manufactured exports is around 13 percent, compared with 30 percent in China, because of the lack of design and R&D content in Indonesian products. The efficient delivery of health and education services is key to having productive human resources; competitive financial services are important for funding investments; and of course, as noted above, efficient and competitive transportation and logistics are key to competitive goods delivery as well as to reduce disparities and wide price divergences between the regions in Indonesia.

Indonesia also needs to have a position on the trading system that would be most conducive for developing countries. In terms of bilateral and regional agreements, Indonesia should focus on ensuring that these agreements are comprehensive, apply the openness principle to allow for the addition of new members, incorporate more liberal rules of origin, and contain capacity-building provisions. Currently, Indonesia is part of the ASEAN Economic Community Agreement with a timeline of 2015, out of which the goods agreement component has advanced to the point where 99 percent of intra-ASEAN trade is already at zero percent. However, there is less progress in the other areas of services and investment. Increasingly countries are seeing ASEAN as a domestic market, and intra-ASEAN human movement is already visa-free. In fact, 46 percent of tourists in ASEAN are intra-ASEAN.

As a member of ASEAN, Indonesia is also a party to the ASEAN+1 free trade agreements with China, Korea, Japan, Australia, New Zealand, and India. In 2011, when Indonesia was chair, ASEAN developed an approach of consolidating these six agreements so that we could move to a higher standard (ratchet up) while allowing for variable geometry in terms of the number of countries participating per issue/sector or overall. This allows for flexibility and time that can be combined with capacity building. There is also a built-in openness and open-accession principle, which will allow for new members to join. This sequential model and ASEAN approach can be contrasted with the Trans-Pacific Partnership approach of negotiating a comprehensive agreement from the start and facing the same difficulties and sensitivities as with the Doha Round negotiations. Time will tell which approach is better, but what Indonesia has tried to do is to lead the way in terms of model principles in regional agreements.

Finally, Indonesia has been active in multilateral WTO negotiations. For the reasons discussed above, we believe that a rules-based system provided by the WTO is still the best way to ensure a fair trading system for developing countries. We also believe that, as part of the WTO trade and development agenda, the role of aid for trade and capacity building should be made more effective and concrete.

2.4 CONCLUSIONS

Most countries still share a vision of a global economy supported by free, fair, and open trade that boosts global growth, drives development, and promotes sustainability. Their hope is for a multilateral trading system and the WTO to drive these outcomes and provide the overarching framework. The benefits of such an outcome are clear for all members, especially developing countries, and for all stakeholders.

To achieve this outcome, it is crucial to safeguard the basic principles and architecture of the multilateral trading system. This can be achieved by continuing to strengthen the current rules-based framework of the WTO, by maximising all efforts to completing the Doha Round multilateral negotiations, and by ensuring that there is coherent and effective capacity building and aid for trade programs. At the same time, the multilateral trading system will have to deal with new challenges and the different approaches toward the process of opening up, which are happening outside of the current WTO negotiations, as well as new issues. Most countries are now involved in bilateral and regional agreements, most of which have a wider coverage of issues beyond the current Doha Round negotiations, have different schedules of opening up with a variety of rules and standards, and are already addressing new issues. There is also a move toward plurilateral agreements. However, there is no framework to ensure that these developments will be 'consistent' with the multilateral trading system.

Of course, to be consistent with the multilateral benchmark, the multilateral trading system also needs to move to come up with the global standards and rules in these new areas. Countries like Indonesia should not lose sight of the vision of a WTO that drives global growth and development through trade. And the simplicity and predictability that comes with a single set of global trading rules that benefits all countries and stakeholders, especially small countries and small businesses that do not have the resources to manage the complexity of dealing with different rules under bilateral and plurilateral trading systems.

This means that there is a need for a vision and political commitment at the highest level to think about best-practice principles regarding these different approaches and also how the WTO should link and interact with sectorals, plurilaterals, and regional/bilateral agreements. Pangestu and Nellor (2014) offer a view about how the G20 could play a role in this regard. The G20 leaders, whose countries comprise 80 percent of world trade, could take the bold and necessary political commitment to ensure that the changes that are needed in the multilateral trading system are taken. This could involve tasking a vision group that can coordinate with the WTO to come up with a renewed vision, principles, and structure for ensuring an effective world trading system. Countries like Indonesia should also factor in these challenges and developments in the way trade and investment is conducted in designing their own unilateral and regional approaches to trade and investment policy. Trade is still going to be an important means to development, no matter how large a domestic market is.

3 From spaghetti bowl to jigsaw puzzle? Addressing the disarray in the world trade system

Jayant Menon

3.1 INTRODUCTION

When Jagdish Bhagwati (1991) famously described the maze of over-lapping free trade agreements (FTAs) as akin to a 'spaghetti bowl', it spawned a host of gastronomical metaphors, some more bizarre than others. When the action on FTAs switched to Asia in the 2000s (Figure 3.1), Richard Baldwin (2004b) dubbed it the 'noodle bowl'. When attention shifted to how to rectify the mess and return order to the world trade system, lasagna and even pizza came onto the menu (Hamada, quoted in Bhagwati 2008). Turning the spaghetti or noodles into lasagna involves consolidating the bilateral FTAs into a regional bloc, while the pizza involves subsequently linking these regional blocs through cross-regional tie-ups, eventually achieving fully multilateral trade. Turning lasagna into pizza is a culinary feat that finds its parallel at the political level in turning the regional blocs into a multilateral one. But both the lasagna and pizza processes are probably better represented by the activity involved in solving different kinds of jigsaw puzzles, as this is what they more closely resemble.

* I am grateful to Prema-chandra Athukorala for comments, and to Anna Cassandra Melendez for excellent research assistance. Parts of this paper draw upon Menon (2013b) and (2014c). The views expressed in this paper are those of the author and do not necessarily reflect the views and policies of the Asian Development Bank, or its Board of Governors or the governments they represent.

Figure 3.1   FTAs by status, total Asia (cumulative), selected years (no.)[a]

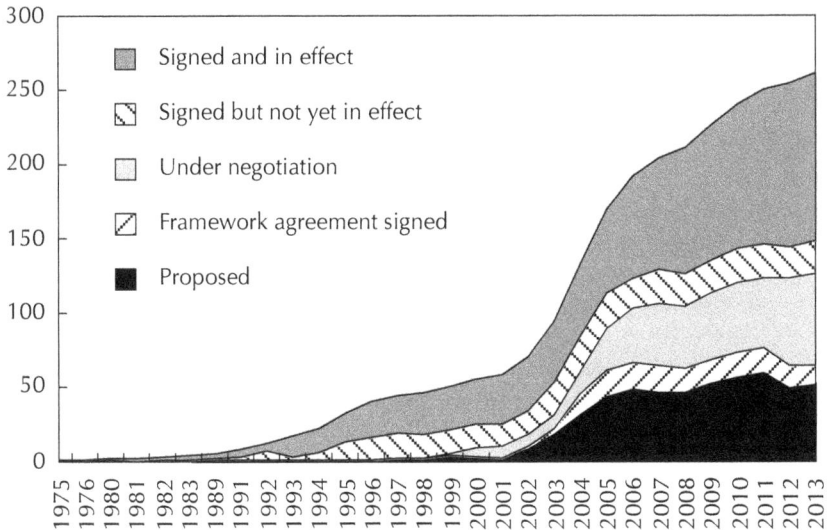

FTA = free trade agreement.

a As of July 2013. 'Proposed' refers to when parties are considering an FTA, establishing joint study groups or taskforces, and conducting feasibility studies to determine the desirability of entering into an FTA. 'Framework agreement signed' refers to when parties are initially negotiating the content of a framework agreement that serves as a guide for future negotiations. 'Under negotiation' refers to when parties begin negotiations without a framework agreement. 'Signed but not yet in effect' refers to when parties sign an FTA after negotiations have been completed. Some FTAs require legislative or executive ratification. 'Signed and in effect' refers to when the provisions of an FTA become effective (for example, when tariff reduction begins).

Source: ARIC FTA database, Asia Regional Integration Center (ARIC).

While the success in Bali in securing a multilateral agreement on trade facilitation, although yet to be ratified, may have resuscitated the World Trade Organization (WTO), it also marked the death knell for the single undertaking. Given that the Doha Round can no longer be concluded as originally intended, these alternative processes — trying to solve the regional and global jigsaw puzzles — are likely to continue. The ASEAN+6 group — consisting of the 10 members of ASEAN plus Australia, China, Japan, Korea, India, and New Zealand — are attempting to create a consolidated bloc called the Regional Comprehensive Economic Partnership (RCEP) by 2015, in order to supersede the various ASEAN+1 FTAs and other internal bilateral FTAs between individual countries (see Menon 2013a). At the same time, the ASEAN countries are aiming to conclude the ASEAN Economic Community (AEC) with the same deadline. Around the world, the US and the EU are pursuing a Transatlantic

Trade and Investment Partnership (TTIP), while the US is also leading a Trans-Pacific Partnership (TPP) southwards that includes seven RCEP members, amongst others. There are several other agreements in place or being pursued around the world.

Can these attempts at regional consolidation succeed and, if they do, will it be possible to link them up to get to global multilateral trade? In other words, will the pieces of the global jigsaw puzzle fall neatly into place, or will the trade landscape disintegrate into fragmented blocs? But before that, the pieces of the puzzle need to be built first, through regional consolidation or cross-regional tie-ups, and this too is like assembling constituent mini jigsaw puzzles. That is, both regional and global jigsaw puzzles will need to be solved, and in that order, if this route is to eventually lead to global free trade. What is the likelihood that such an approach could work and, if it cannot, how do we resolve the disarray in world trade? These are the question we will attempt to answer.

The next section discusses the regional jigsaw puzzles while the following section looks at the challenges associated with solving the global puzzle. A way forward in resolving the trade mess, involving a revival of the unilateral approach but applied to preferences rather than most favoured nation (MFN) tariff rates, is proposed in the subsequent section. A final section concludes this discussion.

3.2   THE REGIONAL JIGSAW PUZZLE

Asia is a latecomer to preferential agreements. Japan and Korea, for instance, had completely ignored the preferential route until recently. Even though ASEAN is one of the longest running regional cooperation arrangements amongst developing countries, it mainly operated as a politico-security pact until the ASEAN Free Trade Agreement (AFTA) in 1992, and even then it has largely remained non-preferential in its implementation of accords by pursuing voluntary multilateralisation of preferences (see Hill and Menon 2012). Despite the late start, Asia has been catching up in the new millennium (Figure 3.1). The past decade has seen more FTAs proposed, negotiated, and ratified in Asia than anywhere else. Within Asia, most of the activity has centered on the East Asian countries or ASEAN+6 (Figure 3.2). There is also a complex web of bilateral FTAs amongst members of the ASEAN+6 group of countries (Table 3.1). Therefore, when considering the regional puzzle, it is only appropriate that we use RCEP as an example.

Like any jigsaw puzzle, we begin with disarray. But the RCEP puzzle is more than just messy — there is no solution because the pieces of the puzzle do not fit together. The pieces of the jigsaw are the ASEAN+1

Figure 3.2   FTAs by status, ASEAN+6 (cumulative), selected years (no.)[a]

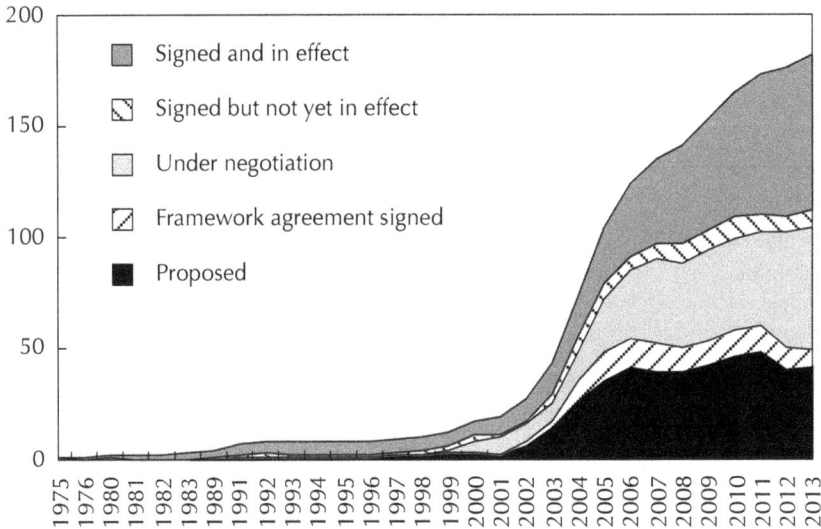

FTA = free trade agreement.

a   As of July 2013. 'Proposed' refers to when parties are considering an FTA, establishing joint study groups or taskforces, and conducting feasibility studies to determine the desirability of entering into an FTA. 'Framework agreement signed' refers to when parties are initially negotiating the content of a framework agreement that serves as a guide for future negotiations. 'Under negotiation' refers to when parties begin negotiations without a framework agreement. 'Signed but not yet in effect' refers to when parties sign an FTA after negotiations have been completed. Some FTAs require legislative or executive ratification. 'Signed and in effect' refers to when the provisions of an FTA become effective (for example, when tariff reduction begins).

Source: ARIC FTA database, Asia Regional Integration Center (ARIC).

and bilateral FTAs, and they come in different shapes and sizes (both width and breadth) as well as density and vintage. Indeed, they can vary depending on the number of items that are up for negotiated liberalisation, and usually just about everything *is*, including rules of origin (ROOs).

With ROOs, for instance, there are at least 22 different types in operation amongst the ASEAN+1 FTAs. This total is arrived at after aggregating ROOs that are similar but not the same, and ignoring the fact that some tariff lines have more than one ROO that needs to be met, which could be added to the tally. Only about 30 percent of tariff lines across these FTAs share common ROOs (Medalla 2011). There are eight different types of ROOs that apply to the electronics chapter alone (Chapter 85 of the Harmonised System (HS)). Even automotive products (HS 87), with just 76 tariff lines at the 6-digit level, have six different types of

Table 3.1   Share of imports from FTA partners in total imports, 2011 (%)

Country	FTA proposed	Framework agreement signed, under negotiation, or signed but not yet in effect	FTA ratified	Total imports from FTA partners as % of total imports
Australia	0.8	32.8	35.0	68.6
Brunei Darussalam	0.0	16.4	82.3	98.7
Cambodia	0.2	2.3	83.7	86.1
China	3.5	22.6	24.6	50.7
India	2.5	46.2	27.7	76.4
Indonesia	6.3	16.1	67.6	90.0
Japan	0.1	60.8	18.2	79.1
Korea	4.4	49.9	36.6	90.9
Lao PDR	0.0	6.3	90.6	96.9
Malaysia	4.4	21.4	61.3	87.0
Myanmar	0.1	1.5	93.2	94.8
New Zealand	0.5	30.6	47.0	78.1
Philippines	10.9	7.4	55.6	74.0
Singapore	0.0	25.3	62.4	87.7
Thailand	1.3	18.0	57.2	76.6
Vietnam	1.0	14.0	70.7	85.8
ASEAN+6 total	**2.6**	**34.2**	**34.9**	**71.6**

Source: Author's calculations. Raw data from *IMF Direction of Trade Statistics*, data as of May 2013.

ROOs. There is significant variation in ROOs not only across products within an FTA, but also across FTAs for the same product.

The 40 bilateral FTAs (Table 3.1) between individual members of RCEP further complicate the picture. Take, for instance, the Japan–India FTA. There are 12 types of ROOs in this FTA, seven of which cannot be found in any of the other ASEAN+1 FTAs. Almost two-thirds of tariff lines use one of these seven new ROOs, and about half have to comply with two ROOs: a change in tariff subheading and a 40 percent domestic content requirement. The ASEAN–India FTA, on the other hand, is the only ASEAN+1 FTA that does not have the *de minimis* provision, which provides for change-in-tariff-classification that facilitates product fragmentation trade.

The sheer number of ROOs, and lack of commonality in their application to tariff lines across FTAs, or variations in the provisions of ROOs across FTAs, raises obvious difficulties in harmonising and consolidating them. But consolidate them they must, if RCEP is to eventuate. The question is how and in what form. The only way to make the pieces fit is to reshape them: either shave them down or build them up. Shaving down the bits can be thought of as a 'race to the bottom', where the lowest common denominator rules, making for an easier fit. Building them up is the opposite, where laggards lift their reform game to meet the standard set by the front-runners.

Details remain sparse, but what we do know from the RCEP's Guiding Principles is that it will add to, rather than replace, existing ASEAN+1 FTAs, while at the same time introducing 'significant improvements' over these agreements. There is, however, an important qualifier in the dreaded 'flexibility' clause: 'RCEP will include appropriate forms of flexibility including provision for special and differential treatment, plus additional flexibility to the least-developed ASEAN Member States'. Pursuing harmonisation, while retaining flexibility, is likely to produce one of two outcomes. Because harmonisation implies consensus, a race to the bottom is likely because the country with the lobby that has the most to lose from the dilution of ROOs is also likely to be the most belligerent, and least likely to compromise. Since the gains to a country looking to retain protection usually outweigh the benefits to others from liberalising ROOs, the incentive structure would favour the former.[1] This follows from Baldwin's (2006b) asymmetric lobbying theory, which explains why potential losers tend to lobby harder. Alternatively, countries exercising flexibility could result in conservatism — approximating the status quo and preserving the current noodle bowl. These outcomes are more likely than the hoped-for 'race to the top' scenario, unless incentives are provided to overcome pressure from the vested interests that lobbied for different ROOs to begin with. The very existence of so many ROOs and exemptions confirms the power of such lobbies. Breaking through these pressures will not be easy, and will require a stronger commitment to reform from all members, big or small, strong or weak (Menon 2013a). The problem is that some countries may not see any carrot — and there is no stick. Almost in desperation, some countries have even identified flexibility itself as the carrot, highlighting the RCEP's commitment not to impose or compel commitment from its members. If this is the carrot, then it cannot be much of one, and comes at the expense of the stick.

---

1 It is not uncommon for the main beneficiaries of such liberalisation to lie outside the bloc, especially if the bloc is not big enough to include the lowest-cost supplier, but then their interests are not represented and do not factor in the calculus.

If either a race to the bottom or minimal change scenario plays out, then the RCEP will be largely redundant. Although cumulation rules may expand through increased membership, this usually amounts to little when product fragmentation trade is significant (Menon 2012). Changing the type of ROO is more important, but also more difficult. The South Asia Free Trade Agreement (SAFTA), a failed attempt at consolidation, illustrates this. Most trade within South Asia continues under more generous bilateral FTAs or under MFN rates (Weerakoon 2008). Sadly, SAFTA's main contribution has been to add another strand to the global spaghetti bowl.

Will the same fate befall the RCEP? Unless there is enough political will to close potential loopholes disguised as 'flexibility' and pursue reforms deeper than those ever before attempted, RCEP's future as a consolidated bloc remains uncertain. The RCEP faces many challenges but this is the fundamental one. Previous assessments of challenges facing the RCEP have failed to recognise this fundamental constraint, and have focused on side issues ranging from the apparent need to address agriculture more fully to even proposing increasing investment in infrastructure (Das 2012; Kawai and Wignaraja 2013). It is difficult to imagine how a preferential agreement can deal with agricultural liberalisation more fully when the greatest distortion in this sector relates to production subsidies, which cannot be removed selectively or preferentially. To suggest that infrastructure investment should be increased in order to make the RCEP or any other FTA more effective is to confuse means and ends. Asia may need more investment in infrastructure but pursuing this need should not be done in order to make a second-best policy appear less so, but rather to promote growth and development for its own sake.

We have discussed the RCEP in some detail in order to illustrate the difficulties associated with regional consolidation. The other important mega-regional agreement in the Asia–Pacific region, the TPP cuts across geographic subregions. Unlike the RCEP, the TPP is not aimed at consolidation since not all members have bilateral FTAs between them or are part of common plurilateral agreements. But where they do exist, there is no intention of preserving any of the bilateral or plurilateral agreements among its members. The TTP is clear in its aim in going further in creating an agreement so deep that it should neutralise any existing agreements by either matching or superseding them. The TPP's agenda is more wide-ranging and ambitious than the Doha Round. In addition to harmonising ROOs and the like, just as with solving the regional puzzle, it purports to address areas that have never been successfully dealt with before by any of the countries involved. And prospects for completion are not looking good. The TPP has already missed three deadlines — the latest one being October 2013.

This is not surprising if one looks closely at what is being attempted, and compares it with the Doha Round experience. Although there are less countries involved in the TPP negotiations compared to the Doha Round, the difficulties that diversity in negotiating positions introduces into the process is not a linear function of the number of countries involved. That is, moving from more than 150 countries to 12 does not reduce diversity in negotiating positions proportionately. There can be as much diversity among 12 countries as there are amongst a group of 150 if the 12 countries have very different positions on key issues. When a grouping includes countries as varied as Vietnam, Brunei, Peru, and the US, then there is sufficient diversity to complicate negotiations being pursued on a single-undertaking basis, especially when the agenda is a highly ambitious one.

For these and other reasons, there is also concern that the TPP is degenerating into a series of bilateral deals, with a US–Japan agreement at its core. Given sensitivities across members on different issues, a variety of exemptions in the form of so-called 'carve-outs' are anticipated, and these can only be accommodated through bilateral arrangements. With renewed uncertainty over the prospects of the Obama Administration securing Trade Negotiating Authority or 'fast track' in the US, the future of the TPP remains uncertain since other members may be reluctant to sign up to an agreement when it remains unclear if the key proponent can actually deliver (Menon 2014b).

In summary, solving the regional jigsaw puzzles is clearly a complicated exercise, and fraught with difficulties. This is true whether it involves consolidating existing agreements, like with the RCEP, or not, like the TPP. In both cases, there is a serious risk of the final outcome being a highly diluted version of the ambition set at the very beginning of negotiations. A meaningful RCEP or TPP will require resolve similar to that which gave birth to the EU – an example of successful FTA consolidation, if nothing else. There does not seem to be such political will in Asia at the moment for the RCEP, or for the TPP given that securing trade promotion authority in the US appears increasingly unlikely. Therefore, unless these challenges are overcome soon, RCEP and the TPP may be seen as serving the geopolitical interests of a few players, to little economic effect.

3.3 THE GLOBAL JIGSAW PUZZLE

Despite the difficulties associated with solving the regional puzzles, it is still only part of the broader issue of addressing the disarray in the world trade system. To illustrate, let us assume that the RCEP succeeds in coming up with a consolidated agreement that supersedes its con-stituent components — that the regional jigsaw puzzled is solved and the resulting image is a better and brighter one than before. Let us also assume that the TPP is concluded as originally intended, as are all the other mega-blocs around the world. If this is the best-case scenario, what does success look like? Not good at all, unfortunately — it would merely substitute the mess at the regional level with one at the global level. We end up with a fragmented world trade system, or one that is carved up into distinct blocs.

Solving the global jigsaw puzzle can be pursued in a number of ways. One often-discussed proposal is to try and tie-up the various regional blocs so that they may be linked together, almost seamlessly. Is this likely?

This approach to solving the global puzzle is naturally bound to encounter all of the problems associated with solving the regional jigsaw puzzle. Furthermore, there are additional complications that arise. Not only are some pieces of the jigsaw puzzle missing (parts of South and Central Asia, the Middle East, and the Pacific Islands are absent), there are also overlapping bits and pieces that are redundant and probably irreconcilable. And unlike with the RCEP for instance, the global puzzle cannot be solved by retaining the regional ones — the intention is for them to disappear. Therefore, for the outcome to approximate multilateral free trade, the link-ups must go at least as far as, or further than, what exists in their constituent parts. But then this is akin to concluding the Doha Round, and there is no reason to expect that link-ups of this nature will make the task any easier. While there are cases of successful regional con-solidation, such as the EU, cross-regional link-ups of mega blocs have no precedent. Although the example of the RCEP highlighted the diversity that can exist between FTAs *within* a regional bloc, the diversity *between* regional blocs are likely to be as high or higher still. Furthermore, it is unclear how the process of global consolidation of the regional blocs will take place. Should it proceed sequentially, or should there be a kind of single undertaking where the different blocs come together to negotiate a comprehensive deal? If the latter sounds like the Doha Round, then it is because it is strikingly similar in terms of process, and likely to be just as difficult to conclude. A sequential bloc-by-bloc, or bottom-up approach, building on open accession clauses of existing agreements may not be much easier either. Assuming that the RCEP can harmonise its services sector, liberalisation or sanitary and phytosanitary (SPS) standards with that of the TTP or TTIP, for instance, will it be able to also merge them with the South American or African blocs, or indeed both? The gulf in the levels of development between these blocs, as well as other forms of diversity, pose obvious difficulties. Furthermore, if services trade is liber-alised, for instance, through mutual recognition arrangements (MRAs), as in ASEAN, rather than harmonisation through regulatory convergence towards a regional standard, then the merging of different blocs is even more difficult. Unless the modality employed for liberalisation is conducive to expansion, the much bandied about 'open accession' clauses will mean little in practice, especially when considering that the countries looking to accede would not have had any input into the negotiated outcome, and would have to fully accept whatever has been agreed.

Proponents of FTAs argue that deeper agreements can be achieved more rapidly on difficult issues when there are only a small number of negotiating partners involved, and there is evidence to support this argument. But many advocates fail to explain how this principle could work within the context of FTA consolidation or indeed in terms of inter-regional tie-ups in solving the global puzzle. That is, no one has addressed the issue of how these deeper accords can suddenly be agreed upon by reversing the process and adding more countries or regions.[2] The experience with the ASEAN+1 negotiation process is that in all of their FTAs, the ASEAN6 (the original five members plus Brunei) have negotiated different terms from the newer members, the CLMV countries (Cambodia, Lao PDR, Myanmar and Vietnam) (see Menon and Melendez 2011). In some of these FTAs, such as the ASEAN–India Free Trade Agreement, the terms vary across almost every member, reflecting the reality that countries always negotiate individually rather than as a group, and a common position is only one of a number of possible outcomes. If this process is replicated when it comes to solving the global puzzle, with individual countries or even coalitions of countries within each region negotiating separately, the process could be an extremely cumbersome and difficult one. Again, the snags with concluding the Doha Round come to mind.

Consolidation at the regional or global level may be just as difficult, if not more so, than starting from scratch, as there are no discrepancies to be resolved or policies to be reversed. Getting a pair of countries to agree on a specific set of terms will not necessarily facilitate similar breakthroughs with third parties. To ignore this is to ignore ground realities and the political economy of FTA negotiations. And anyone who has looked closely at an FTA will know how difficult the task of enmeshing even two similar agreements can be, let alone many different ones. The experience of the Pacific Basin Initiative, involving four Latin American countries — Chile, Columbia, Mexico, and Peru — confirms the point. After several decades of trying to harmonise the bilateral FTAs to arrive

---

2 If access to a bigger market is the lure, enabling the process of adding more countries without diluting accords, then wouldn't the Doha Round be a better, if not easier, process? It may be better. But we know it is not easier.

at a consolidated regional one, they finally gave up and decided to start negotiations almost from scratch, which seemed to work.

3.4   THE WAY FORWARD

There is a sense of *deja vu* about the current state of the world trade system. The last time the world appeared to be disintegrating into regional blocs, it helped conclude a difficult multilateral round of negotiations called the Uruguay Round. Hill (1994) described how deteriorating trade relations among key economies helped rather than hindered the move towards concluding the round, with the EU pressing ahead with its '1992 Agenda', growing interest in an embryonic Asia–Pacific Economic Cooperation (APEC), and the North American Free Trade Agreement (NAFTA) threatening to spread southward. Many hope that the re-emergence of regionalism and trade friction amongst major economies will result in history repeating itself by reviving multilateralism. However, the repeat of history seems less likely now that the single undertaking appears to have been replaced by the cherry-picking process with the passing of the WTO's multilateral agreement on trade facilitation. In any case, the Uruguay Round did not dissolve regionalism around the world — in fact, regionalism continued to grow in its aftermath. The Doha Round could never have addressed the negative consequences of regionalism either. Even if the Doha Round negotiations are successful, there will be a need for regional blocs to address the discrepancies reflecting disparate and independently negotiated outcomes. An obvious and practical solution would be to multilateralise regionalism by offering the negotiated concessions to non-members in a non-discriminatory manner. If all regional blocs can see the benefit of pursuing this course of action, we will have an outcome that is not just as good as that of the Doha Round, but much better.

This outcome could be better than the Doha Round for at least two reasons. First, the Doha Round is, in essence, the world's largest FTA in that concessions are traded reciprocally amongst WTO members, and non-WTO members — of which there are still about 40 — are excluded. Many of these non-members are small, poor, fragile, or land-locked (or isolated in other ways), face high trade costs, and are subject to a host of other vulnerabilities. The benefits from engaging them in greater commercial exchange will be substantial, mostly to them, but also for the rest of the world. Multilateralisation of preferences to all, and not just the WTO membership, would achieve this. It would also eliminate the need for ROOs. Second, and more important, it will do what a Uruguay Round could not, and the Doha Round cannot, and that is to remove as

Figure 3.3   ASEAN+6 imports from FTA partners as a share of total imports, 2011 (%)

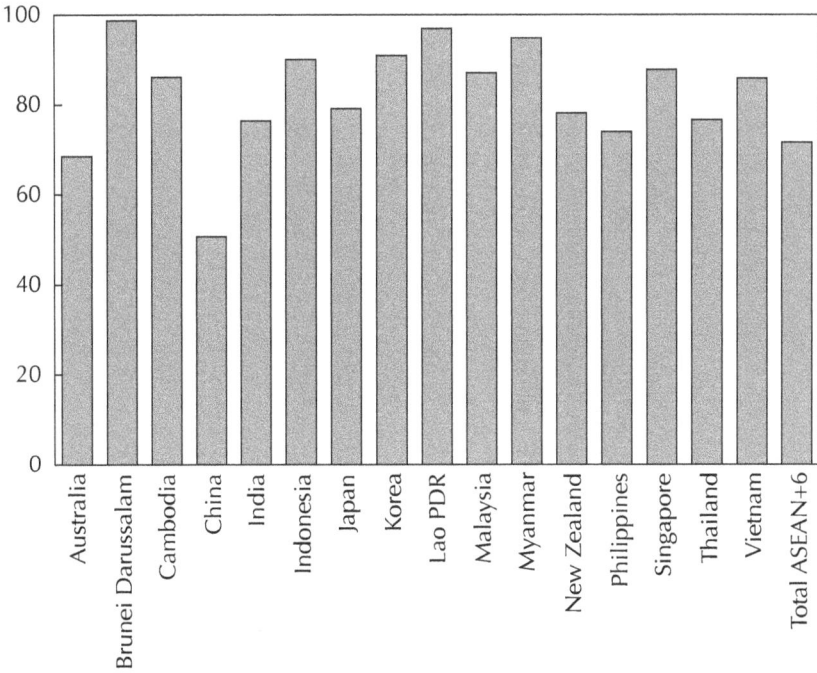

Source: Author's calculations. Raw data from *IMF Direction of Trade Statistics*, data as of May 2013.

opposed to dilute preference discrepancies and other distortions associated with discriminatory arrangements. The contradictions of the jigsaw puzzle will finally be eliminated and the spaghetti bowl emptied of its hazardous content.

In Asia, for instance, more than three-quarters of imports of most of the RCEP countries, except for China and Australia, are already covered or about to be covered by an FTA (see Figure 3.3 and Table 3.2). For ASEAN+6 as a group, more than a third of imports are already covered by FTAs, with another third about to be covered with FTA negotiations ongoing (Menon 2014a). In this context, there is little point in holding out to negotiate reciprocity with a residual set of countries, usually small in terms of trade volumes, especially when full utilisation cannot be assured, but trade diversion and deflection are real risks. When a country X has concluded FTAs with most of its major trading partners, preference erosion necessarily sets in, and there is often little, if any, preference advantage *between* the trading partners in country X's market. The only

Table 3.2   Deviation from baseline, ASEAN+6, 2020 (%)

	Preferential liberalisation, complete utilisation	Preferential liberalisation, incomplete utilisation	Multi-lateralisation of preferences	Multi-lateralisation of preferences, with reciprocity, complete utilisation	Multi-lateralisation of preferences, with reciprocity, incomplete utilisation	Global liberalisation
World real GDP	0.045	0.019	0.119	0.310	0.131	0.346
ASEAN+6 real GDP	0.344	0.108	0.857	1.235	0.388	1.025
ROW (–A+6) real GDP	-0.063	-0.013	-0.147	-0.022	-0.005	0.101
World real GNP	0.029	0.015	0.110	0.273	0.142	0.312
ASEAN+6 real GNP	0.424	0.134	0.536	1.345	0.423	1.019
ROW (–A+6) real GNP	-0.113	-0.027	-0.044	-0.112	-0.027	0.059
World real exports	1.075	0.241	1.818	2.939	0.658	3.726
ASEAN+6 real exports	3.406	0.779	5.495	6.833	1.563	6.362
ROW (–A+6) real exports	-0.104	-0.031	-0.041	0.970	0.293	2.392

ASEAN = Association of Southeast Asian Nations; GDP = gross domestic product; GNP = gross national product; ROW = rest of the world.
Source: Author's calculations.

significant advantage that FTA partners have is over the countries that do not have an FTA with country X. When the non-FTA partners as a group do not supply a significant share of country X's imports, there is likely to be much less resistance from FTA partners to the multilateralisation of preferences. In other words, the proliferation of FTAs is not only erod-ing preferences between FTA partners, it will also eventually lead to a situation where the perceived cost (to FTA partners) of multilateralising preferences (to non-FTA partners) starts to diminish, and particularly in relation to the rising cost (to country X) of maintaining multiple FTAs and implementing their rules of origin.

But this is already happening. Globally, only 15 percent of trade flows are conducted under preferential terms, while the costs of try-ing to implement largely unused preferential arrangements continue to increase. In Asia, the trade-weighted preference utilisation rate of intra-ASEAN trade in 2008 was a mere 2.3 percent, while 72.9 percent of trade travelled at a zero MFN rate (WTO 2011). The fact that preference uti-lisation rates are generally very low needs to be taken into account in quantifying the impacts of FTAs, and in assessing the relative merits of pursuing non-reciprocal modalities of liberalisation, such as the multi-lateralisation of preferences. Previous studies on the impacts of FTAs in East Asia for instance have assumed full utilisation of preferences. The evidence suggests that this assumption is seriously in error, with the estimated uptake particularly low in this region. In assessing the impact of tariff liberalisation in the case of RCEP, our regional puzzle example, Menon (2013b) assumes a more realistic utilisation rate of 25 percent and then compares impacts under various scenarios. These scenarios include solving the regional puzzle (RCEP) with complete (Scenario 1 or S1) and incomplete (25 percent) utilisation (S2); multilateralisation of preferences by RCEP members (S3); an attempt at moving towards solving the global puzzle by linking the RCEP with a rest-of-the-world (ROW) FTA, but again with complete (S4) and incomplete (S5) utilisation; and finally a global free trade scenario (S6), which could be achieved by successfully solving the global puzzle or by all countries pursuing multilateralisation of preferences.

From Table 3.2, comparing preferential liberalisation with multi-lateralisation of preferences, we find that the latter is superior in all cases, and especially when incomplete utilisation is taken into account. We find that actual utilisation rates significantly diminish the benefits from pref-erential liberalisation, but in a non-linear way. In general, when members extend their preferential reductions to non-members on a non-discrimi-natory basis, welfare is enhanced because of three primary effects: (i) the extent of the liberalisation is greater, (ii) the broader liberalisation undoes the welfare-reducing trade diversion resulting from the preferential liberalisation, and (iii) the productivity of scarce resources within each member country is allocated more efficiently across its industries.

Scenarios S4 and S5 are akin to cross-regional tie-ups of FTAs, whereby the ROW grouping reciprocates by reducing its tariffs on exports from ASEAN+6. As noted, this would be a stylised example of how we could go about solving the global jigsaw puzzle. The benefits to members when reciprocity is introduced are greater than S3 only when there is full utilisation of preferences (S4). If utilisation is incomplete (S5), then members benefit more from multilateralisation of preferences (S3). However, the gross national product (GNP) of ROW falls by 0.15 percent under S4 (with much smaller declines under S5). These are the largest reductions for non-members under any of the scenarios. The additional gains to members in this scenario, with full utilisation of preferences, appear to occur at the expense of non-members. This raises the potential for possible retaliatory actions by non-members, reducing the benefits to the world as a whole. If the maximum gains to members accrue at the expense of potential retaliatory actions, then the possibility of trade deflection raises the likelihood of low utilisation rates. Since tariffs between large trading blocs such as NAFTA and the EU, and other significant groupings such as South America and Africa remain unchanged, there are significant opportunities and benefits from trying to deflect trade in order to obtain duty-free access.

In the final scenario of global liberalisation, which is most likely to be achieved by all countries pursuing multilateralisation of preferences, the GNP of all member countries would be increased. For RCEP members, there is little difference to the welfare effects of global liberalisation (S6) versus multilateralisation of preferences (S3). This finding has important implications for policy. It suggests that it is very much within the control of member countries to initiate actions that will produce almost the best welfare outcomes from trade liberalisation. There is really no need to wait for an unlikely global liberalisation solution for members to reap the benefits from it. It also appears that there is little to be gained from reciprocity, given time delays, negotiating costs, and uncertainty in the magnitude of benefits if utilisation is incomplete.

Surely multilateralisation deserves more serious consideration than ever before, and should no longer be dismissed as being 'pie in the sky'. After all, this kind of unilateral action had accounted for more than two-thirds of all trade liberalisation by developing countries in the two decades leading up to 2003 (World Bank 2005). There is also a host of other evidence,[3] including that of Vézina (2010), which shows that it

---

3 For more examples, ranging from Australia and New Zealand to India and Central Europe, refer to the two-volume publication edited by Jagdish Bhagwati (2002), and summarised in his introduction.

was unilateral actions that played the overwhelming role in the trade liberalisation of the original ASEAN members, and in drawing in FDI to these countries to supplant the regional supply chain. In this way, the rise in regionalism may eventually be the most compelling factor in contributing to its own demise by revitalising multilateralisation, if not the multilateral system. As Hill and Menon (2008) put it, the proliferation of bilateral and plurilateral FTAs may eventually lead to them collapsing under their own weight.

While the application of the multilateralisation approach is relatively straightforward, when it comes to tariffs and other similar technical barriers, it is also an approach naturally suited to non-tariff barriers and difficult sectors such as services. Although bilateral or regional negotiations can play a role in having a non-tariff barrier (NTB) removed, once they are removed, it may be difficult or costly to exclude third parties from sharing in the benefits. The removal of many NTBs share public good characteristics in that they are non-excludable and non-rival in consumption. That is, once they are provided (this provision may involve removing a constraint), then it is difficult, if not impossible, to avoid free riding. In other words, unlike tariffs, it is either costly — often prohibitively so — or impractical to remove NTBs in an exclusive or preferential manner. Similarly, if services liberalisation is pursued through harmonisation of standards rather than mutual recognition arrangements, non-members can easily accede. In either case, the possibility of multilateralising harmonised rules and regulations or mutually recognised requirements are present, although it is more easily done with the former than with the latter.

3.5 CONCLUSION

The rise of mega regionals, such as the RCEP, the TPP and the TTIP, suggests that the world trade system is appearing more like a jigsaw puzzle than a spaghetti bowl these days. There are both regional and global jigsaw puzzles to be solved, and in that order, if order is to return to a fragmented world trade system. But both the regional and global puzzles may remain just puzzles, given the difficulties associated with resolving the problems at each level. The difficulties of FTA consolidation at the regional level have been widely documented, while piecing together the blocs around the world to form a coherent whole is even more challenging, and has never been attempted. In this context, a way forward is to return to the most widely used modality of trade liberalisation — unilateral actions — but this time involving the multilateralisation of preferences rather than unreciprocated reductions in tariff rates. As more and more FTAs are negotiated, preference erosion sets in, reducing the resistance of FTA partners to multilateralisation. Its application to tariffs and other technical barriers is straightforward, but it is also an approach naturally suited to non-tariff barriers and difficult sectors such as services. The removal of many NTBs share public good characteristics that make it either costly or impractical to be discriminatory or exclusive. Similarly, if services liberalisation is pursued through harmonisation of standards or mutual recognition arrangements, the possibility of multilateralisation exists. If harmonisation is achieved through regulatory convergence, for instance, rather than through MRAs, it will facilitate multilateralisation because it will be easier for non-members to accede. Therefore, multilateralisation of preferences, whether tariff or non-tariff, appears to present a practical way forward in addressing the disarray in the world trade system.

4   Agricultural trade consequences of Asia's economic growth: a case study of wine

*Kym Anderson**

Hal Hill has been an avid student of Asian economic growth and trade throughout his career. While that has not led him to do research specifically on trade in farm products, his fondness for conversing over shared meals with good food and wine is well known. Hence the agricultural focus of this chapter, with a particular application to Asia's trade in wine.

Rice wine is common in Asia of course, but wine made from grapes has had a very minor role traditionally. Prior to this century, grape wine was consumed only by Asia's elite and produced only in tiny quantities mostly in just Japan and, from the late 1980s, China.[1] However, income growth and a preference swing towards this traditional European product have changed the consumption situation dramatically. China is also expanding its area of vineyards and is now the world's fifth largest producer of grape wine (hereafter called just wine), up from fifteenth as recently as 2001. That supply expansion has not been able to keep up with China's growth in demand, so wine imports have surged. Nor are those imports only of low quality. The average current US$ price of wine imports grew at 7 percent per year between 2000 and 2009 in Asia, compared with only 5.5 percent in the rest of the world. By 2009 that Asian

---

*   Thanks are due to Glyn Wittwer for extracting additional modelling results, and to the Australian Grape and Wine Authority for research funds.
1   Wine grape production in China may have begun more than two millennia ago, but it would have been only for the ruling elite's pleasure (McGovern 2003, 2009). For developments in East Asian wine markets to the turn of this century, see Findlay et al. (2004).

average import price was nearly 80 percent higher than the world average, and more than four times higher in the case of Hong Kong and Singapore. Even the unit values of China's imports of both bottled still wines and sparkling wines were above the global average by 2009 (Anderson and Nelgen 2011). Meanwhile, after removing its tariff on wine imports in February 2008, Hong Kong has become the world's most important market for ultra-premium and iconic wines.

What is the future of Asia in the world's wine markets? Will China's wine production eventually exceed its consumption domestically? How important will wine demand be in the four next-most-populous Asian countries (India, Indonesia, Pakistan, and Bangladesh)? Who else will satisfy Asia's growing thirst? How will the various wine quality categories develop in Asia? Which wine varieties will Asians prefer? What roles will excise and import taxes play? What is the future of the austerity drive China introduced in 2014 that has dampened conspicuous consumption of luxuries such as expensive wines?

This chapter seeks to address these types of questions. It first draws on comparative advantage theory, then looks at the recent history in more detail before presenting some projections for the next five years under various assumptions about economic growth rates and real exchange rates. It concludes that China is by far the most dominant player in Asia, and that it is set to continue to change global markets for wines dramatically, just as it has been doing and will continue to do for many other products.

4.1   DETERMINANTS OF COMPARATIVE ADVANTAGE IN WINE

According to the workhorse theory of comparative advantage developed in the 20th century, we should expect agricultural trade to occur between relatively lightly populated economies that are well-endowed with agricultural land and those that are densely populated with little agricultural land per worker (Krueger 1977). Leamer (1987) develops this model further and relates it to paths of economic development. If the stock of natural resources is unchanged, rapid growth by one or more countries relative to others in their availability of produced capital (physical plus human skills and technological knowledge) per unit of available labour time would tend to cause those economies to strengthen their comparative advantage in non-primary products. By contrast, a discovery of minerals or energy raw materials would strengthen that country's comparative advantage in mining and weaken its comparative advantage in agricultural and other tradable products, ceteris paribus. It would also boost national income and hence the demand for non-tradables, which would cause mobile resources to move into the production of non-tradable goods and services, further reducing farm and industrial production (Corden 1984). As ports and other infrastructure are developed and costs of trading internationally fall for the country, more products would move from the non-tradable to the tradable category (Venables 2004).

At early stages of development of a country with a relatively small stock of natural resources per worker, wages would be low and the country is likely to have an initial comparative cost advantage in unskilled labour-intensive, standard-technology manufactures. Then, as the stock of industrial capital grows, there would be a gradual move towards exporting manufactures that are relatively intensive in their use of physical capital, skills, and knowledge. Natural resource-abundant economies, however, may invest more in capital specific to primary production and so would not develop a comparative advantage in manufacturing until a later stage of development, at which time their industrial exports would be relatively capital intensive.

The above theory of changing comparative advantage has been used successfully to explain Asia's resource-poor first- and second-generation industrialising economies becoming more dependent on imports of primary products from their resource-rich trading partners (see for example Anderson and Smith 1981). It also explains well the 20th century's flying geese pattern of comparative advantage and then disadvantage in unskilled labour-intensive manufactures as some rapidly growing economies expand their endowments of industrial capital per worker relative to the rest of the world, with the classic example being clothing and textiles (Ozawa 2009).

But how helpful is that theory for explaining comparative advantage in wine? Grape-based wine is dependent on wine grapes as an input, and they are too perishable to be transported internationally without at least the first stages of processing. The lowest-quality wine grapes and wine can be produced in less-than-ideal regions and sold as an undifferentiated commodity without a great deal of knowhow, but only at prices barely above the cost of production for most vignerons. To produce a higher-quality product that can be differentiated from other wines by consumers, and thus attract a higher price, requires far more technological knowledge and skills in grape growing, wine making and wine marketing in addition to access to high-quality vineyard land or at least grapes from these regions. To be economically sustainable, the producer also needs ready access to financial capital to cover the very considerable up-front establishment costs and to finance the years when receipts fall short of outgoings, including the first seven years before cash income begins to exceed cash outlays. Secure property rights over the vineyard land are essential as well, since the lifetime of vines is at least 30 years and can be much longer.

Of particular importance as determinants of a country's competiveness in producing wine, rather than other farm products, are the three Ts: terroir, technology, and tradition.

Terroir refers to various pertinent aspects of climate, topography, soils, and geology that determine the quality of the vine's growing conditions. Vineyard site selection, therefore, is crucial. Experience has determined the best sites and most-suitable grape varieties in long-established regions, whereas in new regions science has to be used to speed the process of approaching the potential of any region to produce quality wine grapes. The conventional wisdom is that wine grapes grow best between the 30° and 50° temperate latitude bands north and south of the equator, and where rain is concentrated in the winter and summer harvest times are dry. Lower latitudes typically result in lower-quality wine grapes, although moving to higher altitudes can help because temperatures decline about 5°C per 1,000 metres of elevation (Gladstones 1992; Ashenfelter and Storchmann 2014).

Traditions determine not only how a product is produced but also the extent of local consumer demand. This is important for wine because typically local demand is the easiest and least costly for producers to satisfy, as there are relatively high fixed costs of entry into new export markets (Friberg, Paterson, and Richardson 2011). Stigler and Becker (1977) argue that economists should begin by assuming tastes are stable over time and similar among people and then focus on explaining differences in consumption patterns using standard determinants such as relative prices and real incomes. That view is supported for food even in the poorest settings. For example, recent studies in both India and China demonstrate that introducing subsidies to rice and wheat consumption does almost nothing to boost nutrition, as consumers tend to eat the same amount of nutrients but do so by switching from less-preferred coarse grains to now-subsidised rice and wheat (Jensen and Miller 2011; Kaushal and Muchomba 2013). Social norms and religion can also influence interest in consumption of alcoholic beverages.

Also, when preferences are non-homothetic, trade patterns can be affected by growth in domestic demand (Markusen 2013). Wine typically has an income elasticity of demand of greater than one. Hence as a country's per capita income rises, there would be a decline in its comparative advantage in wine, unless its wine productivity grew sufficiently faster than income, other things equal.

As for technologies, there is always potential to improve on traditional production, processing, entrepreneurship, and marketing, be that by trial and error of practitioners over the generations or via formal investment in private and public research and development (R&D). The New World wine-producing countries have been more dependent on newly developed technologies and less on terroir than have producers in Western Europe, although both sets of countries have made major R&D investments — and expanded complementary tertiary education in viticulture, oenology, and wine marketing — over the past half-century (Giuliana, Morrison, and Rabellotti 2011). Those technologies are potentially transferrable to other countries and can even become globalised, as has happened with grain technologies (Olmstead and Rhode 2007). That process has been greatly accelerated over the past two decades through two mechanisms. One is the emergence of fly-in, fly-out viticulturists and winemakers from wine-producing countries of both the Old World (i.e. Western Europe) and the New World (the Americas, South Africa and Australasia — see Williams 1995). The decline in airfares has made it far more affordable for young professionals to work in both hemispheres each year, doubling their vintage experiences and learning and spreading new technologies quickly. The other mechanism is via foreign direct investment joint ventures: by combining two firms' technical and market knowledge, the latest technologies can be diffused to new regions more rapidly.

How important modern technologies are relative to terroir in determining comparative advantage is a moot point. One recent statistical study suggests terroir is not as dominant as is commonly assumed — even in regions as established as Bordeaux (Gerguad and Ginsburg 2008). Another study of vineyard sale values in Oregon finds that while appellation reputation has some economic value, each location's physical attributes are not closely related to wine prices (Cross, Plantinga, and Stavins 2011). A recent book by Lewin (2010) begins its section on wine regions with the New World rather than the Old World, to emphasise the point that wines almost everywhere are manipulated by winemakers as they endeavour to make use of available knowledge to produce the products most desired by their customers. What they choose to produce is increasingly being affected by how they can maximise profits through satisfying consumer demand, rather than by what they prefer to make with their available resources.

New technologies in agriculture have long tended to be biased in favour of saving the scarcest factor of production, as reflected in relative factor prices. Hayami and Ruttan (1985) emphasise that the focus of R&D investments has been driven in part by changes in factor prices, and in particular by the rise in real wages. That has resulted in the development and adoption of labour-saving technologies such as mechanical harvesters and pruners for vineyards and super-fast bottling and labelling equipment for wineries in viticultural land-abundant, labour-scarce countries. The adoption of labour-saving technologies has helped countries with rapidly rising real wages retain their comparative advantage in what traditionally had been (at least at the primary stage) a labour-intensive industry. This in turn means poorer countries need to find sources of comparative advantage other than just low wages.

Relative factor endowments affect the comparative advantage of a country also in terms of the quality of its exported products. New trade theory suggests richer, capital-abundant countries will export higher priced, higher-quality goods (Fajgelbaum, Grossman, and Helpman 2011; Nayak 2011).

A further set of influences on comparative advantage that can be important at certain times relates to currency exchange rate movements. A macroeconomic shock such as Argentina's devaluation by two-thirds in late 2001, or a doubling in the Australian–US dollar exchange rate over the subsequent decade due largely to Australia's mining boom, have had major (and opposite) impacts on the international competiveness of wineries in those two Southern Hemisphere countries (Anderson and Wittwer 2013).

4.2   ASIA'S WINE PRODUCTION, CONSUMPTION, AND TRADE TO DATE

The previous section provides plenty of reasons for not expecting much wine-grape production in most Asian countries: there is almost no tradition of wine consumption domestically; most people's incomes until very recently have been too low for wine to be a priority; there are very few regions with suitable terroir, especially where it is not hot and humid; and in numerous Islamic Asian countries their religion frowns on alcohol. It is therefore not surprising that the only Asian countries with a significant area of grapevines (of which only a fraction is used in wine making) are parts of Japan, Korea, and China. About 1 percent of South Korea's small crop area has been devoted to vines over the past two decades, and just 0.4 percent of Japan's small crop area since the 1970s, with little change in either country over those periods. By contrast, the share of crop area under vines in China has been growing rapidly, doubling since the turn of the century. Even so, the share in China is still not quite as high as in Japan, which suggests there is scope for substantially more expansion without encroaching very much on land used for food production, bearing in mind that quality wine grapes grow better on poor slopes than on fertile, flat land. China has been open to foreign direct investment in vineyards and wineries, and has welcomed flying vignerons as consultants. China even seems to have found ways to provide adequate property rights for investors, notwithstanding the fact that farmland cannot be privately owned in China. Its vineyards are heavily focusing on red varieties (considered by Chinese people to be best for their health), especially varieties originating in France.[2]

While it is true that India, Thailand, and even Myanmar have some vineyards and have begun producing wine from them, the volumes are as yet insignificant.

China's volume of wine production has been growing more than twice as fast as its area under vines. This has been possible not just because the share of grapes destined for wine has risen, but also because China imports a lot of wine in bulk and blends it with wine made from Chinese grapes. This is feasible because national labelling laws are such that a bottle marked 'Product of China' is required to have only 10 percent local content.

Turning to consumption, there are only five Asian countries, plus Hong Kong and Taiwan, where per capita grape wine consumption has yet to exceed 0.2 litres per year. In each of those countries, the level in 2012 is well above that of 2000, but the most dramatic increase has been in China (Figure 4.1(a)). Since China is also the most populous country, its growth has overwhelmingly dominated Asia's overall increase in wine consumption, which has nearly quadrupled since 2000 (Figure 4.1(b)). China accounted for barely half of Asia's wine consumption in 2000, but now it accounts for all but one-fifth. Similarly populous India, by contrast, has a wine industry that is less than one-fiftieth that of China's, notwithstanding the industry's double-digit growth there during the past decade.

During the first decade of this century, wine has doubled its share of Asia's recorded consumption of alcohol, bringing it to just 3 percent, or only one-fifth, of wine's global share of recorded alcohol consumption. The same handful of Asian countries are the only ones in which wine's share is above the Asian average (Figure 4.2).

So, despite the recent rapid growth in wine consumption in Asia, the potential for further expansion remains enormous, given the current very low level of per capita consumption and share of wine in total alcohol purchases. The rapid aging and educating of the populations in Asia's emerging economies also lends itself to a continuing expansion of demand for wine there. Certainly the new Chinese government's austerity drive has discouraged consumption of expensive wines and other luxuries in 2014, but that influence is likely to fade over time and

---

2   In 2010 96 percent of China's winegrape area was planted to red varieties, and the country of origin of 97 percent of the varieties is France (Anderson 2013).

Figure 4.1   Per capita and total consumption of grape wine in Asia, 2000–2012[a]

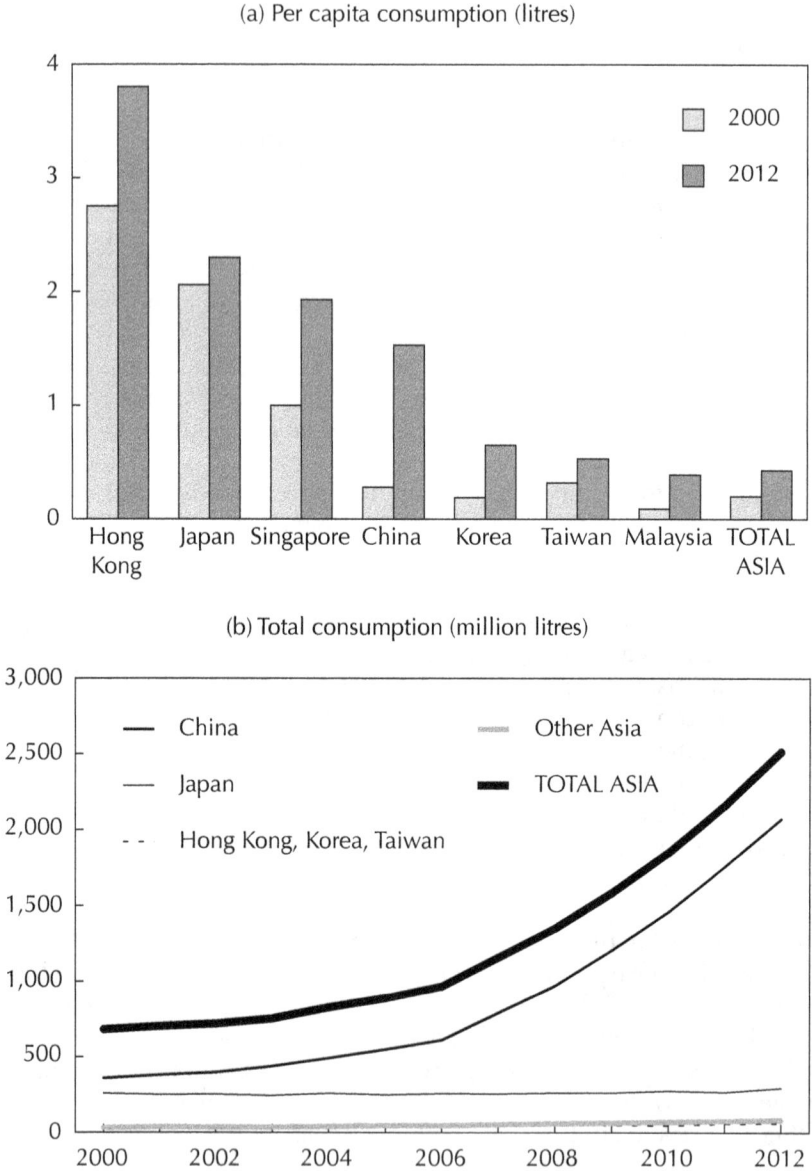

(a) Per capita consumption (litres)

(b) Total consumption (million litres)

a   All other Asian countries consume less than 0.2 litres per capita per year.
Source: Anderson and Nelgen (2011), updated using Euromonitor International.

Figure 4.2   Share of wine in total alcohol consumption in Asia, 2000 and 2009 (%)[a]

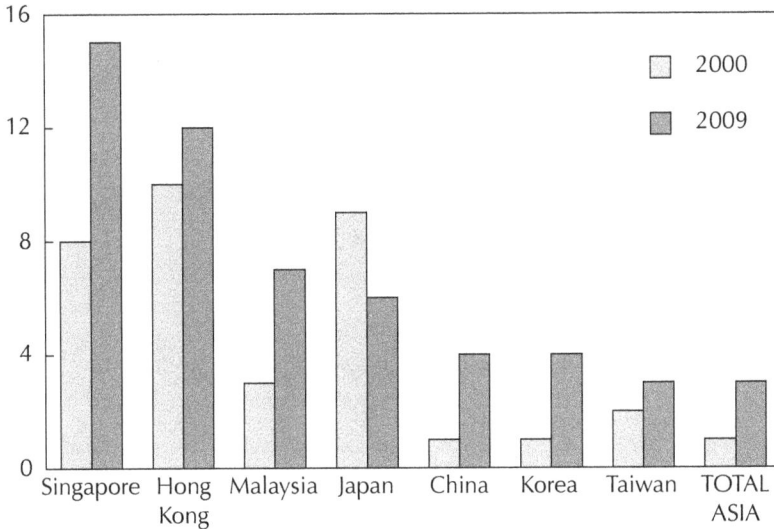

a   For all other Asian countries, the share of wine in total alcohol consumption is less than 3%.
Source: Anderson and Nelgen (2011).

it impacts much less on lower-quality wines, which are by far the most voluminous (Table 4.1).

No Asian country has yet produced grape wine for export in notice-able quantities. As for import dependence, it varied in 2009 from 15 per-cent in China (up from 8 percent in 2000–2005) to 68 percent in Japan, 96 percent in Korea, and 100 percent for all other Asian countries (Anderson and Nelgen 2011, Table 54). Thus China's share of Asian wine imports is much less than its share of consumption, especially when expressed in value terms because the unit value of China's imports in 2009 was only half the Asian average. Even so, China, together with Hong Kong which re-exports at least one-fifth of its wine imports to China, dominate Asia's aggregate wine imports (Figure 4.3).

One needs to be careful not to diminish the role that some other Asian countries play as significant importers of high-quality wine. As is seen in Figure 4.3, the shares of those countries in the value of world imports far exceed their volume shares, reflecting the fact that the average price of their imports is well above that of most other countries. For small pro-ducers of super-premium wines, especially in nearby Australia, they are important and profitable markets.

Table 4.1   *China's wine production, consumption and trade by quality category, 2009*

	Production (million litres)	Imports (million litres)	Consumption (million litres)	Self-sufficiency (%)
Non-premium	600	80	680	88
Commercial-premium	344	86	430	80
Super-premium	18	7	25	72
Total	**962**	**173**	**1,135**	**85**

Source: Anderson and Nelgen (2011, Section VI).

Figure 4.3   *Share in the volume and value of global wine imports, developing Asia, 2009 (%)*[a]

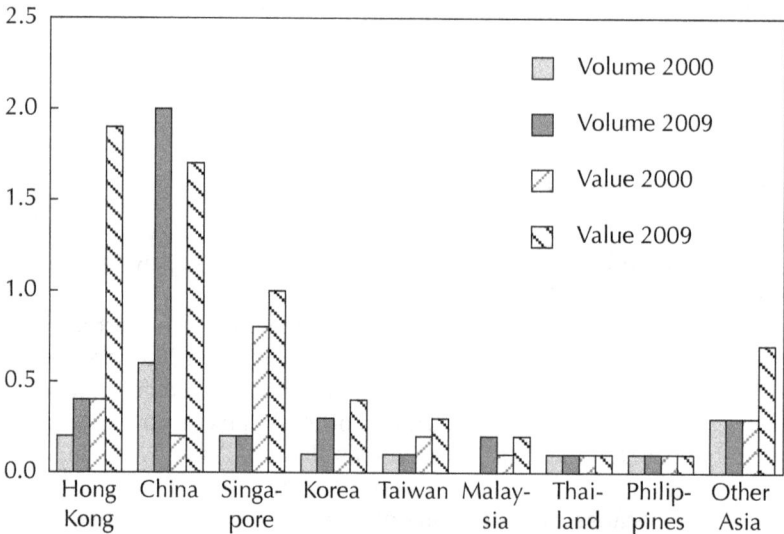

a   The volume (value) shares of Japan are 5.8% (5.3%) in 2000 and 3.9% (2.1%) in 2009.
Source: Anderson and Nelgen (2011).

Needless to say, Asian wine imports would be considerably larger if import tariffs and excise taxes on wine were less. In numerous Asian countries wine imports exceed those for beer and spirits on a per litre of alcohol basis (Table 4.2). The decision by Hong Kong to eliminate its tariff on wine imports in early 2008 is partly why its imports in Figure 4.3 are so much higher by the end the previous decade than they were at the beginning of that decade.

Table 4.2   Ad valorem consumer tax equivalent[a] of excise plus import taxes on alcoholic beverages, 2008 (%)

	Non-premium wine (A$2.50/litre)	Commercial-premium wine (A$7.50/litre)	Super-premium wine (A$20/litre)	Beer (A$2/litre)	Spirits (A$15/litre)
Japan	32	11	4	0	12
Hong Kong	0	0	0	0	100
India	165	155	152	100	151
Korea	46	46	46	124	114
Philippines	22	12	9	10	35
Taiwan	23	14	12	2	23
Thailand	232	117	81	51	52

a   At the prices shown in the column headings (expressed in Australian dollars).
Source: Anderson (2010).

Even without any reforms of those taxes, consumption and imports of wine in Asia are destined to rise over the years to come. How much they might rise, and how much domestic wine production might expand to satisfy at least some of that demand increase, is not easy to predict. A recent study nonetheless has focused on projecting the world's wine markets over the next five years. The next section reports on its findings as they relate to Asia.

4.3   MODELLING THE WORLD'S WINE MARKETS TO 2018

Anderson and Wittwer (2013) have revised and updated a model of the world's wine markets that was first published by Wittwer, Berger, and Anderson (2003). In it, wine markets are disaggregated into non-premium (including bulk), commercial-premium, and super-premium wines.[3] Two types of grapes are specified: premium and non-premium. Non-premium wine uses non-premium grapes exclusively, super-premium wines use premium grapes exclusively, and commercial-premium wines use both types of grapes. The world is divided into 44 individual nations and seven composite regions.

---

3 Commercial-premium wines are defined by Anderson and Nelgen (2011) to be those between US$2.50 and US$7.50 per litre pre-tax at a country's border or wholesale.

The model's database is calibrated initially to 2009, based on the comprehensive volume and value data and trade and excise tax data provided in Anderson and Nelgen (2011, Sections V, VI and VII). It is projected forward in two steps. The first step involves using actual aggregate national consumption and population growth between 2009 and 2011 (the most recent year for which data were available for all countries when the study began), together with changes in real exchange rates (RERs). The second step assumes aggregate national consumption and population grow from 2011 to 2018 at the rates shown in Appendix Table A4.1, and that RERs over that period either (a) remain at their 2011 levels or (b) return half-way to their 2009 rates (except for China, whose RER is assumed to continue to slightly appreciate, by 2 percent per year between 2011 and 2018). In each of those steps, a number of additional assumptions are made regarding preferences, technologies, and capital stocks.

Concerning preferences, there is assumed to be a considerable swing towards all wine types in China as more Chinese earn middle-class incomes. Since aggregate wine consumption is projected by the major commodity forecasters to rise by 70 percent rise over that seven-year period, the increase in China's consumption is calibrated to that in the more-likely scenario in which exchange rates revert halfway back from 2011 to 2009 rates. That implies a rise in per capita consumption from 1.0–1.6 litres per year. This may be too conservative. Per capita wine consumption grew faster than that in several Western European wine-importing countries in recent decades, and Vinexpo claims China's 2012 consumption was already 1.4 litres per year Braithwaite (http://asiapacific.vinexpo.com/en/). With the number of middle class in China currently around 250 million and growing at 10 million per year (Kharas 2010; Barton, Chen, and Jin 2013), and with grape wine still accounting for less than 4 percent of alcohol consumption by China's 1.1 billion adults, large increases in volumes of wine demanded are not unreasonable to expect. However, if China's income growth grows slower than the rate assumed in the base case, and if that means China's RER does not continue to appreciate slightly, wine import growth would be slower. For the rest of the world, the long-trend preference swing away from non-premium wines is assumed to continue now that recession in the North Atlantic economies has bottomed out.

Both grape and wine industry total factor productivity is assumed to grow at 1 percent per year everywhere, while grape and wine industry capital is assumed to grow net of depreciation at 1.5 percent per year in China, but zero elsewhere. This means that China's production rises by about one-sixth, one-quarter, and one-third for non-premium, commercial-premium, and super-premium wines between 2011 and 2018, which in aggregate is less than half that needed to keep up with the modelled growth in China's consumption. Of course if China's wine production from domestic grapes were to grow faster than the rate assumed in the base scenario, wine imports would increase less.

Given the uncertainty associated with several dimensions of developments in China's wine markets, the more likely of our two main scenarios to 2018 (in which RERs for all but China revert half-way back from 2011 to 2009 rates, called Alternative 1) is compared with a third scenario (called Alternative 2) in which three dimensions are altered. China's aggregate expenditure growth during 2011–18 is reduced by one-quarter (from 7.5 percent to 5.6 percent per year),[4] its RER does not change from 2011 instead of appreciating at 2 percent per year over that period, and its grape and wine industry capital is assumed to grow at 3 percent instead of 1.5 percent per year. Each of those three changes ensures a smaller increase in China's wine imports by 2018 in this Alternative 2 scenario. However, this scenario should be considered a lower-bound projection because, even if China's growth in GDP, industrialisation, and infrastructure spending were to slow down more than assumed in the Base and Alternative 1 scenarios, and less conspicuous extravagance and iconic gift-giving by business and government continued through to 2018, Chinese households nonetheless are being encouraged to lower their extraordinarily high savings rates and consume more of their income. In addition, grape wine is encouraged as an alternative to the dominant alcoholic beverages of (barley-based) beer and (rice-based) spirits because of its perceived health benefits and because it does not undermine food security by diminishing food grain supplies.

This global model has supply and demand equations and hence quantities and prices for each of the grape and wine products and for a single composite of all other products in each country. Grapes are assumed to be not traded internationally, but other products are both exported and imported. Each market is assumed to have cleared before any shock, and to find a new market-clearing outcome following any exogenously introduced shock. All prices are expressed in real (2009) terms.

To project global wine markets forward, it is assumed that aggregate national consumption and population grow from 2011 to 2018 at the rates

---

4 According to one of China's most prominent economists and former Senior Vice-President of the World Bank, 'China can maintain an 8 percent annual GDP growth rate for many years to come ... China's per capita GDP in 2008 was 21 percent of per capita GDP in the United States. That is roughly the same gap that existed between the United States and Japan in 1951, Singapore in 1967, Taiwan in 1975, and South Korea in 1977 ... Japan's average annual growth rate soared to 9.2 percent over the subsequent 20 years, compared to 8.6 percent in Singapore, 8.3 percent in Taiwan, and 7.6 percent in South Korea.' (Lin 2013).

Table 4.3   Projected change in volume of grape and wine output for China, 2011–2018 (%)

	Base	Alternative 1	Alternative 2
Non-premium wine	18	17	24
Commercial-premium wine	26	25	35
Super-premium wine	29	28	39
Premium grapes	20	20	31
Non-premium grapes	18	17	27

Source: Anderson and Wittwer (2013).

shown in Appendix Table A4.1 and that preferences, technologies, and capital stocks continue to change as described above, plus that RERs over that period either remain at their 2011 levels (the Base scenario) or return half-way to their 2009 rates, except for China (Alternative 1 scenario). The latter RER changes began to happen in mid-2013, so the Alternative 1 scenario is more likely to be representative of the real world by 2018 than the Base scenario. Alternative 2 scenario presents a lower-bound projection of what might happen to Chinese wine import demand if China's economy slows by one-quarter, its RER ceases to appreciate, and simultaneously its domestic grape and wine production capital grows twice as fast.

Table 4.3 suggests China's production of grapes and wine would grow at similar rates in the first two scenarios: by one-sixth for non-premium wine and a bit over one-quarter for premium wines. In the third scenario those rises increase to one-quarter for non-premium wine and to more than one-third for premium wines.

The income, population, and preference changes together mean that Asian consumption volumes grow dramatically over the period to 2018 except in Japan where the increase is confined to super-premium wine (Table 4.4). For China, the increase in consumption is around two-thirds in the first two scenarios and a little less than one-half in the slower growth scenario, whereas for other emerging Asian countries they increase consumption only one-seventh or one-sixth over the period to 2018. Given the vast differences between Asian countries in their 2011 consumption levels, China dominated the volume growth globally while Western Europe sees a decline in its consumption, which somewhat dampens global consumption growth (Figure 4.4). The fall in Europe is mainly due to the hefty weight in its consumption of the declining non-premium wine subsector.

Table 4.4   Projected change in volume of wine consumed in Asia, 2011–2018 (%)

	China	Japan	Other Asia
Base scenario (assuming no RER changes from 2011)			
Non-premium wines	29	–14	0
Commercial-premium wines	87	–3	10
Super-premium wines	87	9	27
All wines	**62**	**–1**	**17**
Alternative 1 (assuming RERs return half-way from 2011 to 2009 rates)			
Non-premium wines	31	–14	–1
Commercial-premium wines	95	–4	9
Super-premium wines	100	9	24
All wines	**70**	**–2**	**14**
Alternative 2 (assuming also slower Chinese import growth)			
Non-premium wines	26	–14	–1
Commercial-premium wines	73	–3	10
Super-premium wines	69	9	25
All wines	**46**	**–1**	**14**

Source: Anderson and Wittwer (2013).

When combined with the changes projected in production, it is possible to get a picture of what is projected to happen to wine trade. Table 4.5 provides projections for the main wine-trading regions. In terms of volumes, world trade expands 6 percent by 2018 in the Base scenario, and 7 percent in the Alternative 1 scenario in which RERs change. Virtually all of that increase in those two scenarios is due to China's import growth. In the Alternative 2 scenario, in which China imports less, global trade also expands less (by only 4 percent). In terms of the real value of global trade, however, the upgrading of demand elsewhere means that China accounts for smaller fractions of the growth in the global import value, namely 36 percent, 43 percent, and 30 percent in the Base, Alternative 1, and Alternative 2 scenarios respectively. In all three scenarios, China dominates Asian import growth, and the value of global wine trade rises by about one-sixth (last row of Table 4.5).

Figure 4.4   Projected change in consumption of all wines, 2011–2018 (million litres)

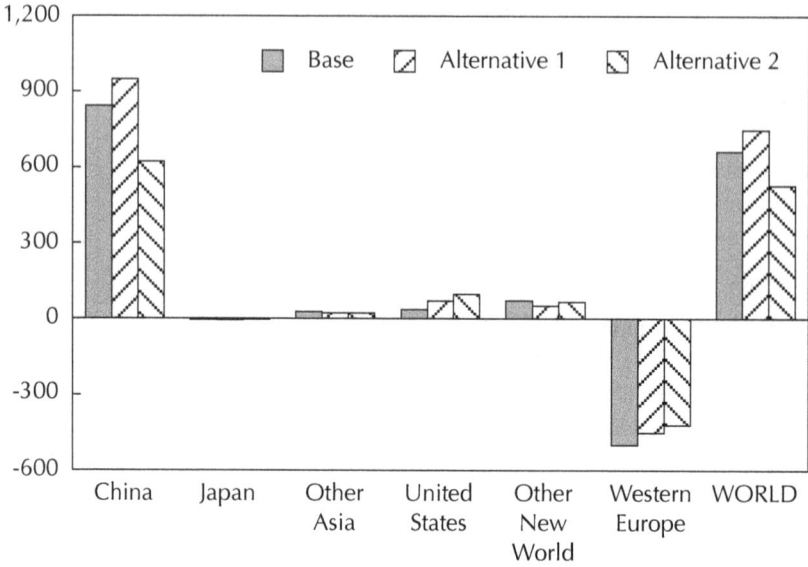

Source: Anderson and Wittwer (2013).

It is not surprising that China is such a dominant force in these projections, given the dramatic growth in its wine consumption over the past dozen years (Figure 4.1); the expectation of continued high growth in its income over the next five years (albeit somewhat slower than in the past five years); and the assumption that China's wine grape production growth cannot keep pace with domestic demand growth. As a result, China's share of consumption supplied domestically falls from its 2009 level of 85 percent to 57 percent, 54 percent and 67 percent in 2018 the Base, Alternative 1, and Alternative 2 scenarios for 2018 respectively.

France is projected to become even more dominant in imports by China in the Base scenario where exchange rates remain at 2011 levels. However, in the more-likely Alternative 1 scenario with a part-reversal of recent exchange rate movements, the increase in China's imports from Australia is almost the same as that of France in value terms, and they lose equally if China's import growth slows further as in the Alternative 2 scenario. In volume terms, Chile enjoys the greatest increase in sales to China in the two alternative scenarios. The impacts of these changes on the shares of different exporters in sales to China are summarised in Figure 4.5. In the Base scenario, France increases the dominance it had in 2009, in the Alternative 1 scenario Australia almost catches France, and

Table 4.5   *Projected change in global wine import and export volume and value, 2011–2018*

	Volume (million litres)			Value (US$ million)		
	Base	Alt. 1	Alt. 2	Base	Alt. 1	Alt. 2
Imports						
United Kingdom	−54	−36	−29	98	174	93
North America	−23	11	37	961	1,097	1,015
Other Europe	−122	−162	−140	1,012	646	552
China	627	739	334	1,948	2,305	1,178
Japan	−10	−13	−10	262	235	230
Other Asia	30	27	26	615	553	539
Other developing	152	133	141	498	311	318
World	**600**	**696**	**359**	**5,394**	**5,321**	**3,925**
Exports						
Australia	0	90	59	336	933	675
Other New World	78	219	75	469	954	597
Old World	538	412	263	4,370	3,489	2,653
World	**600**	**698**	**359**	**5,394**	**5,321**	**3,925**
	(6%)	(7%)	(4%)	(17%)	(17%)	(15%)

Source: Authors' model results.

in the Alternative 2 scenario Australia slightly overtakes France. Meanwhile, all other exporters' shares remain less than half those of Australia and France.

Projected bilateral trade changes more generally are summarised in Table 4.6 for the most-likely Alternative 1 scenario. All major wine-producing regions benefit from China's burgeoning demands. In volume terms, this demand is slightly at the expense of growth in their exports to other regions, although not in value terms because of the modelled upgrading of quality in those other markets. For Australia and other Southern Hemisphere exporters, projected growth in real export values in local currency terms is even larger than in the US$ terms shown in Table 4.6 due to the modelled real depreciation of the currencies of this group. For example, Australia's export value growth of US$933 million converts to an Australian dollar increase of A$1360 million. Australia's projected volume growth in this scenario is an extra 21ML of wine per

Figure 4.5   Share of China's wine import value by source, 2009 and projected 2018 (%)

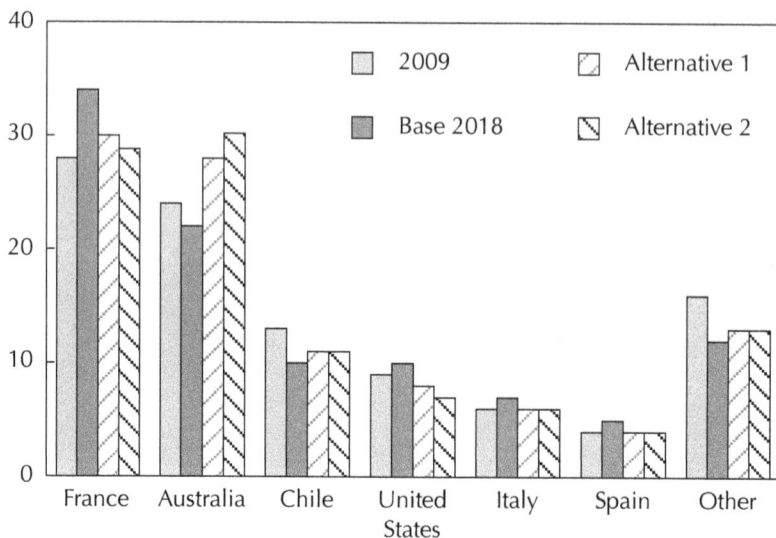

Source: Anderson and Wittwer (2013).

year being exported to China during 2011 to 2018. That should be manageable, as it is the same rate of increase in Australia's sales to the United States during the first decade of this century.

4.4   SUMMARY AND IMPLICATIONS

China has already become by far the most important wine-consuming country in Asia, and the above projections point to the enormous speed with which China may become an even more dominant market for wine exporters, with a projected extra 620–940 ML to be added by 2018 to its consumption of 1,630 ML in 2011. Since China's domestic production is projected to increase by 'only' about 210–290 ML by 2018, its net imports are projected to rise by between 330 and 740 ML.

While the recent and projected rates of increase in per capita wine consumption in China are no faster than what occurred in several northwestern European countries in earlier decades, it is the sheer size of China's adult population of 1.1 billion — and the fact that grape wine still accounts for less than 4 percent of Chinese alcohol consumption — that makes this import growth opportunity unprecedented. It would be somewhat less if China's own wine grape production increases faster,

Table 4.6   Change in export volume and value of wine-exporting
countries under Alternative 1 scenario, 2011–2018

	Exporter				
	Australia	Other Southern Hemisphere	United States	Western Europe	Other
Volume of imports (million litres)					
United Kingdom	−25	−10	−8	7	−1
United States	−14	−4	0	32	0
Canada	−4	−3	−4	8	0
New Zealand	−2	0	0	0	0
Germany	−3	−13	−4	−44	−12
Other Western Europe[a]	−9	−17	−4	−6	−7
China	147	242	53	266	31
Japan	−1	−3	−3	−5	−1
Other Asia	1	3	3	21	−1
Other countries	0	5	−8	112	−17
Total world	**90**	**200**	**25**	**391**	**−8**
Value of imports (US$ million)					
United Kingdom	42	60	−27	107	−8
United States	115	167	0	542	17
Canada	33	46	−9	187	−2
New Zealand	9	0	0	4	−2
Germany	0	−4	−10	−65	−15
Other Western Europe[a]	27	30	−13	643	−43
China	649	356	191	948	161
Japan	4	9	−4	201	21
Other Asia	50	53	16	427	11
Other countries	4	81	−19	414	−84
Total world	**933**	**798**	**125**	**3408**	**56**

a   Other Western Europe = Belgium, Denmark, Finland, Ireland, the Netherlands, Sweden and Switzerland.

Source: Authors' model results.

as in the Alternative 2 scenario, but certainly in as short a period as the next five years that is unlikely to be able to reduce the growth in China's wine imports very much, especially at the super-premium end of the spectrum.

Of course these projections are not predictions. Where exchange rates move, and how fast various countries' wine producers take advantage of the projected market growth opportunities in Asia will be key determinants of the actual changes in market shares over the coming years. Not all segments of the industry are projected to benefit, with non-premium producers facing falling prices if demand for their product continues to dwindle as projected in the scenarios examined. But those exporting firms willing to invest sufficiently in building relationships with their Chinese importer/distributor—or in grape growing or winemaking as joint venturers within China—may well enjoy long-term benefits from such investments, just as others have been doing and will continue to do for so many other products besides wine.

Meanwhile, the super-premium wine market in several other emerging Asian economies will remain an important and growing area of profitable sales for exporters such as Australia. The three largest Islamic countries in Asia—Bangladesh, Indonesia, and Pakistan—by contrast, are far more remote possibilities. India potentially could be more important sooner, but trade restrictions and high taxes have to date confined the rapid growth in sales (but from a very low base) to domestic firms.

Table A4.1   Aggregate consumption and population growth, 2011–18 (%)[a]

	Aggregate consumption	Population growth		Aggregate consumption	Population growth
France	10.0	0.7	Australia	17.8	7.3
Italy	10.0	0.7	New Zealand	15.4	5.9
Portugal	10.0	0.7	Canada	14.2	5.6
Spain	10.0	0.7	US	15.5	5.2
Austria	10.0	0.7	Algeria	30.0	4.9
Belgium	10.0	0.7	Brazil	27.3	3.8
Denmark	10.0	0.7	Chile	23.4	5.0
Finland	10.0	0.7	Mexico	22.0	4.6
Germany	10.0	0.7	Uruguay	25.6	7.3
Greece	10.0	0.7	Other Latin America	25.6	7.3
Ireland	10.0	0.7	South Africa	23.1	3.0
Netherlands	10.0	0.7	Turkey	31.8	9.1
Sweden	10.0	0.7	North Africa	31.8	9.1
Switzerland	10.0	0.7	Other Africa	55.8	15.1
UK	10.0	0.7	Middle East	31.8	9.1
Other Western Europe	10.0	0.7	China	69.0	2.7
Bulgaria	23.1	1.9	Hong Kong	23.7	4.7
Croatia	23.1	1.9	India	63.1	7.0
Georgia	23.1	1.9	Japan	7.1	−1.3
Hungary	23.1	1.9	Korea	22.0	0.7
Moldavia	23.1	1.9	Malaysia	34.4	8.2
Romania	23.1	1.9	Philippines	34.4	9.8
Russia	20.6	−1.7	Singapore	18.6	5.6
Ukraine	23.1	1.9	Taiwan	34.6	2.3
Other Central Europe	23.1	1.9	Thailand	36.0	2.6
			Other Asia-Pacific	32.2	11.2

a   Average annual growth rates.
Source: Projections from global economy-wide modelling by Anderson and Strutt (2012).

PART 2

Development

5 Economic relations between China, India and Southeast Asia: coping with threats and opportunities

Anne Booth

5.1 INTRODUCTION

This chapter examines how economic links between the ASEAN countries and the two Asian giants, China and India, have changed over the past two decades. The first section summarises the literature on the rise of China and India, and the implications of this rise for the global economy. This section also examines the literature on the threats posed by China to both ASEAN and other parts of the developing world, and the implications for ASEAN of the growth of 'Factory Asia'. The second section examines the statistical evidence on patterns of ASEAN merchandise trade, investment flows, and migration between ASEAN and other parts of Asia. The third section of the chapter discusses the implications of the free trade agreement between ASEAN and China and ASEAN and India for patterns of trade and investment across Asia. The main conclusion of the paper is that the ASEAN countries have benefited from increased economic links with China and to a lesser extent India. But economic links within ASEAN and between ASEAN and other OECD countries remain very important. The free trade agreements between ASEAN and both India and China became fully operational in 2010; in neither case do they appear to have led to a dramatic increase in bilateral trade or investment flows.

*Table 5.1   Real per capita GDP (PPP-adjusted $ 2005 prices) for the
ASEAN countries and China, 1996, 2004 and 2010[a]*

Country	1996	2004	2010
Singapore	32,746	39,879	55,839
Brunei	53,905	50,713	44,543
Malaysia	9,063	10,173	11,962
Thailand	6,256	6,734	8,066
China (2)	**2,631**	**4,458**	**7,746**
China (1)	**2,102**	**3,915**	**7,130**
Indonesia	3,052	3,079	3,966
India	**1,639**	**2,317**	**3,477**
Philippines	2,431	2,715	3,194
Vietnam	1,288	1,912	2,779
Laos	1,235	1,605	2,620
Cambodia	830	1,338	1,890

a   The Penn World Tables do not give data for Myanmar. Data refer to real GDP (PPP adjusted) in 2005 prices, derived from the growth rates of consumption, government and investment expenditures. Two different series are given for China.

Source: Heston, Summers and Aten (2012).

5.2   THE RISE OF CHINA AND INDIA AND THE 'THREAT' TO SOUTHEAST ASIA

The Asian crisis and its aftermath

In 1996, the ASEAN-6 all had per capita GDP above both China and India, with the possible exception of the Philippines (Table 5.1).[1] Four of these six countries had achieved more than three decades of sustained economic growth, and were selected for inclusion in the World Bank's 1993 'Asian Miracle' report (Singapore, Malaysia, Thailand and Indonesia). The World Bank, and many other observers, argued that these countries had 'got their policies right' and should be taken as models by less successful economies in other parts of the developing world. The 1993 report, written in the aftermath of the violence in Tiananmen Square, did not include China as one of the Asian miracles, although there was

---

1   The Penn World Tables give two series for China. For further details see Heston, Summers, and Aten (2012).

some discussion of the 'growth spillover' from Hong Kong into southern China. At that time there was still doubt about the growth potential of Vietnam, Laos, Cambodia, and Myanmar given that their governments had not made unequivocal commitments to economic reform, and were still far from fully integrated into the regional and international economies. Although India had also embarked on economic reforms in the 1980s and early 1990s, its impact on longer-term growth was also still not certain.

Even in the latter part of 1996, when the financial press was already pointing to signs of trouble in some of the miracle economies, especially in Thailand, few expected that the economies in Southeast Asia would be in any way 'threatened' by either China or India.[2] The financial crisis that hit much of the region in the latter part of 1997 and the ensuing capital outflow triggered a growth collapse in 1998 in several countries. In 2001, there was a further growth slowdown, especially in Malaysia and Singapore, as a result of falling world demand for electronics exports. By contrast, the Chinese economy was, at least according to the official data, booming.[3] Growth was also accelerating in India and in Vietnam, Laos, and Cambodia. But in Thailand and Indonesia, the two economies that had experienced the most severe growth collapse in 1998, the pace of economic recovery was slow, and the pre-crisis level of per capita GDP was only regained in 2003 in Thailand and 2004 in Indonesia. Thereafter, economic growth accelerated in both countries, but by 2010 per capita GDP (in 2005 prices) in all the ASEAN economies with the exception of Singapore, Brunei, and Malaysia was near or below China. Per capita GDP in India had overtaken the Philippines and had narrowed the gap with Indonesia (Table 5.1).

The rise of China and its implications for ASEAN

In the early 2000s, a number of studies emerged that suggested that China's membership of the World Trade Organization (WTO) would pose both opportunities and threats to other economies, both in Asia and in other parts of the world. In the Asian context, there were several strands to this argument (Ianchovichina, Suthiwart-Narueput, and Zhao 2004, 22). The main opportunity was seen in terms of the rapidly growing Chinese economy, which would suck in imports from ASEAN countries

---

2 See *The Economist*, 24 August 1996 and *The Financial Times*, 5 December 1996.

3 In recent years several scholars have argued that the Chinese growth figures are overstated, and that the domestic impact of external shocks has not been fully reflected in the official figures. See Wu (2014) for a summary of the evidence.

and elsewhere. Chinese growth would also lead to increased Chinese investment into ASEAN, especially in those sectors producing natural resources for which demand in China was growing rapidly. A further opportunity was offered by China's rapidly developing capital goods industries, which could provide plant and equipment in sectors such as textiles, telecommunications, and power generation more cheaply than firms in Japan, Europe, or the US.

On the threat side, it was feared that Chinese exports of a range of labour-intensive manufactures (textiles, garments, footwear, toys, low-end electronics) would out-compete those from the ASEAN economies in the major OECD markets, and in the domestic ASEAN economies. When an ASEAN–China free trade agreement was first proposed by the then Chinese premier, Zhu Rongji, in November 2000, there were worries that Chinese imports would flood into the ASEAN economies, putting the local industries under further pressure. Many in the ASEAN economies worried that both these trends could lead to a sharp slow-down in growth in the manufacturing sectors. It was argued that, given 'the broad similarity in trade structures and the fundamentally competitive nature of Sino–ASEAN economic relations', it was more likely that China and ASEAN would compete, rather than complement one another (Wong and Chan 2003, 523).

In addition, as a result of China's abundant supplies of cheap labour, huge investments in infrastructure and improvements in the legal and regulatory environment, ASEAN countries were worried that foreign investment would flood into China at the expense of other parts of developing Asia. As per capita GDP grew and a large middle class emerged, it was also argued that more foreign investment in China would be oriented to the domestic market rather than to export production. But in either case, there were fears that investment flows to the ASEAN countries would be affected (Wong and Chan 2003, 517). Not just would new foreign direct investment (FDI) be increasingly directed to China rather than to the ASEAN economies, but large multi-nationals that had established export bases in Malaysia, Thailand, and Indonesia would be tempted to relocate to China to take advantage of lower production costs, better logistics, and the large domestic market.

In the early years of the 21st century, there seemed to be more evidence to support the pessimists who worried about threats from China, than the optimists who stressed the opportunities. Ianchovichina, Suthiwart-Narueput, and Zhao (2004, 36) argued that with the abolition of quotas in the global textile and garment trade, China would become a formidable competitor for other Asian exporters. Studies using computable general equilibrium (CGE) models or other quantitative techniques showed that China would continue to take market share in a number of labour-intensive products from other developing countries, including those in ASEAN (Tongzon 2005, 194). Unsurprisingly, Tongzon found that the product categories where Chinese competition would be most fierce were textiles and garments, footwear, and some electrical products. In common with other analysts, Tongzon pointed out that the main source of China's competitive advantage was low unit labour costs; he also stressed that China's large and rapidly growing domestic market allowed firms to achieve economies of scale, which further lowered costs compared with many other developing countries.[4]

Tongzon acknowledged that the rapidly growing China market presented opportunities for exports from ASEAN into China. But he pointed out that, even after its entry into the WTO, there remained a range of non-tariff barriers in China, including inefficient customs administration and weak enforcement of rules and regulations governing imports at the regional level. Other studies published between 2004 and 2007 also found that labour-intensive export industries in the ASEAN countries, with the exception of Vietnam, would tend to contract while agricultural and resource-based exports would expand (Holst and Weiss 2004, 1273; Coxhead 2007, 1110). But some simulation studies also stressed that the rapid growth of China's foreign trade created benefits for many economies in terms of improved volume of trade and improved terms of trade. This was especially the case for agricultural, mineral, and other resource-based products (Yang 2006, 54).[5]

The rise of India

In spite of India's improved growth performance, there was little fear in the ASEAN countries that it posed a threat in the same way that China did. This position reflected the fact that while merchandise exports from India were growing as a result of reforms in trade policy over the 1990s, India was still a long way behind China in terms of the volume and value of exports. India's performance in increasing exports of services, including IT services, was impressive; by 2007 it was claimed that India was the tenth largest exporter of services in the world (Pal and Dasgupta 2008, 10). But these exports did not directly compete with exports from most parts of ASEAN, which remained a net importer of services in spite of growth

---

4 In fact the post-MFA period has seen several Asian countries, including Bangladesh and Cambodia, increase their garment exports by exploiting niche markets such as casual wear in the case of Cambodia.

5 Most of these studies depended on CGE models, and the results were, to a considerable extent dictated by the parameters chosen. For a critique of these models see Ravenhill (2010 1935).

Table 5.2   Top 10 trading partners of the ASEAN nations as a share of their merchandise exports and imports, 1996 and 2012 (%)

Country/ region	Exports		Imports	
	1996	2012	1996	2012
ASEAN	25.0	25.8	18.3	22.8
China	2.3	11.3	2.6	14.5
Japan	13.3	10.1	20.9	11.2
EU-28[a]	14.5	10.0	16.4	9.7
United States	18.4	8.6	15.1	7.5
Hong Kong	3.3	6.4	1.5	1.2
Korea	2.9	4.4	3.8	6.2
Australia	1.9	3.6	2.5	1.9
India	1.2	3.5	0.8	2.3
Taiwan	n.a	2.8	n.a	5.0
Other	17.2	13.5	18.1	17.8
Total	**100.0**	**100.0**	**100.0**	**100.0**

a   EU-15 in 1996.

Source: 1996: *ASEAN Statistical Yearbook 2001*, pp. 58–63. 2012: ASEAN Statistics, Table 20 (www.asean.org/images/resources/2014/Jan/StatisticUpdate, accessed 11 February 2014).

in sectors such as tourism, air transport, logistics, and financial services. Merchandise exports and imports between India and the ASEAN countries grew between 1996 and 2012 as a percentage of total ASEAN trade, but in 2012 India was still a minor trading partner compared with China, Japan, the European Union, and the United States (Table 5.2). Viewed from the Indian side, in 2012/13 the ASEAN countries accounted for 11 percent of Indian exports, compared with around 8 percent in 2002.

Crowding out or linking in? ASEAN and the rise of Factory Asia

The debates about the impact of the rise of China on the rest of Asia, and indeed on the rest of the developing world, took place in tandem with another discussion about the growth of 'Factory Asia', where 'billions of different parts and components from plants spread across a dozen nations' are assembled and dispatched to markets all over the world (Baldwin 2006a). By the early 21st century, trade in parts, components, and accessories (intermediate goods) had become the most dynamic part of international trade; in 2009 trade in intermediate goods accounted for more than half of non-fuel merchandise trade.[6] According to one analysis, trade in intermediate products encourages 'specialization of different economies, leading to a "trade in tasks" that adds value along the production chain' (WTO and IDE/JETRO 2011, 4). As early as 2001, parts and components accounted for as much as half of total trade in the Philippines, and a lower but still significant component in Malaysia, Thailand, and Vietnam (Haddad 2007, 11).

Some researchers have used the evidence on the growth of trade in intermediate goods to refute the argument that China's rise would 'crowd out' exports from other parts of Asia. It has also been argued that, to the extent that exports of textiles, footwear, and garments have been stagnating or even falling in recent years, it has happened mainly in the high-wage Asian economies as a result of their own changing comparative advantage (Haddad 2007, 21; Athukorala 2009, 260). Haddad argued that many of the products that have been negatively affected by competition from China have tended to be intermediate and high-technology products including electronics, communication equipment, and machinery. Producers of these products in countries such as Japan, South Korea, and Germany have thus been more affected by competition from China than the ASEAN countries. Other researchers have argued that, over the first decade of the 21st century, there had been a 'sustained shift from parts and components towards final goods' in the composition of China's imports from other parts of Asia. The implication is that China is 'becoming more of a consumer and less of an assembler' (Park and Shin 2010, 179–180).[7]

The rise of China, and the robust growth of the global economy as a whole until 2008, presented at least some of the ASEAN economies with a number of opportunities to integrate themselves into global production networks. These opportunities led to the rapid growth of plants, many Japanese-owned, producing vehicles and vehicle parts, and computer components in Thailand. In the Philippines, exports of electronic products increased rapidly, mainly as a result of investment by Japanese and American multinationals (Haltmaier et al. 2007, 32–35). Indonesia, in contrast to the Philippines, Thailand, Malaysia, and Singapore, has been criticised for 'not participating vigorously' in the new regional production networks that were evolving across East Asia and Southeast

---

6 The Factory Asia literature has tended to define trade within production networks as only covering parts and components. This definition excludes trade in assembled products that account for an increasing share of total trade in Asia.

7 This argument can be criticised on the grounds that China is still the final assembly location for many parts and components procured elsewhere in Asia and beyond, and that many of these final products are then exported.

Asia (Gill and Kharas 2007, 29; see also Aswicahyono, Narjoko, and Hill 2008, 18; Lipsey and Sjoholm 2011, 56–57). Although Indonesia's share of world manufactured exports increased between 1994/95 and 2006/07, its share of several categories was below those of Malaysia and Thailand (Athukorala and Hill 2010, Table 7).

The blame for Indonesia's supposedly poor performance has been placed on poor infrastructure and logistics and cumbersome customs procedures, as well as inadequate investment in education and skills training. Some Indonesian commentators have been blunter, and point out that corruption has become worse than under Suharto. On a range of economic, social and governance indicators, it has been argued that Indonesia has been falling behind not just China but also economies such as Vietnam and India, which in the early 1990s had been well behind Indonesia. But, in fact, in nominal dollar terms, Indonesian exports were growing strongly between 2003 and 2010. The main reason was the rapid growth in both volume and prices of exports of coal, LNG, palm oil, and rubber, reflecting Indonesia's continuing comparative advantage in these commodities. China has become an important market, but in 2012 only about 11 percent of Indonesia's exports were going to China. Other destinations included other ASEAN countries, South Asia, Japan, and the European Union. The Indonesian experience in the decade up to 2012 shows that export growth can be rapid, even in a country that has not been able to link into the Factory Asia networks.

The Indonesian experience can be contrasted with that of Thailand where exports of primary products accounted for around 40 percent of all Thai exports to China in 1995, but had dropped to just over 20 percent in 2012 (Lee 2013, 4). In recent years, manufactured goods have dominated Thai exports to China, and manufactures also account for most Chinese exports to Thailand. This trade in parts and components, as well as in final goods, also accounts for a growing share of Chinese trade with the Philippines, Malaysia, and Vietnam. But this trade is vulnerable to fluctuations in markets where the assembled goods are sold, and the main markets are still in North America and the EU. With the onset of the global economic crisis in 2008, trade between China and Thailand contracted, reflecting the sharp fall in demand in the leading OECD economies.

Asian drivers of global trade?

Recent work by Kaplinsky has discussed the impact of the 'Asian drivers' on the economies of the developing world. This work examines the impact of China and India on global trade and investment flows; in one paper, Kaplinsky and Messner (2008, 197) claim that the global economy 'is undergoing a profound and momentous shift' because of the rise of

China and India, which has caused a 'critical disruption to the global economic and political order'. Kaplinsky and Messner (2008) discuss a number of factors that are pushing both countries into global dominance, including their size, their relatively low wages, their large labour force, and their hunger for a range of resource-based products, which China and India are increasingly dependent on world markets to supply. They also emphasise that in both countries the state plays an important role in the allocation of resources between sectors of the economy. Kaplinsky and Messner (2008) acknowledge that these two countries have pursued different development strategies: China has integrated rapidly into regional and global production networks, while India has adopted 'stand alone' strategies. But both economies are now in a position to play a greater role in global economic and political governance, commensurate with their growing power.

Critics point out that some of the claims of this literature are exaggerated. While the growing influence of China in world trade is obvious, to what extent can it be claimed that China is now 'driving' the economic development of the ASEAN countries? Economic historians can point out that there have been several momentous shifts in trade patterns in most Asian countries over the twentieth century, both before and after independence. For example, the rise of Japan as an important trading power in the early decades of the twentieth century had important implications for many Asian colonies, whether British, French, or Dutch. After independence, the role of the colonial powers declined and the role of the United States and Japan increased. The next section of the paper will argue that the recent statistical evidence does not support the view that, in the ASEAN context, China and India are poised to supplant the more mature economic powers either as trading partners or as sources of investment and technology.

5.3   ASEAN TRADE, INVESTMENT, AND MIGRATION LINKS WITH OTHER ASIAN COUNTRIES

Merchandise trade patterns

How has ASEAN merchandise trade evolved from the mid-1990s to 2012? In 1996, total ASEAN merchandise exports and imports amounted to almost US$674 billion. The severe economic crisis of 1997/98 caused a fall in merchandise exports from and imports into the main ASEAN economies, but by 2000 the total value of exports and imports had regained the 1997 level (ASEAN 2010a, 58–63). Between 2003 and 2008, export and import growth was rapid; in 2008 the total value of imports and exports was US$1.9 trillion, which was close to three times the 1997 level. The

Table 5.3   Share of total ASEAN trade within ASEAN and with China,
2002–2012 (%)

Year	Intra-ASEAN	China
2002	22.2	6.0
2003	25.1	7.2
2004	24.3	8.3
2005	24.9	9.3
2006	25.1	10.0
2007	25.0	10.6
2008	24.8	10.4
2009	24.5	11.6
2010	25.4	11.3
2011	25.0	11.7
2012	24.3	12.9

Source: As for Table 5.2.

global recession caused a fall in 2009, in 2010 there was a sharp recovery, and by 2012 the total value of exports and imports from the ASEAN-10 was over US$2.47 trillion.

The rapid growth in the total value of ASEAN merchandise trade since the mid-1990s can be ascribed to several causes. First, the total value of world trade was growing rapidly over these years, at least partly as a result of China's growing participation in the global economy.[8] Second, the ASEAN countries' trade with China grew rapidly, both in absolute terms and as a percentage of their total trade. In 1996, exports to China accounted for only about 2.3 percent of total exports from ASEAN countries. By 2012, this percentage had jumped to 11.3 percent. China's share of total imports into ASEAN increased from 2.6 percent to 14.5 percent over this sixteen-year period (Table 5.2). Third, intra-ASEAN trade was also growing; in 1996 about 21.5 percent of the total trade of the ASEAN countries took place within ASEAN and by 2002 this had increased to 22.2 percent. Since 2005, the ASEAN share has been fairly stable at around 25 percent (Table 5.3). The rise in China's share of ASEAN's import and

---

8   According to the Direction of Trade Statistics (DOTS), the value of world merchandise exports and imports grew from US$10.67 trillion to US$36.174 trillion over the fifteen years from 1996 to 2011. Even allowing for the impact of the 1997/98 crisis, growth in the value of ASEAN trade was slightly faster than this.

Table 5.4   Breakdown of increase in merchandise exports and imports to/from ASEAN, 2002–2012 (%)

Country	Exports	Imports
ASEAN	27.2	23.0
China	14.1	17.3
Japan	9.4	9.3
United States	5.3	5.4
European Union	7.9	8.5
Korea	4.5	6.9
India	4.1	2.7
Australia	4.2	1.9
Other	23.3	25.0
Total	**100.0**	**100.0**

Source: As for Table 5.2.

export trade was offset by a fall in the relative share of Japan, the EU, and the US, although, in absolute terms, ASEAN trade with all three of these countries continued to expand.

If we look at the percentage breakdown of the increase in ASEAN merchandise trade by value over the decade from 2002 to 2012, intra-ASEAN trade accounted for 27 percent of the increase in exports and 23 percent of the increase in imports (Table 5.4). China accounted for 14 percent of the increase in exports and 17 percent of the increase in imports. Intra-ASEAN trade was thus a more important factor in driving the growth in total ASEAN trade over this decade than was increased trade with China.[9] Japan accounted for around 9 percent of the growth in exports and imports over these years. Looking at the ASEAN figures as a whole, it is clear that growth in trade with China was an important factor in total growth of both exports and imports over this decade, but by no means the only cause. Trade with India accounted for only a small share of the growth in both merchandise exports and imports.

It is also important to note that there was, by 2012, substantial variation in the extent to which the ASEAN-10 countries were trading with

---

9 This is not to deny the importance of external factors in the growth of intra-ASEAN trade. To the extent that much intra-ASEAN trade is in parts and components, its continued growth will depend on demand for final products in other segments of the global economy.

Table 5.5   Share of merchandise trade taking place within ASEAN, 2012
(%)

Country	Exports	Imports	Total
Myanmar	36.5	44.9	40.7
Laos	44.1	33.3	37.9
Cambodia	13.3	37.0	27.6
Malaysia	26.8	28.0	27.3
Singapore	31.8	21.0	26.6
Indonesia	22.0	28.1	25.1
Philippines	18.9	22.9	21.1
Thailand	24.7	17.3	20.9
Brunei	13.2	43.6	19.8
Vietnam	15.2	18.4	16.8
ASEAN-10	**25.8**	**22.7**	**24.3**

Source: ASEAN Statistics, from ASEAN Secretariat (www.asean.org).

one another, with China, and with other parts of the world. Myanmar was conducting 40 percent of total trade with its ASEAN partners, and Laos 38 percent, while in Brunei and Vietnam the percentage was under twenty (Table 5.5). Laos is land-locked, so most of its export and import trade has to pass through neighbouring countries, while the sanctions imposed by most OECD countries meant that Myanmar has had to trade mainly with other parts of Asia. The percentage of trade with ASEAN partners in Myanmar will probably fall as sanctions are eased. All the larger ASEAN economies were conducting less than 30 percent of their trade with one another in 2012. The implications of this for an ASEAN single market are discussed further below.

Turning to ASEAN trade with China, the Direction of Trade (DOT) data for 2012 show that the various countries of Southeast Asia have reacted to the challenges posed by the rise of China in very different ways. Countries such as Myanmar, Cambodia, and Vietnam were sending only a relatively small proportion of their total exports to China because their main exports (labour-intensive manufactures, rice, and other agricultural products) compete with those from China. But on the import side, China was a more important source for both Myanmar and Vietnam (Table 5.6). Brunei, entirely an exporter of oil and gas, sent only a small proportion of its exports to China, probably because it is locked into long-term contracts with other countries outside developing Asia, although it sourced

Table 5.6 Share of total exports and imports from ASEAN countries going to/sourced from China and Developing Asia, 2012 (%)[a]

Country	Exports to:		Imports from:	
	China	Developing Asia	China	Developing Asia
Myanmar	13.3	69.8	36.9	68.8
Cambodia	2.5	12.9	19.5	71.7
Laos	21.5	71.7	16.2	86.7
Vietnam	11.2	26.3	25.8	40.3
Philippines	10.8	28.0	11.8	22.2
Indonesia	11.4	32.1	15.3	32.1
Thailand	11.7	34.9	14.8	29.7
Malaysia	12.6	31.5	15.1	32.0
Brunei	2.7	20.6	21.3	39.4
Singapore	10.7	47.7	10.3	35.1

a   Countries are ranked by per capita GDP from lowest to highest. The DOTS totals are used for exports and imports from individual countries, rather than the IFS totals, where the two diverge. Developing Asia includes all Asian countries except Japan, Taiwan, Korea, Singapore and Hong Kong.

Source: International Monetary Fund, *Direction of Trade Yearbook 2013.*

around 20 percent of its total imports from China. Singapore, Indonesia, Thailand, Malaysia, and the Philippines were sourcing 15 percent or less of exports and imports from China in 2012.

Who is running surpluses/deficits with whom?

A source of confusion in recent analyses of ASEAN–China trade is the issue of merchandise trade surpluses and deficits. It is well-known that China has run a large trade surplus with some parts of the world, including the US, and this has been a source of friction in the bilateral relations between the two countries. The ASEAN countries as a group have also run large trade surpluses with the rest of the world; in 2010 and 2011 these surpluses were around US$96 billion, according to the ASEAN Secretariat, although they fell to US$33.3 billion in 2012. But with China, the ASEAN Secretariat data show that the ASEAN-10 have consistently run trade deficits since the 1990s. In other words, ASEAN exports to China have been less than their imports from China, and the size of the trade deficit has been increasing over time. Over the five years from 2002 to 2006, the average size of the deficit between ASEAN countries and China, according to the ASEAN Secretariat data, was US$6.1 billion. By 2012 this had increased to US$35.7 billion.

But the Chinese figures on trade with the ASEAN countries have shown in recent years a rather different trend. The Chinese trade data, published in the *China Statistical Yearbook 2012*, show that in 2010 and 2011, China has been running a large trade deficit with the ASEAN countries; in other words, it is importing more from ASEAN than it is exporting.[10] According to the Chinese figures, the deficit amounted to US$29.4 billion in 2011, while the ASEAN Secretariat data show imports from China exceeding exports to China by some US$24.6 billion in that year. Why did the two sets of data show such a different result? The ASEAN figures are derived from national government sources so they could reflect problems in the trade data in at least some of the 10 member states. But the largest disparities are found for Singapore, Thailand, and Malaysia, all countries that have fairly reliable trade data.

Two explanations can be put forward to explain the differences. The first relates to the fact that a significant part of China's trade with the rest of the world, including some of the ASEAN countries, still goes through Hong Kong. For example, although the Thai data on exports from Thailand to China are much lower than the Chinese figures on imports from Thailand, when Thai exports to Hong Kong are added to Thai exports to China, the difference is much less and can be explained by transport and other costs. The Thai trade statistics use the first port of destination rather than final destination, while the Chinese import data use the port of origin rather than the port through which the goods are transshipped (usually Hong Kong). A second explanation that has been put forward recently is that the Chinese firms engaged in international trade have been deliberately mis-invoicing exports and imports in order to circumvent capital controls. According to this argument, two types of mis-invoicing have been used in China and in other countries using capital controls. One relates to export under-invoicing and the other to import over-invoicing.

According to one recent estimate, mis-invoiced trade between Chinese companies and the US rose from US$48.8 to US$59 billion between 2000 and 2011 (Kar and Freitas 2012). But these figures have been challenged by other studies that argue that many of the anomalies can be explained by the shipping of both imports and exports through Hong

---

10   Park and Shin (2010, Table 1), using data from a Hong Kong source, claim that China was running a trade deficit with ASEAN of over US$26 billion in 2007. The ASEAN data present a very different story; they show that ASEAN was running a deficit with China of US$15.2 billion.

Kong (Kessler and Borst 2013, 2). But these authors acknowledge that there does appear to be a problem with the Chinese import data where over-invoicing appears to have been used as a means of sending capital out of the country. It is thus possible that part of the difference between the ASEAN trade data and the Chinese data are the result of mis-invoicing, although the extent of the problem is difficult to determine.

The evidence on investment flows

The share of the main Southeast Asian economies in total capital inflows into ASEAN plus China and Hong Kong contracted sharply after 1998, and had not recovered by 2004 (Ravenhill 2006, 656). The contraction was especially severe in Indonesia where inflows were negative for most years between 1999 and 2003. Much of this fall was due to the impact of the Asian financial crisis and the ensuing political and economic instability, rather than to competition from China. After 2002, inflows of FDI into the ASEAN economies did begin to grow again, especially in Singapore, Malaysia, and Thailand (ASEAN 2010a, 106–107), although with the onset of the global financial crisis in 2008, there was a fall in flows to ASEAN as a whole.

The figures from 1997 to the early years of this century led some commentators to conclude that China was diverting flows from Southeast Asia, and that this trend was likely to continue. In fact, the years from 2004 saw an improvement in the growth performance of most ASEAN countries, and an acceleration of investment flows into ASEAN to the point where the six largest ASEAN economies (Indonesia, Malaysia, Singapore, Thailand, Vietnam, and the Philippines) have been attracting inflows not much below those going to China. In 2011 and 2012, investment flows into the Southeast Asian economies were estimated to be US$109 billion and US$111.3 billion compared with US$124 billion and US$121 billion flowing into China (UNCTAD 2013, 214). In per capita terms, and relative to GDP, the ASEAN economies attracted more inward FDI than China in these two years. Whether these trends will continue can be debated, but they do suggest claims that the ASEAN countries have been 'losing out' to China in FDI inflows are rather premature.

Considerable attention has also been given to capital outflows from China in recent years, both to ASEAN and to other parts of the world. In fact, the data compiled by the ASEAN Secretariat show that only a small part of the capital inflow into the ASEAN countries came from China between 2002 and 2009, around 2 percent, although the percentage was slightly higher for the CLMV countries (Cambodia, Lao PDR, Myanmar and Vietnam) (ASEAN 2010a, 116–117). In 2011, the ASEAN Secretariat reported that 6.7 percent of total FDI came from China, compared with more than 16 percent from within ASEAN itself. These figures might appear to contradict the estimates of Scissors (2011), which shows that cumulative, non-bond committed investment from China to Indonesia in the years from 2005 to 2010 amounted to US$9.8 billion. This made Indonesia the eighth largest recipient of Chinese non-bond investment over these years, after Australia, the US, Nigeria, Iran, Brazil, Kazakhstan, and Canada. But these data refer to commitments, not implemented investment projects. In terms of commitments, Indonesia received more investment than any other ASEAN country, including Singapore.[11] Most of these commitments were in the power, gas, energy, and steel sectors.[12] Inflows of foreign investment from India to Southeast Asia, while increasing in recent years, are still a small proportion of total flows. In 2009–2011, inflows of foreign investment accounted for only 0.8 percent of the total.

Less attention has been paid to Indian investment in the ASEAN countries, although in 2010 the ASEAN Secretariat figures showed that Indian investment was higher than that of China (US$3.4 billion compared with US$2.5 billion from China). Preliminary data for 2011 and 2012 show some drop in Indian flows into ASEAN. Several ASEAN countries have themselves become important exporters of capital in recent years, including Singapore, Malaysia, Thailand and Indonesia. In 2012, total outward investment from Southeast Asia was almost US$61 billion compared with US$84 billion in outward flows from China and US$8.6 billion from India (UNCTAD 2013, 214). In Malaysia, capital outflows have exceeded inflows for the period from 2007 to 2012; in Thailand outward flows exceeded inward flows in 2011 and 2012. Although

---

11 Chinese outward investment data are extremely difficult to interpret, given the fact that a high percentage goes to Hong Kong, the Cayman Islands and the British Virgin Islands. It is widely suspected that much of this investment goes back to China. For a discussion of the data see Schuler-Zhou and Schuller (2009). While some of the investment to Hong Kong, may end up in Southeast Asia, it has also been argued that in Vietnam and Cambodia, some investment registered as Chinese is in fact owned by companies in Taiwan, Hong Kong or Macao (see Kubny and Voss 2010). The estimates given by Scissors (2011) refer to commitments only; he stresses that the amount actually implemented could be much lower.

12 For a complete breakdown of all Chinese overseas investment deals between 2008 and 2010 see Salidjanova (2011, Appendix 1). More recent data are given in Scissors (2012), who claims that Chinese investment commitments to Indonesia up to mid-2012 amounted to US$23.3 billion, compared with only US$8.8 billion to Singapore. One assumes that much of this is not yet implemented.

Singapore has been the largest exporter of capital in ASEAN in recent years, it still manages to attract even larger inflows.[13]

Should the net outflows of capital from Malaysia and Thailand be seen as a sign of failure in that these economies are no longer providing profitable opportunities for investment at home for either domestic or foreign capital? Or is it a sign that Malaysian and Thai firms, together with those from Singapore and Indonesia, are becoming more outward looking and successful in investing abroad in profitable businesses? There is some truth in both these arguments, but the net outflows from Malaysia do seem to indicate that the Malaysian government should make further reforms to improve the investment climate, including opening up sectors of the economy, which until now have been dominated by local business groups linked to the United Malays National Organisation (UMNO). In Thailand, the net outflows in 2011 and 2012 are the result of the political instability. In China in recent years, the official government view is that increasing outward flows of capital are a sign of China's growing power in the world economy, but in fact they might also reflect a dearth of profitable investment opportunities at home.[14]

Flows of people between ASEAN countries and abroad

Over the past decade, much has been written about growing movements of labour from the developing countries of Asia, and the associated remittances. In 2010, India and China were receiving in excess of US$50 billion in remittances and the three largest labour-exporting countries in ASEAN (Philippines, Vietnam, and Indonesia) a further US$35 billion (Jha and McCawley 2011, 17). Although the evidence on destinations of migrant workers from and to East Asia and Southeast Asia is far from complete, most migrants head for the higher-income countries in their immediate vicinity, or to high-income countries where they have some historical or religious ties. Migrants from Myanmar go to Thailand, Indonesians go to Malaysia and to Saudi Arabia, Filippinos to Malaysia, Singapore, and Hong Kong, as well as to the US and the EU, and Vietnamese

---

13 One study has found that FDI inflows into Malaysia have been positively correlated with those into China, which suggests that there is complementarity rather than competition in FDI-led industrial development between the two countries (Athukorala and Wagle 2011, 126).

14 The official Chinese attitude to outward investment was well caught in a recent press article, proclaiming that China had in 2012 vaulted to the world's third largest investor. It was argued that the increasing outward investment testified to the growing competitiveness of Chinese industry. The article did not mention where the FDI flows were going.

to Taiwan, Korea, and also the US.[15] There are thought to be large numbers of migrants from both China and ASEAN in Japan but the data are not considered to be very accurate.

As far as can be ascertained from the published figures, there are not large numbers of Chinese or Indian citizens working in the ASEAN-6, except in Singapore. Countries such as Malaysia and Indonesia are hostile to in-migration from China or India, as they have been ever since independence. There are thought to be large numbers of Chinese in Myanmar, especially in Mandalay and northern towns, although the numbers are not easy to establish.[16] The flow of people from China to ASEAN, which has been growing in recent years and is easier to quantify, relates to tourism. In 2009, tourist arrivals to ASEAN reached a record 65.75 million people, of whom 4.1 million came from China. This made China the largest single source of tourists to ASEAN from outside the ASEAN region, overtaking Japan, Australia, and Korea (ASEAN 2010a, 146). Given that all the ASEAN countries have ambitions to increase their tourism sectors, it is likely that arrivals from China will continue to grow.[17]

5.4   FREE TRADE AGREEMENTS WITH CHINA AND INDIA, AND ASEAN 2015

The ASEAN–China Free Trade Agreement

Discussions about enhanced economic cooperation between China and ASEAN began in 2000, at the ASEAN–China summit in that year. It was decided to move towards a formal free trade area, incorporating six of the 10 ASEAN countries in 2010, with Vietnam, Laos, Cambodia, and Myanmar joining in 2015. The formal commencement of the ASEAN–China Free Trade Agreement (ACFTA) on 1 January 2010 was greeted with enthusiasm at the official level in China and in some multilateral bodies. The official Chinese view was that 'China and ASEAN enjoy geographic advantage in their economic cooperation, and their economies

---

15 A migrant stock matrix for 2010 shows that around 12.8 million people born in Southeast Asia were living outside their countries of birth. Around 3.96 million were in other parts of Southeast Asia while the rest were in North America, the Middle East, the EU, and Oceania (ADB 2012, 29).

16 Some sources quote figures of two million, but they are impossible to verify. The government now appears to be taking a harder line towards both migrants and investment from China, so many migrants may be repatriated.

17 In recent years, Malaysia has attracted the largest numbers of tourist arrivals in ASEAN: in 2009, 23.6 million tourists or 36 percent of the ASEAN total. But Myanmar had the fastest rate of growth between 2002 and 2009 (see ASEAN 2010a, 144).

are highly complementary to each other'. Senior officials in the Asian Development Bank were quoted as arguing that ACFTA was an important vehicle for trade-led recovery in the Asia–Pacific region. It was also pointed out that it presented an opportunity for the ASEAN countries to 'latch onto China's production networks' and sell to Chinese consumers (Macan-Markar 2010). The reaction in ASEAN was more muted, although the ASEAN Secretary-General stated that the free trade area 'will benefit both sides and help lift the world economy out of the crisis'.

In one sense, the official enthusiasm around a free trade area between China and the ASEAN-6 might seem rather odd, given that by 2010 all these countries were already WTO members and, as such, supposedly committed to non-discriminatory free trade. Most of the supporters of ACFTA have made little attempt to spell out exactly what the benefits would be, either to China or to the various ASEAN countries. Indeed, some commentators have suggested that the business communities in ASEAN and China played little role in creating ACFTA, which appeared to be driven largely by political factors (Ravenhill 2010). At the same time, voices were raised in the ASEAN region that were much less supportive of ACFTA. In the Philippines, fears were expressed that it would simply legalise the widespread smuggling of footwear, garments, shoes, and other manufactures and agricultural products, which has already placed considerable pressure on domestic producers (Bello 2010).[18] The Indonesian government, no doubt concerned about the domestic implications of ACFTA, formally lodged a letter on 14 January 2010 asking the ASEAN-10 nations to defer its implementation until January 2011, although this did not happen.

Part of the concern in both Indonesia and the Philippines resulted from a fear that there might be a repeat of the Thai experience of the so-called 'early harvest' experiment during the period when Thaksin was in power. This caused problems for Thai farmers when tariffs on around two hundred fruits and vegetables between Thailand and China were removed. The removal of tariffs resulted in a flood of products from China into Thailand, but Thai farmers found that exports of their products into China were still being subject to various tariff and non-tariff barriers. As tariffs were reduced or removed on a much broader range of agricultural and manufactured products, there was an expectation in several ASEAN countries that China would continue with what has been termed China's 'half-open' model. This implied that China would

---

18 In his contribution to Flick (2011), Mendoza claims that there was a large amount of 'smuggled or hoarded' low-cost Chinese goods in the Philippines, which were not included in the official trade data, which suggests that the Philippine trade surplus with China shown in the official data may be overstated.

flood the ASEAN countries with Chinese products sold at extremely low prices, while only taking in return those products, mainly unprocessed raw materials, which were needed for China's accelerated industrialisation. The fact that many Chinese producers had by early 2010 large unsold stocks of manufactures as a result of slowing world demand, adding to the concerns in ASEAN that these products would be dumped in Southeast Asia at below-cost prices.

While it is easy to dismiss some of these claims as attempts by high-cost local producers to claim protection against cheaper imports, whether from China or elsewhere, the problem of dumping cannot be dismissed out of hand. At the same time there were fears, especially in Indonesia, that their traded goods sectors were uncompetitive. An opinion piece in Indonesia's leading English-language newspaper, *The Jakarta Post*, published in October 2010, stated that 'most people are of the opinion that Indonesia's agricultural products and manufacturing goods are extremely uncompetitive against China's' (27 October 2010). It went on to argue that instead of seeing ACFTA as an instrument to strengthen the interdependence of the ASEAN region with China, many Indonesians see it as leading to 'cutthroat competition that will have negative impacts on the development of Indonesian economic capabilities in the long term'. Other commentators viewed Chinese policies as essentially neo-colonial; in its hunger for raw materials, China is in effect seeking to re-impose colonial patters of trade on Southeast Asia.

These views appeared to reflect widely held beliefs in Indonesian business, media, and political circles, as well as in other ASEAN nations. But how realistic are they? The evidence on the growth in Indonesia's merchandise exports since 2002 indicates that, in fact, Indonesia's traded-goods sectors still can compete in international markets, while in other parts of ASEAN there has been robust growth in a range of export activities from parts and components to tourism. It has already been pointed out that much of the increase in Thai exports to China since the late 1990s has been in parts and components, rather than in primary products. What does seem clear is that China's growing export power has forced Indonesia, and other ASEAN countries as well, to re-evaluate their longer-term comparative advantage, away from labour-intensive manufactures and towards a range of primary exports, including coal and natural gas, as well as towards more sophisticated manufactures and traded services.[19]

---

19 More evidence on the growth of China-Indonesia trade is given in Booth (2011). By 2009, exports from Indonesia were dominated by mineral fuels, coal, and vegetable oils, while imports from China were dominated by manufactures and machinery.

The ASEAN–India Free Trade Agreement

The ASEAN–India Free Trade Agreement was signed in 2009, and became operational in 2010. This agreement appears to have attracted much less attention within ASEAN than ACFTA, although there have been several appraisals of the agreement by Indian researchers. The initial focus of the free trade agreement was on tariff liberalisation: all parties to the agreement pledged to reduce tariff rates on a large number of tariff lines and non-tariff barriers were also to be eliminated. Tariff lines were divided into four broad heads, with provision for a sensitive list where tariffs would be lowered to five percent, and an exclusion list (Pal and Dasgupta 2009, 11–12). These authors stressed that, given the large trade deficit India has been running with the ASEAN bloc since the late 1990s (over US$6 billion in 2007), there were concerns within India that the ASEAN countries would benefit more than India. The authors also pointed out that India already had trade agreements with Singapore and Thailand, and with Myanmar through the Bay of Bengal initiative. The ASEAN–India Free Trade Agreement thus boiled down to improved market access to Indonesia, Malaysia, the Philippines, and Vietnam (Pal and Dasgupta 2009, 13).

There were particular concerns with agricultural products, including animal and vegetable oils and fats, coffee, tea, and spices where Indonesia, Malaysia, and Vietnam were already significant exporters to India (Francis 2011, 49). Francis argued that some manufacturing sectors would also be adversely affected, although those Indian companies already active in ASEAN, especially in chemicals and iron and steel could benefit from greater market access (Francis 2011, 55). Other studies have produced more optimistic results for trade creation resulting from the free trade agreement. Chandran and Sudarsan (2012, 70) concluded that the fisheries sector would probably not be adversely affected by the agreement, and some products would benefit from tariff-free entry into ASEAN markets. More broadly, Pal and Dasgupta (2009, 14) argued that there should be 'significant complementarity' between India's export-oriented service sector and the ASEAN agricultural and manufacturing sectors. Broadening the free trade agreement from trade in goods to trade in services should therefore be a priority.

ASEAN 2015

Any evaluation of the future of ASEAN–China and ASEAN–India economic ties should take into account the stated aim of the ASEAN-10 countries to form a full economic community by 2015. This includes the formation of a single market and production base, together with other initiatives to deepen and broaden economic integration (ASEAN 2010b,

21). All tariff and non-tariff barriers will be eliminated by 2015 in the ASEAN-6 countries and by 2018 for the CLMV countries. There will, however, be some exemptions for 'sensitive' products. It is also proposed to remove restrictions on trade in services for transport, healthcare, tourism, and logistics, and remove most other restrictions on trade in services, including financial services by 2015. It is also proposed to establish a free investment regime and facilitate freer flows of capital. Controls on the movement of skilled labour will also be removed.

While there is still some skepticism about the extent to which these goals will be reached for all ASEAN countries, it is clear that there has already been considerable progress, at least in the ASEAN-6 group.[20] Whether we look at trade and investment flows, or flows of people as both tourists and migrant workers, the interaction between the diverse peoples of the ASEAN region has greatly increased over the past four decades. ASEAN has also been quite successful as a negotiating group in international economic organisations such as the WTO, and will become more influential to the extent that its own integration process is viewed as successful by the rest of the world. Skeptics will point out that intra-ASEAN trade reached 25 percent of total trade among the ASEAN-10 in 2003, but does not seem to have increased between 2003 and 2012 (Table 5.3). They also argue that well under half of all trade conducted within ASEAN takes advantage of ASEAN free trade area preferences, mainly because the bureaucratic procedures are too costly (Ravenhill 2010, 196–197). On the other hand, it has also been argued that the rise of China and the formation of ACFTA has acted as a spur to further ASEAN integration (Rajan 2008, 188).

5.5   CONCLUDING COMMENTS

A key finding of this paper is that the merchandise trade patterns of the ASEAN countries are quite diversified by region and that no single country or trading block dominates. The proportion of total ASEAN trade conducted with China reached 11.6 percent in 2009, and has increased only slightly since the implementation of ACFTA in January 2010 (Table 5.3). The ASEAN–India Free Trade Agreement does not as yet seem to have had a major impact on trade flows. Although there has been some increase in India's share of ASEAN exports and imports, the country

---

20 Barriers to integrating trade in services are especially difficult to overcome. According to a number of independent studies, the EU has still a considerable way to go in achieving a single market, especially in the service sectors. Language is a major barrier, as it is in the ASEAN states.

remains a minor trading partner. Neither China nor India are important sources of investment for the ASEAN countries as a whole. Most capital flows into the ASEAN-10 still come from Japan, the EU, and other parts of the world economy. There are considerable variations across the 10 member states of ASEAN in the extent to which they trade with other ASEAN countries, or with China and India. But for ASEAN as a whole, there are few signs of 'tectonic shifts' in their patterns of trade and investment. The changes have been incremental, rather than dramatic.

In the decade from 2002 to 2012, intra-ASEAN trade accounted for a larger share of the growth in ASEAN export and import trade than did trade with China. If the progress towards a single market within ASEAN continues, it is likely that intra-ASEAN trade as a proportion of total trade of the ASEAN countries will increase. That is not to deny that China in particular will continue to play an important role as a trading partner of the ASEAN countries in coming years. But it is unlikely to become a dominant partner. There can be little doubt that most ASEAN governments, and many civil society groups, harbour suspicions about the motivations of Chinese foreign economic policy. In some countries, there are concerns that China is treating ASEAN governments in the same way that it has dealt with several regimes in Africa whose governments have granted China access to oil, mineral resources, and even agricultural land on terms that are not always very favourable to the host countries, and that cause severe dislocation for local populations.

The details of China's aid and investment projects are often opaque, and the longer-term benefits to the host countries are far from clear. The widely publicised termination of the dam project in northern Myanmar in 2011 suggests that even those governments that in the past have been friendly to China have to consider the costs of Chinese-financed projects to local populations. There is also some evidence that even the more developed ASEAN economies, such as Thailand, feel that they must, for longer-term strategic reasons, agree to contracts with China for infrastructure development (in the Thai case railways) even when companies from other countries can offer better terms (Lee 2013, 9–10). Trade and investment policies are never formulated in a political and strategic vacuum, and this is likely to be especially true of China's, and India's relations with the ASEAN countries in coming years. But the argument that either country is in some sense 'driving' the economic development of the ASEAN countries is an exaggeration. What is clear is that the rise of the two Asian giants has encouraged the 10 member states of ASEAN to accelerate the pace of their own economic integration.

6 Revisiting the growth acceleration episodes of Indonesia and India: a political economy reading

Kunal Sen

6.1 INTRODUCTION

Indonesia and India are the world's most populous nations, and are known for their diverse ethnic, linguistic, and religious mix (Nehru 2013). Apart from population and ethnic diversity, they also share one other important attribute—both countries witnessed rapid economic growth for well over a decade, and are seen as growth successes, at least for a part of their recent history (Indonesia for 1967–1996 and India for 1993–2010). Rapid, sustained economic growth is not a feature we witness in many developing countries—in fact, the Commission for Growth and Development (2008) finds that only ten countries from the developing world have experienced sustained growth in the post-World War II period: Botswana, Brazil, China, Hong Kong, Indonesia, Korea, Malaysia, Singapore, Taiwan, and Thailand. India would be added to this list if more recent growth data were available. What is also common to the growth experiences of Indonesia and India is that the period of rapid economic growth came to an end—in 1996 for Indonesia and in 2010 for India.

This chapter examines whether there were common causes for the end of rapid growth in these two very disparate countries. It does so by situating the growth experiences of these two countries within a wider understanding of the nature of economic growth in developing countries. In recent years, there has been a realisation that the emphasis in the previous growth empirics literature on long-run growth or levels of income is not compatible with the 'stylised facts' of economic growth (Pritchett 2000). Massive discrete changes in growth are common in developing countries, and most developing countries experience distinct growth episodes: growth accelerations and decelerations or collapses (Jerzmanowski 2006). If this is the case, it is not surprising that Indonesia and India had rapid growth episodes that eventually came to an end. While the East Asian financial crisis is seen as the catalyst for the end of rapid growth in Indonesia, and the 'policy paralysis' of the ruling government and the global slowdown are seen as the proximate causes of the growth slowdown in India, we argue in this chapter that there are deeper institutional factors that can explain the end of the rapid growth episodes in these two countries that are broadly similar.

We first provide an argument for why we see what we call 'boom and bust' growth in developing countries, drawing from the institutional economics literature and our own earlier work. We then provide a summary of the growth experiences of Indonesia and India. We then apply our argument to Indonesia and India respectively.

6.2 A FRAMEWORK FOR UNDERSTANDING BOOM AND BUST GROWTH

As the recent empirical literature on economic growth shows, economic growth in many developing countries involves discrete and quantitatively massive transitions between periods of high growth, periods of negative growth, and periods of stagnation (Kar et al. 2013a). To fix our ideas on transition paths around growth regimes, we provide a simple sketch of these transition paths in Figure 6.1. Using a rough and ready way to demarcate growth regimes, we classify growth regimes into four categories: (i) a growth regime that we call 'miracle growth' where the average increase in per capita income is 5 percent per annum or more; (ii) a growth regime that we call 'stable growth', where the average increase in per capita income is between 0 and 5 percent per annum; (iii) a growth regime that we call 'stagnant growth', where the average increase in per capita income is around 0 percent per annum; and (iv) a growth regime that we call 'growth crisis' where the average change in per capita income is negative. Figure 6.1 makes clear that a complete characterisation of the growth process in any particular country needs an understanding of the factors that lead to growth acceleration — that is, the transition from stagnation or crisis to stable growth or miracle growth — as well as the factors that lead to the avoidance of growth collapses and the maintenance of positive growth — that is, the ability of the country to stay in stable growth or miracle growth in period t +1 if it has experienced the same in period t. It is not obvious that the factors that lead to growth acceleration will lead to growth maintenance as well, as Rodrik argues:

Figure 6.1   Transition paths between growth phases

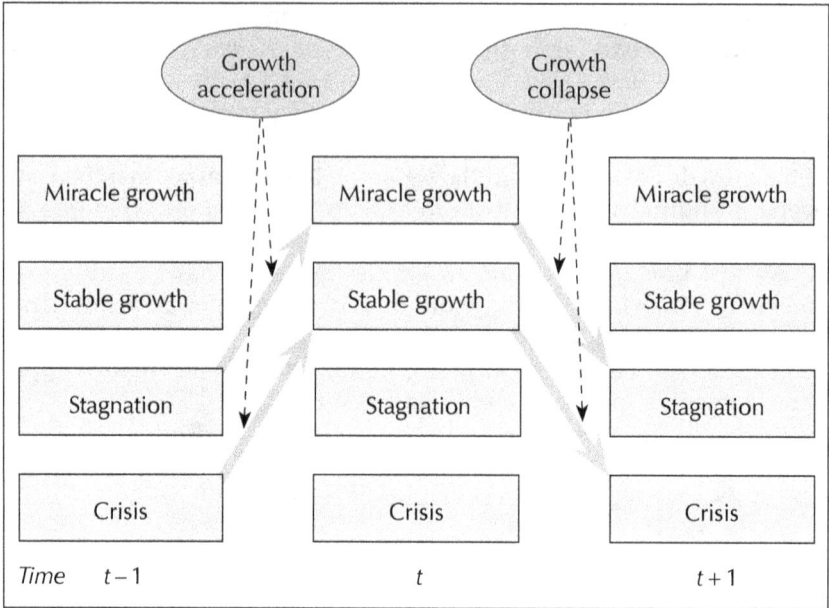

Source: Author's illustration.

Igniting economic growth and sustaining it are somewhat different enterprises. The former generally requires a limited range of (often unconventional) reforms that need not overly tax the institutional capacity of the economy. The latter challenge is in many ways harder, as it requires constructing a sound institutional underpinning to maintain productive dynamism and endow the economy with resilience to shocks over the longer term (Rodrik 2005, 3).

Once we view economic growth as transitions between the above growth phases, and in particular, the transitions from crisis/stagnant growth to stable/miracle growth, the key issues that need to be addressed are (i) what are the institutional determinants of growth acceleration, and (ii) how are they different from the institutional determinants of growth maintenance? We turn to these two questions next.

The institutional determinants of boom and bust growth

A recent set of papers has tried to go beyond the proximate determinants of economic growth (such as macroeconomic stability and trade openness) to study the fundamental causes of economic growth across countries and, in particular, the importance of economic and political institutions (most notably, Acemoglu, Johnson, and Robinson 2001).

These papers have mostly focused on the institutional determinants of economic growth, and have not distinguished between different phases of economic growth and, in particular, between growth acceleration and growth maintenance. Here, we briefly review the literature on institutions and growth and explore the possible implications of this literature for our understanding of the institutional determinants of boom and bust growth.

Acemoglu and Robinson (2008, 2012) have provided an influential theoretical argument on why institutions can be seen as fundamental causes of economic growth. In their theory, economic growth may accelerate initially under extractive economic institutions, such as insecure property rights and regulations that limit entry to markets, and extractive political institutions that concentrate power in the hands of a few with limited checks and balances. However, it is unlikely for economic growth to be maintained and to be broad-based without the emergence of inclusive economic and political institutions. Inclusive economic institutions are secure property rights for the majority of the population (such as smallholder farmers and small firms); law and order; markets that are open to relative free entry of new businesses; state support for markets (in the form of public goods provision, regulation, and enforcement of contracts); and access to education and opportunity for the great majority of citizens. Inclusive political institutions are political institutions that allow broad participation of the citizens of the country and uphold the rule of law, and place constraints and checks on politicians along with the rule of law. Once inclusive economic and political institutions emerge, economic growth may be maintained for a long time. However, political and economic elites may not have a strong incentive to change extractive institutions if they personally benefit from the presence of those institutions. In contrast, inclusive economic and political institutions will be more likely to prevail once they emerge because, with the emergence of such institutions (e.g. democratisation and secure property rights for the majority of the population), strong economic performance will be likely to result, reinforcing the welfare-enhancing effects of these institutions. The persistence of extractive institutions may explain why developing countries see boom and bust growth, because these institutions are not likely to lead to long-run sustained growth (Acemoglu, Johnson, and Robinson 2005). While Acemoglu, Johnson, and Robinson (2005) provide a powerful argument on why institutions matter for economic growth, they do not provide a convincing argument on why economic growth often dies out once it has been initiated (see Sen (2013) for a critique of their theory).

Sen (2013) and Pritchett and Werker (2013) provide a framework explaining why economic growth, once accelerated, often is not maintained. They argue that the movement from one growth regime to

Figure 6.2   The deals space

		Closed deals	Open deals
Kick-starting growth	Disordered deals	Only those with political connections get to make deals, and even they cannot be certain that officials will deliver	Anyone can make a deal, but no one is certain that officials will deliver
	Ordered deals	Only those with political connections get to make deals, but they can be confident that officials will deliver	Anyone can make a deal, and they can be certain that officials will deliver
	Maintaining growth		

Source: Author's illustration, based on Pritchett and Werker (2013).

another (e.g. growth stagnation to growth acceleration, or from incipient growth maintenance to mature growth maintenance) is a function of the quality of institutions. Pritchett and Werker (2012) postulate that the set of institutions that would be crucial to growth acceleration are the movement from disordered to ordered deals, where deals are defined to be: 'a *specific* action between two (or more) entities in which there is actions that are not the result of the impersonal application of a rule but rather are the result of *characteristics* or *actions* of specific individuals which do not spill-over with any precedential value to any other future transaction between other individuals', where ordered deals are deals that, once negotiated, are honoured, while disordered deals are not. Pritchett and Werker (2012) also postulate that the move from growth acceleration to growth maintenance would depend on the movement in the institutions space from closed to open deals, where open deals are widely available and closed deals are limited to an elite. We set out the deals space in a 2x2 matrix, as in Figure 6.2, and show how it relates to different phases of growth. As we have argued, a shift from disordered deals to ordered deals is associated with growth acceleration and a shift from closed ordered to open ordered deals is associated with growth maintenance.

Thus, for economic growth to be maintained, formal institutions need to emerge and/or be properly enforced, and the personalised relationships between politicians and investors should not be confined to a few investors, but be available to a wider set of investors (Pritchett and Werker (2013) call this a move from 'closed' to 'open' deals). However, there is nothing pre-ordained in the evolution of institutions to suggest that the move from closed to open deals or from informal to formal institutions is linear. As economic growth originates in a country, there are feedback loops that occur from the growth process to institutional quality. These feedback loops can be either positive or negative—in other words, whether with further economic growth institutions improve or deteriorate. As Pritchett and Werker (2013) argue, in many developing countries as the growth process evolves, deals may become more closed over time, especially if the sources of growth are the natural resource or infrastructural sectors (which are high-rent sectors) and political elites have an incentive to enter into crony capitalist deals with the business elite. Also, in weak institutional environments, and especially in political systems that have limited checks on the executive (as in an autocracy), with economic growth, crony capitalism may emerge over time. Therefore, if the deals become closed over time, and institutions deteriorate, economic growth can come to an end. In most developing countries, with weak formal institutions or the lack of ability to enforce them, and where informal institutions underpin much of economic activity, economic growth is very likely to be episodic (Sen 2013).

To what extent can our framework explain the growth experiences of Indonesia and India? To address this question, we provide a summary of these two countries' growth experiences and their respective institutional environments as background to a deeper analysis of the political and institutional drivers of their growth episodes.

6.3   IDENTIFYING GROWTH EPISODES FOR INDONESIA AND INDIA

Before we examine the causes of boom and bust growth in Indonesia and India, we first need to periodise Indonesia's and India's growth and, in particular, establish when their growth accelerations and decelerations occurred. We follow our own procedure that we have set out in Kar et al. (2013b). This procedure differs from previous approaches that have attempted to time India's growth acceleration, which either have been ad hoc in that they have simply eyeballed the data to establish the timing of the break (such as DeLong (2003) or Sen (2007)) or have used a statistical method (Bai and Perron 1998) in a mechanistic way. Our approach combines the statistical approach with an economic filter to provide a more unified way of establishing breaks in GDP per capita data. We use Penn

World Tables (version 7.1) GDP per capita in purchasing power parity data from 1950 to 2010 (wherever available) for 125 countries (Kar et al. 2013a).[1]

In the case of Indonesia, our procedure identifies 1967 as the beginning of the growth acceleration episode and 1996 as the end of the episode, and the beginning of a growth deceleration episode. According to our estimates, GDP per capita growth in Indonesia accelerated in 1967 to 4.71 percent per annum (ppa) versus a predicted rate of 1.22 ppa from an average of 1.66 ppa in 1960–1966.[2] This growth acceleration episode lasted 29 years and was followed by a growth deceleration episode, with a growth rate of 1.42 ppa in 2002–2010, as compared to a predicted growth rate of 3.07 ppa. This implied that GDP per capita (GDPPC) was 101 percent higher at the end of the 1967–1996 episode than it would have been using the predicted growth rate of 1.22 ppa, and GDPPC was 23 percent lower in 2010 than it would have been using the predicted growth rate of 3.07 ppa (Pritchett et al. 2013). Indonesia's 1967 growth acceleration led to a GDP gain of US$1,119 billion PPP dollars in net present value terms for the duration of the episode and a cumulative increase in income per person of US$9,712 PPP dollars (see Pritchett et al. (2013) for more details of how these estimates were arrived at). We plot Indonesia's economic growth in Figure 6.3 (five-year moving average to smooth out spikes in growth rates). We see high growth rates in the 1967–1996 episode, followed by a sharp fall during the East Asian financial crisis, followed by slower growth compared to the 1967–1996 period.

In the case of India, our procedure identifies 1993 as the beginning of the first growth acceleration episode, and 2002 as the beginning of the second growth acceleration episode. GDP per capita growth in India accelerated in 1993 to 4.23 ppa versus a predicted rate of 2.34 ppa, and then accelerated again in 2002 to 6.29 ppa versus a predicted rate of 2.91 ppa. The net present value (at a 5 percent discount rate) of the additional output from the 2002 growth acceleration was US$2.65 trillion PPP dollars, adding to the US$1.05 trillion net present value (NPV) of output gain from the 1993 acceleration for a total NPV gain from the two growth accelerations of US$3.7 trillion dollars. Taken together, India's two

---

1 Since our periodisation of growth ends in 2010, and our minimum period for a growth episode is eight years (see Kar et al. (2013b) for more details), the decline in growth rates brought about by the global financial crisis of 2007–2008 would not count as a growth deceleration episode in our periodisation for any specific country.

2 We calculate the predicted growth rate using a regression for each country/episode to allow 'predicted' growth to depend on a country's initial GDP per capita, the episode-specific world average growth and a flexibly specified regression to the mean. See Pritchett et al. (2013) for more details.

Figure 6.3   *Indonesia's economic growth (% annual change in per capita GDP), 1961–2010, five-year moving average*

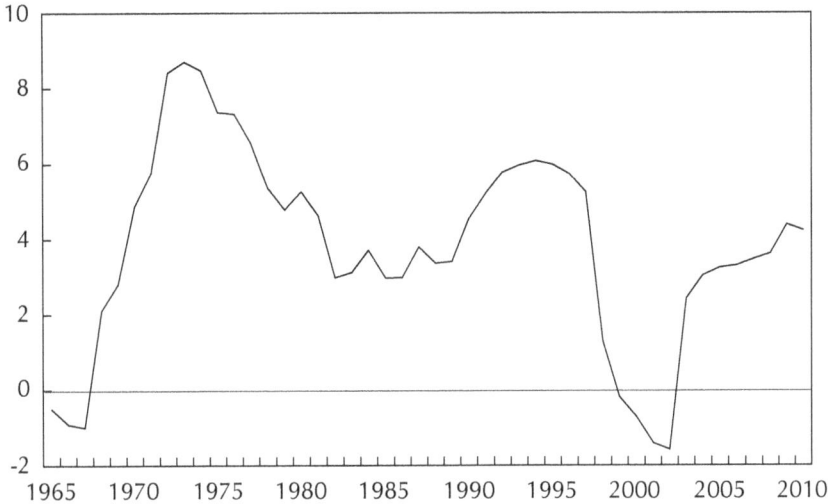

Source: World Development Indicators, author's calculations.

growth accelerations added about US$4,000 in PPP terms to the average Indian's income, as compared to the level of income predicted by the counter-factual rate of growth (see Pritchett et al. 2013).

We plot India's real GDP per capita growth in Figure 6.4 (five-year moving average to smooth out spikes in growth rates). As is clear from the figure, economic growth increases steadily from the 1990s to 2010. However, economic growth declines sharply in the period 2010–2013 (the most recent year for which we have GDP data), and the average for these three years is 3.35 percent compared to 6.33 percent in 2002–2010. While the economic growth slowdown may be temporary, we will argue later in the chapter that the decline in economic growth may be medium term and thus constitute a growth deceleration phase.

Evolution of political and economic institutions in Indonesia and India

While both Indonesia and India have been growth successes in the past, their political institutions have differed greatly in their respective growth acceleration episodes, and indeed for much of their post-independence histories. As Figure 6.5 shows, India has remained a democratic country for its entire post-independence period. Indonesia had an autocratic political system for much of its post-independence history, under

Figure 6.4   India's economic growth (% annual change in per capita GDP), 1961–2013, five-year moving average

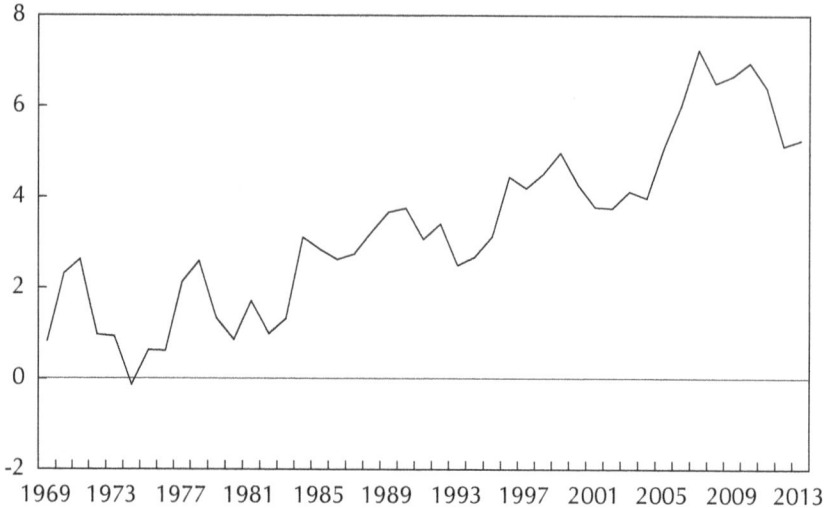

Source: World Bank, World Development Indicators 2014, for 1960–2012, and IMF's World Economic Outlook for 2013, author's calculations.

Suharto's New Order government, which came to power in 1967. Indeed, the duration of autocracy in Indonesia coincides almost perfectly with its growth acceleration episode. With the resignation of President Suharto on 21 May 1998 and with elections being held in 1999, there was a robust transition to democracy in the 2000s. In fact, by 2010, there was little difference between the two countries in their measures of inclusiveness of political institutions.

To look at the differences in economic institutions between the two countries, we look at the protection of property rights and the degree of corruption for the years 1984–2010 (data are not available for these measures prior to 1984). Examining the evolution of property rights institutions first, in Figure 6.6 we find that the quality of Indonesia's property rights institutions is better than India's in the early 1990s, but that the risk of expropriation increases in Indonesia closer to the end of the Suharto regime. It improves again in the democratisation phase. In India, the risk of expropriation improves significantly in the 1990s and early 2000s, but declines in the second half of the 2000s. With respect to corruption, Figure 6.7 shows that the level of corruption was much higher in Indonesia than in India in the 1980s (though Indonesia was growing much faster than India during this period). The level of corruption had become very similar in these two countries in the 1990s. However, in the 2000s, India's

Figure 6.5 Evolution of political institutions in Indonesia and India (*Polity 2 score*)[a]

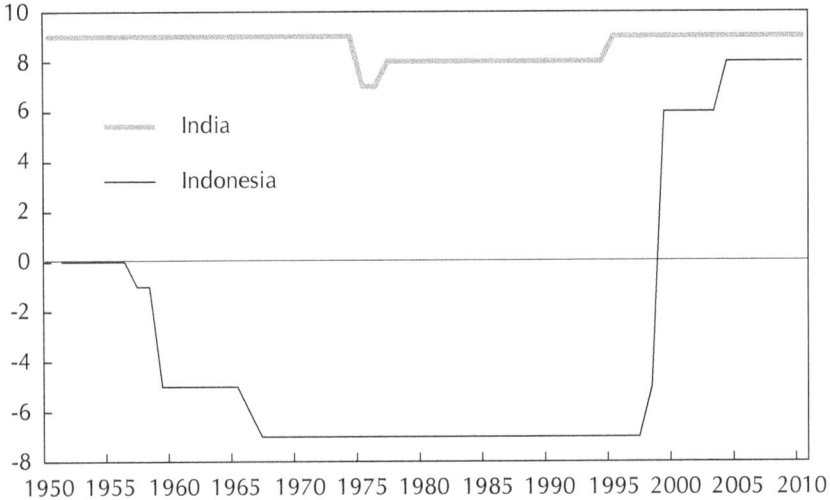

a   The Polity 2 score measures the level of democracy for all independent states with greater than 500,000 total population and covers the years 1800–2011, based on an evaluation of that state's elections for competitiveness, openness, and level of participation. For each year and country, a 'Polity Score' is determined which ranges from –10 to +10, with –10 to –6 corresponding to autocracies, –5 to 5 corresponding to anocracies, and 6 to 10 to democracies.

Source: Polity IV database (http://www.systemicpeace.org/polity/polity4.htm, accessed 1 February 2014).

corruption levels had now exceeded Indonesia's. We will now assess what this implies for the growth experiences of the two countries.

6.4   UNDERSTANDING THE INDONESIAN GROWTH EXPERIENCE

As observed earlier, Indonesia witnessed a growth acceleration episode, beginning in 1967 and then ending in 1996. There is an extensive literature on the Indonesian growth experience that we will not summarise here (see Hill 1996). Our purpose in this section is to highlight the applicability of our framework to the Indonesian case, before we move on to a more extensive discussion of the Indian case.

Indonesia's growth experience provides a case study of a country where 'ordered' deals around informal institutions of credible commitment underpinned the acceleration of growth. However, there was not a sufficiently large move to open deals to formal institutions of credible

Figure 6.6   Evolution of protection of property rights institutions in Indonesia and India (risk of expropriation)[a]

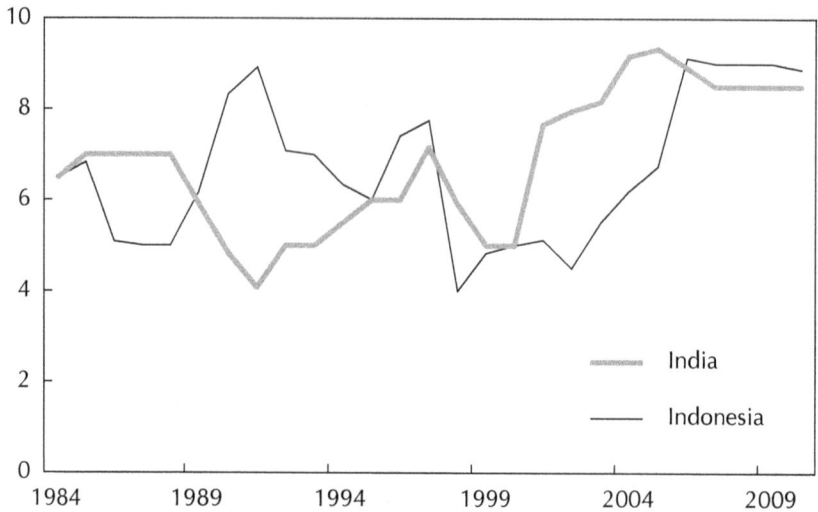

a   Higher values imply better protection of property rights.
Source: ICRG database, author's calculations.

Figure 6.7   Evolution of control of corruption in Indonesia and India[a]

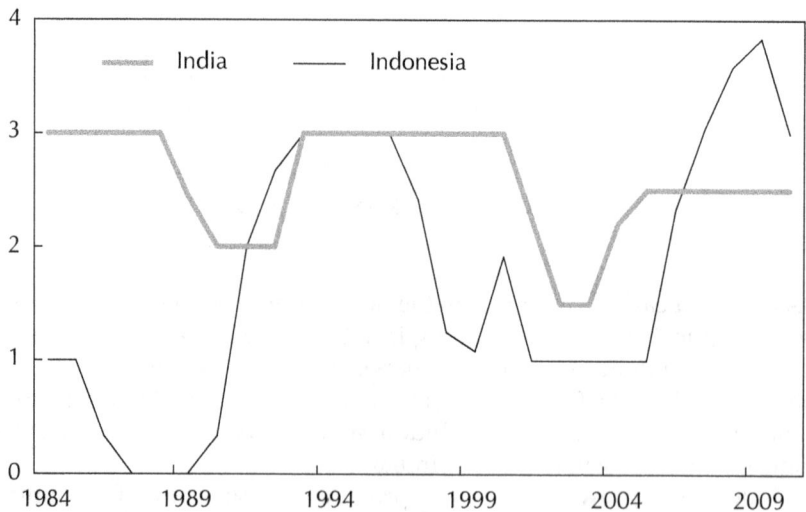

a   Higher values imply lower corruption.
Source: ICRG database, author's calculations.

commitment even after three decades of positive growth, which may have contributed to the growth collapse in the late 1990s.

After the 'New Order' government of Suharto came to power in 1965, the proximate causes of economic growth in the first decade and a half of the Suharto regime were sound macroeconomic management and the promotion of rice agriculture and light industry in national development plans. State-owned enterprises were the dominant corporate force within the economy, making substantial investments in a range of capital- and technology-intensive industries, such as aircraft and shipbuilding (Rosser 2002). The oil boom of the 1970s allowed bureaucrats access to funds that financed the growth of these state-owned enterprises. However, the state intervention of the Suharto regime in the early years of positive economic growth did not resemble the more strategic industrial policies witnessed in Korea, Singapore, and Taiwan, but was principally followed to increase the number of business clients for the state (Robison 1986). As Robison and Hadiz (2004, 53) argue, 'larger strategic objectives were routinely subsumed by the search for extra-budget funding to sustain the political institutions and patronage networks of Indonesia's rules and their own personal enrichment'.

With the fall in oil prices in the first half of the 1980s, there was a need to mobilise new sources of investible resources from the private sector as well as to develop export industries, particularly in the manufacturing sector (Rosser 2002). Thus, the state ownership and public monopolies and the pervasive and protective trade and financial regimes that provided the basis for the patron–client networks that existed between politico-bureaucrats and domestic capitalists in the early stages of economic growth in Indonesia were no longer sustainable in the form in which they had existed prior to the 1980s. In a series of reform packages beginning in the mid-1980s, the Indonesian government deregulated trade and financial regimes, relaxed foreign investment restrictions, and opened a range of former state monopolies to private investment (Hill 1996). The crisis of the early 1980s could, therefore, have been the trigger for the emergence of more inclusive economic institutions in Indonesia, as well as the development and enforcement of formal institutions such as competition law and regulations underpinning transactions in financial markets.

While some progress was made in this regard, the deregulation process seems to have further entrenched the emerging 'politico-business' oligarchies, and the patron–client networks that sustained these oligarchies (Robison and Hadiz 2004). Thus, the families that owned domestic conglomerates as well as the politico-business class in Indonesia moved into the sectors of the former state monopolies, such as banking, finance, and infrastructure. These families also successfully concentrated their presence in sectors that were largely untouched by deregulation, such as natural resource industries and domestic trading monopolies. In addition, they diversified their sources of funds from oil revenues to largely unregulated commercial bank loans and equity in international capital markets. Finally, they preserved their authority over the 'strategic gate-keeping institutions of the state', ensuring that they maintained control over the allocation of rents.

In this way, the patron–client networks that were there because of politico-bureaucrats and oligarchic capitalists since the early years of the Suharto regime, were significantly strengthened in the 1980s to early 1990s. Figure 6.6 shows that corruption levels in Indonesia were relatively high. The entrenchment of these patron–client networks and 'the harnessing of the state to the unconstrained interest of this privileged group of oligarchies' (Robison and Hadiz 2004, 11) can explain both the nature of the financial crisis in the late 1990s in Indonesia, with its widespread bankruptcies and debt defaults among these oligarchs, and the stagnation in economic growth in the post-crisis period. Institutional quality deteriorated in the 1990s, as the political elite's commitment to deals that was evident in the earlier decades was no longer credible, and investors were increasingly concerned about the risk of expropriation of their investments (as we noted in the previous section, there was a fall in the measure of protection of property rights during this period).[3] Indonesia, therefore, provides a clear example of why economic growth can unravel if informal institutions that underpin growth accelerations remain in place and become predatory in nature, and move from open to closed, as the economy moves further along the growth process (Hofman, Gudwin, and Thee 2010; Pritchett 2011).

6.5   UNDERSTANDING THE INDIAN GROWTH EXPERIENCE

India's political economy had already been supportive of pro-business and pro-growth policies since the 1980s (Kohli 2012; Mehta and Walton 2014). When Indira Gandhi returned to power in 1980, the promotion of economic growth was the focus of the government's economic policy,

---

3   Malaysia and Thailand also suffered a growth deceleration episode after the onset of the financial crisis (Kar et al. 2013a). In contrast, Korea did not observe a growth deceleration episode after the crisis, and economic growth recovered rapidly in the aftermath of the crisis our estimates show that there was no structural break in economic growth in Korea in 1996 as there was for Malaysia, Indonesia and Thailand. A possible reason for this is that the quality of institutions were much higher in Korea than in the other East Asian countries to absorb the crisis and consequently to revive growth (Sen 2013).

leading to a growing alliance between the political and economic elites. As Kohli (2012, 30–31) notes, 'just after coming to power in January 1980, … Indira Gandhi let it be known that improving production was now her top priority. In meeting after meeting with private industrialists, she clarified that what the government was most interested in was production'. Therefore, beginning in the 1980s, the Indian state signalled its intention clearly to the domestic capitalists that it was credibly committing to an environment where private enterprise would be supported and growth-enhancing policies followed. This was reflected in changes in economic policies, such as the slow but steady liberalisation of import controls, especially on capital and intermediate goods. The shift in the relationship between political and economic elites from one of mutual distrust to a more collaborative and synergistic relationship (Cali and Sen 2011) was further accentuated with Rajiv Gandhi coming to power in 1985. Rajiv Gandhi took particular interest in modern sectors such as information technology and engineering, and tried to bring new economic elites from these emerging sectors into the relationship the political elite had with the business sector. In addition, there was a growing diversification of business ownership with the rise of non-traditional business groups in southern and western India, leading to a broadening of the political connectivity of the business elite (Mehta and Walton 2014).

Therefore, the deals environment at the macro level had already become distinctly 'ordered' by the late 1980s, as well as more open with the emergence of new economic elites both in modern sectors as well as in regions outside the industrial heartlands of Gujarat and Maharashtra.

The 1993 growth acceleration episode

There were two further developments in the early 1990s that led to a strengthening of the ordered nature of the deals environment, particularly at the micro level. Firstly, the dismantling of the industrial licensing system[4] in 1991 removed an important source of 'disorder' in the deals environment at the micro level. The approval of applications that firms made to the government for expansion or for new firms to enter the industrial

---

4 For the first four decades after independence, the government intervened in almost all aspects of the activities of formal manufacturing firms. Industry in India was subject to rather formidable legal barriers to entry. Investments, in terms of both the expansion of capacity of existing firms and the creation of new firms, was controlled by the government through its licensing policies, which were in turn determined according to plan priorities. Although the purported objective of the licensing regime was balanced growth, it effectively led to a more monopolistic structure and significantly encouraged rent-seeking by corporations entrenched with public powers (Bhagwati 1993).

sector during the previous licensing regime, no longer depended on individual bureaucrats. Secondly, the removal of the import-licensing system in the early 1990s for most commodities also meant that the highly discretionary and case-by-case nature of imports that were not on Open General Licence was abolished. As Bhagwati (1993, 50) noted, 'the industrial-cum-trade licensing system ... had degenerated into a series of arbitrary, indeed inherently arbitrary decisions, where for instance one activity would be chosen over another simply because the administering bureaucrats were so empowered and indeed obligated to choose'.

The growth acceleration of 1993 was, in great part, due to the 'ordered deals' environment that had already taken shape in the 1980s, and this was further enhanced by the dismantling of the industrial-cum-trade licensing system in 1991. These deals were to a large extent open in nature, with removal of entry barriers in many industries, and this was reflected in the entry of new firms in manufacturing and services, especially in pharmaceuticals and information technology (Alfaro and Chari 2009). At the same time, the collusive relationship that the Indian state had with certain sections of the business elite in the pre-reform period remained in place, and may have been accentuated with the rise of increasingly powerful regional business groups who were closely connected with regional political elites (Mehta and Walton 2014). Thus, during the 1990s, closed deals existed side by side with open deals, and as a consequence, many of the traditional industries (such as consumer durables) were still dominated by the entrenched business groups that had emerged in the license raj (Alfaro and Chari 2009).

There is evidence from detailed firm-level analysis that in 1990 there was a significant degree of dynamism in the corporate sector. Harrison, Martin, and Natraj (2012) find that there was a large allocation of market share from less productive firms to more productive firms in the first half of the 1990s, but not in subsequent years. Mody, Nath and Walton (2011) find significant entry of new firms in virtually all industrial sectors in the early to mid-1990s, which stops in the late 1990s, with very little new firm entry in the 2000s.[5] Kathuria, Raj and Sen (2013) show that the improvement in productivity performance in the manufacturing sector in the 1990s was not confined to the formal sector, but encompassed the informal sector as well.

The dynamism in the private sector in the 1990s is also reflected in indicators of growth and structural transformation (Sen, Kar, and Sahoo 2014). Thus, in the 1993–2002 growth acceleration phase, economic

5 However, as Goldberg et al. (2010) show, much of the product churning that occurs in the 1990s was due to product additions rather than product shedding. In this sense, India's experience of the 1990s with 'creative destruction' was more of 'creative' and less of 'destruction'.

growth was mostly driven by competitive exporting sectors such as IT and chemicals, and domestically oriented sectors such as plastics.

India's per capita economic growth in the 2002–2010 episode was even faster at 6.42 percent per annum as compared to the period 1993–2002 when the average rate of per capita growth was 4.15 percent per annum. However, there was a shift in the pattern of growth towards non-tradable sectors such as construction, communications, banking and insurance, and real estate (Sen, Kar, and Sahoo 2014). There was also a shift in India's exports towards more resource-intensive sectors such as refined petroleum and minerals, along with a decline in the Hausmann-Hidalgo measure of structural transformation. Thus, economic growth in the second growth episode was qualitatively different from that in the first episode, in that it relied more heavily on 'rentier' sectors such as mining and petroleum as well as other high-rent sectors such as telecommunications and real estate.

There was also a shift in the deals environment in this period from relatively open to closed deals. This was most evident in the increasing level of 'crony capitalist' deals that political elites struck with economic elites in 'high-rent' natural resource sectors such as bauxite, coal, iron ore, manganese ore, and natural gas, at both the national and regional levels. For example, there was a succession of scams highlighted by the media in various ore-rich states such as Jharkhand, Karnataka, Goa and Odisha, where influential, politically well-connected business elites systematically underpaid mining royalties to state agencies, along with over-extraction of iron and bauxite in excess of the amounts stipulated by the leases that the private mining firms held with the state governments. The Commission headed by Justice M.B Shah (of the Supreme Court of India) constituted by the central government in 2010 to investigate irregularities in the extraction, trade, and transportation of iron ore and manganese ore across the country found that 'there is enormous and large-scale, multi-stage illegal mining of iron ore and manganese ore running into thousands of crores of rupees every year' (Shah Commission 2012a, 1). The Shah Commission also found clear evidence of collusion between ruling politicians at the state and national levels and the private mining firms, stating that: 'the State has "gifted" property of thousand of crores in the hands of private companies/firms/individuals' (Shah Commission 2012b, 604). There were similar concerns in the allocation of licences for coal deposit blocks to private firms by the central government in the period 2004–2011, which was done preferentially at lower than market rates, instead of through a competitive bidding process, according to investigations on the nature of the allocation process by the Comptroller and Auditor General (CAG). Finally, in natural gas, there were allegations of crony capitalist deals in the award of a production-sharing contract in the exploration and production of natural gas in Krishna Godavari Basin of Karnataka to a politically influential Indian business group, as well as in the nature of the contract and its subsequent revisions.

The existence of 'closed deals' was not confined only to natural resource sectors, but was also evident in telecommunications as well. Telecommunications witnessed impressive growth in the 1993–2002 growth episode, driven by high demand for mobile phones among a rapidly expanding middle class. In 2008, the Department of Telecommunications, under the aegis of the Ministry of Telecommunications (MOT), decided to allocate second-generation (2G) spectrum licences to mobile phone operators on a first-come, first-served (FCFS) basis, at a price significantly below the market price. Later investigation by the CAG found clear evidence of insider information being passed to select private firms on the timing of the FCFS announcement, as well as a very short time given to submit the applications. The CAG (2011) also found irregularities in the MOT's selective interpretation of the recommendations of the telecommunications regulator, the Telecom Regulatory Authority of India (TRAI) on the process of allocating licences to mobile phone operators, which led CAG not to conduct a competitive bidding process for the 2G licences (the CAG estimated the loss to the Indian exchequer due to the under-pricing of 2G licences at over Rp176,000 crores).

Three factors contributed to the emergence of 'closed deals' in the 2002 growth episode, compared to the more open deals environment in the earlier growth episode. First, with increased demand for minerals originating from China, there was a sharp increase in the price of several minerals in the early to mid-2000s. This is evident for iron ore, as shown in Figure 6.8. The price of this commodity increased rapidly from 2005 to 2010, before declining in 2011–2013. In the natural resource sectors the state had the power to allocate licences for production to private firms, in contrast to manufacturing or service sectors such as information technology, where licences were no longer required to start operations after the 1991 economic reforms. As a consequence, there were clear incentives for political elites to preferentially allocate licences to select economic elites on terms that were not transparent, or were not the most economically competitive, in return for extra-legal monetary rewards. Second, as the rapid economic growth in the previous growth episode spurred an increase in demand for infrastructure sectors such as telecommunications, which by its nature is oligopolistic and characterised by high rents, political elites entered into rent-sharing arrangements with business groups that were awarded contracts to operate in these sectors. There was a similar surge in demand for commercial real estate with strong private sector growth, and there were increasing signs of 'closed deals' between political elites and real estate developers in the allocation of land for commercial real estate (Nagaraj 2013). This

Figure 6.8   World price of iron ore, monthly, 1999–2013 (US$)

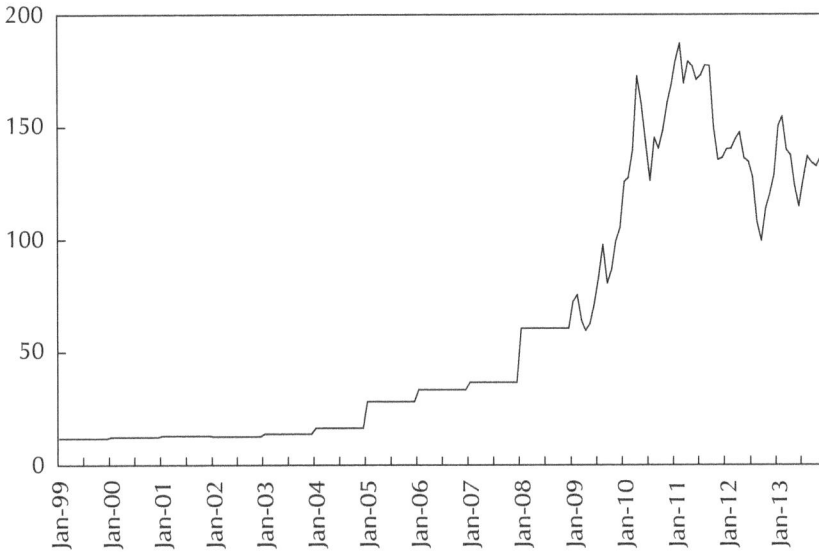

Source: http://www.indexmundi.com/commodities/?commodity=iron-ore, accessed 1 February 2014.

is evident from Figure 6.9, where one observes a clear increase in the proportion of wealth of Indian billionaires originating in the rent-thick sectors (primarily real estate, construction, mining, and infrastructure) as compared to other sectors (manufacturing, information technology), from 2002 onwards. An observed increase in corruption in this period was noted previously. Third, with the increased fractionalisation of the political system at the national level (see Figure 6.10), and the growing importance of regional political elites in the coalition governments of the 2000s, 'closed deals' between these elites and powerful economic interests at both the national and regional levels became more prevalent in the post-2002 period (Sen, Kar, and Sahoo 2014). This was accentuated by the rapid turnover of governments and closely contested elections, at both the national and regional levels, which led to a shortening of the time horizon of political elites, who were more interested in finding ways to extract rents via crony capitalist deals to finance costly elections that they would have to fight in the immediate future.

However, as media accounts of corruption became widespread, and there was growing popular discontent at the flagrantly excessive levels of rents that were shared between political and economic elites in these deals, it became clear that state legitimacy was gradually being eroded towards the end of the growth episode. There was strong social and

*Figure 6.9   Distribution of wealth of billionaires by source of wealth,
India, 1996–2012*

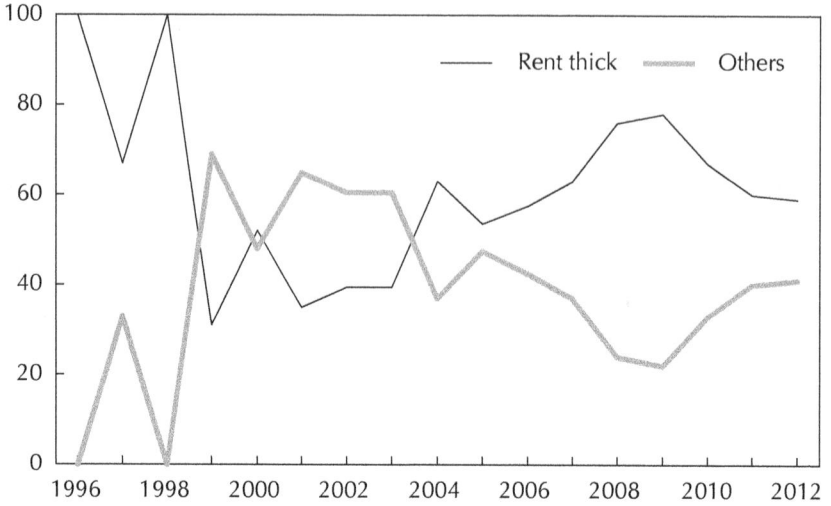

Source: Gandhi and Walton (2012).

*Figure 6.10   Measure of total fractionalisation and proportion of seats
won by the majority party, national elections, India,
1975–2009*

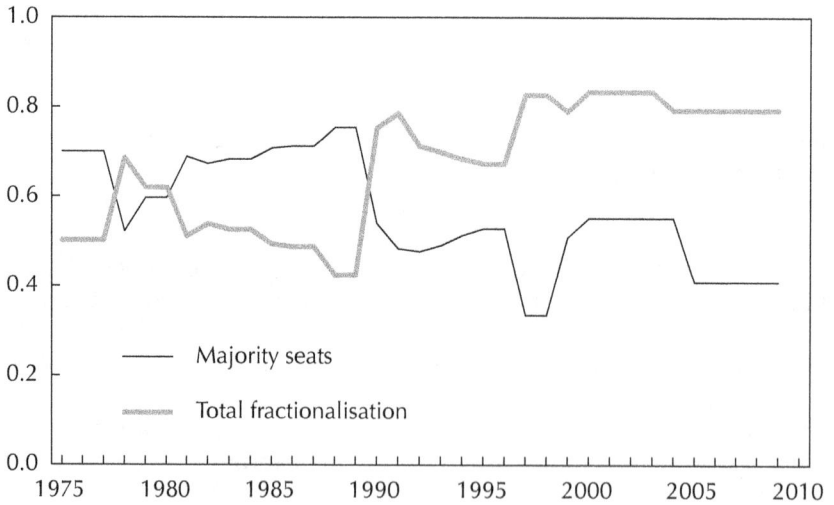

Source: Quality of Government Database, Gothenburg University, accessed 1 February 2014.

Figure 6.11   Evolution of probability of contract viability, India,
1982–2013

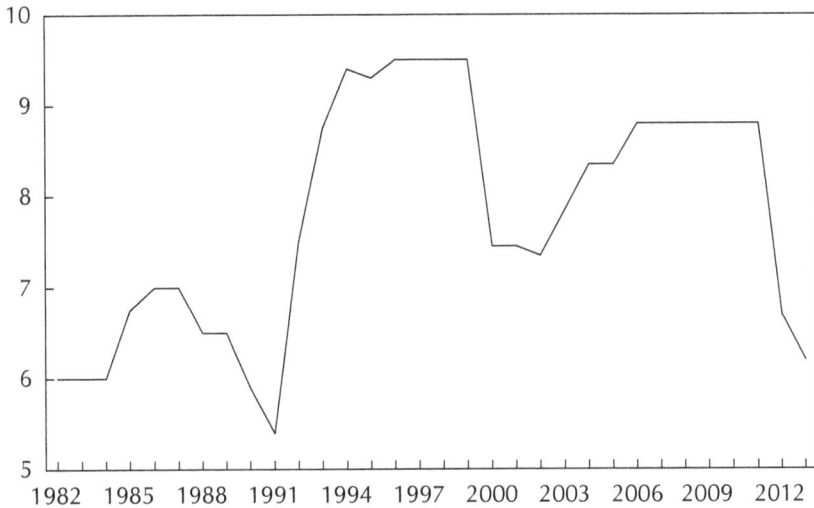

Source: Author's calculations from ICRG database.

political mobilisation of the masses against the attempts by the political elite in states such as Odisha and West Bengal to obtain land through extra-legal and often coercive means for mining or for providing land to large business groups to set up manufacturing plants. In addition, there was strong push-back from accountability institutions, including a ban on iron ore exports by the Indian Supreme Court and the investigations of corruption in the allocation of 2G and coal block licences by the Comptroller and Auditor-General of India. All these developments made the 'closed deals' environment unsustainable towards the end of the first decade of the 2000s. In addition, with the increasing uncertainty on the nature of deals, and where the ruling party at the centre had the authority to credibly commit to new deals in the face of both popular and legal challenges, deals became increasingly disordered as well (see Figure 6.6). This is evident from the behaviour of the International Country Risk Guide (ICRG) measure of the probability of repudiation of contracts, which started moving in an adverse direction in the 2000s, suggesting that investors were increasingly concerned about the credibility of deals (Figure 6.11).

Thus, the post-2002 episode was qualitatively different from the 1993–2002 episode in that the deals environment had shifted decisively from open to closed deals and, as we progressed into the 2000s, from ordered to disordered deals as well. This was also reflected in the increas-

Figure 6.12   Gross fixed capital formation, public sector, private corporate sector, and household sector, India, 1950–2010 (% of GDP)

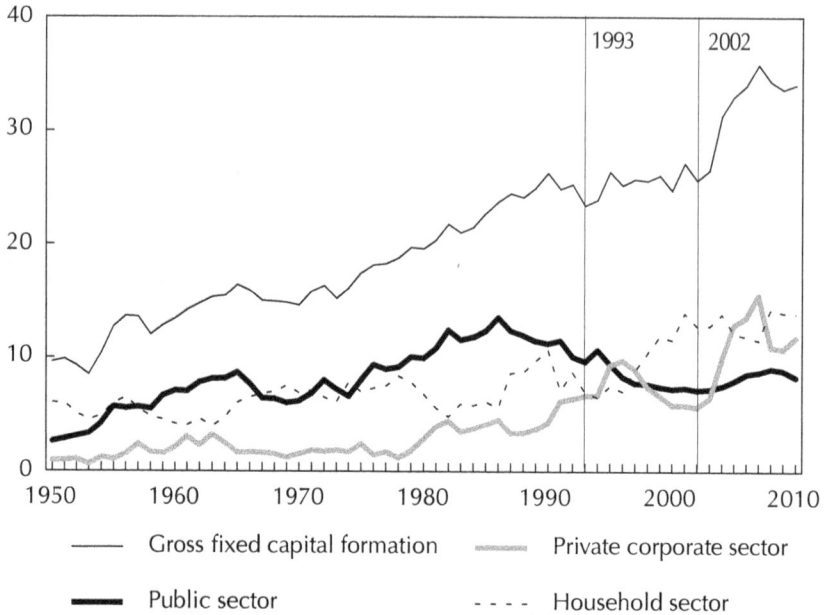

Gross fixed capital formation — Private corporate sector

Public sector — Household sector

Source: National Income Accounts of the Central Statistical Organisation, India, author's calculations.

ing importance of natural resource sectors in India's export basket, the importance of sectors such as construction in India's economic growth, and a decline in structural transformation (Sen et al. 2014). As investor uncertainty increased, there was a fall in private corporate investment in the second half of the 2000s, and the rapid economic growth of the 2000s rapidly came to an end in 2010 (Figure 6.12). While it is premature to identify the slow growth period of 2010–2013 as the beginning of a growth deceleration episode, as there may well be a turnaround in economic growth in the post-2013 period, our discussion of the causes of 'boom and bust' growth in developing countries suggests that the decline in economic growth may well be permanent, and not temporary.

6.6   CONCLUDING REMARKS

Sustained rapid economic growth of well over a decade is a feature that we do not observe frequently in developing countries. Indonesia and

India have both experienced rapid economic growth, among the fastest in the world in their respective growth episodes, though at different periods in their history. Indonesia's 1967 growth acceleration led to a cumulative GDP gain of US$1,119 billion PPP dollars in net present value terms for the duration of the episode and a cumulative increase in income per person of US$9,712 PPP dollars. India's economic growth added US$3.7 trillion dollars in net present value terms cumulatively to India's GDP. Taken together, India's two growth accelerations added about US$4,000 in PPP terms to the average Indian's income. These are staggering gains in income and among the highest in the world in the post-World War II period (Pritchett et al. 2013).[6]

Yet Indonesia's growth acceleration episode came to an end in 1996, and there are clear signs that India's growth acceleration episode came to an end in 2010. In this chapter, we have examined the political and institutional causes of the end of these two growth episodes. We have shown that while these two countries had very different political systems at the end of their respective episodes, one autocratic and the other democratic, the underlying causes of the end of the growth miracles were not very different, and were related to a deterioration of institutional quality, and a shift of the deals that political elites struck with economic elites from being more 'open' to being more 'closed'. This led to negative feedback loops from the growth process to institutions that eventually brought Indonesia's and India's rapid growth episodes to an end.

The wider implication of our analysis is that economic growth in most developing-country contexts remains episodic and prone to collapse, as institutions do not evolve over the growth process, and in many instances deteriorate. In contrast to the argument of North, Wallis, and Weingast (2009), our analysis suggests that the move from limited-access to open-access orders or from growth processes that rely on informal institutions to growth processes that rely on formal institutions is not pre-determined, or linear. Shifts back and forth from good transitions in growth to bad transitions in growth are common in developing countries with weak formal institutions, and sustained rapid economic growth that can take a country from low-income to middle-income status still remains a distant possibility in many country contexts.

---

6 India's income gains during its two growth acceleration episodes and Indonesia's income gain during its 1967–1996 growth episode are among the six largest cumulative income gains for any country, developing or developed, in the post-1950 period. See Pritchett et al. (2013) for more details.

7 Exporting, education, and wage differentials between foreign multinationals and local plants in Indonesian and Malaysian manufacturing

*Eric D. Ramstetter**

7.1 INTRODUCTION

Until recently, Lipsey and Sjöholm's (2004a) study of manufacturing plants in Indonesia in 1996 was one of the few studies of wage differentials between foreign multinational enterprises (MNEs) and local plants, which accounted for the fact that MNEs tend to hire relatively larger shares of workers with higher education.[1] They found that MNEs paid

* The author gratefully acknowledges financial and logistic support from a joint research project of the Asia Pacific Institute of Research and Doshisha University 'Higashi Ajia no yushutsu shikougata kougyouka no otoshiana [Pitfalls of East Asia's export-led industrialisation]' and from a research project of the International Centre for the Study of East Asian Development (ICSEAD) 'Multinationals, wages, and human resources in Asia's large developing economies'. I also thank Shigeyuki Abe, Kenta Goto, Niny Khor Akihiro Kubo, Dionisius Narjoko, Yoko Ueda, Ganeshan Wignaraja, as well as other participants in an Asian Development Review Conference (Manila 1-2 August 2013), an Asian Development Bank Institute seminar (Tokyo 25 October 2013), and an ICSEAD staff seminar (Kitakyushu 14 January 2014) for comments on related research. Responsibility for all opinions expressed and any remaining errors or omissions is the author's alone.
1 These authors also examined other aspects of wage differentials and how they change over time in Lipsey and Sjöholm (2004b, 2005, 2006) and Sjöholm and Lipsey (2006).

significantly higher wages than local, private plants even after accounting for the educational background of the plant's workforce and other plant-level characteristics, and that these conditional wage differentials were larger for white-collar workers than for blue-collar workers. Recently, Ramstetter and Narjoko (2013) re-examined the 1996 evidence and added evidence for 2006, obtaining qualitatively similar results for both years when all manufacturing plants are combined in one sample, though industry-level evidence was weaker. In addition, similar evidence for Malaysian plants in 2000–2004 (Ramstetter 2013) also suggests the existence of positive, MNE–local wage differentials after accounting for both worker education and occupation, in addition to other plant characteristics, both when all industries are combined and at the industry level.

However, none of these studies account for the potentially important effect of a plant's export status on MNE–local wage differentials. As Athukorala and Devadason (2012, 1503) explain in their study of foreign labour's effect on Malaysian wages: 'export-oriented firms generally operate under greater demand pressure compared to domestic-market oriented firms which enjoy both policy-induced and natural protection'. Similarly, factor endowments-based theories of international trade imply that exporters are more likely to experience a tendency toward factor price equalisation than non-exporters. In the case of relatively labour-abundant economies like Indonesia and Malaysia, this would suggest that ratios of wages to capital costs should be higher in exporters than in non-exporters. Another body of literature emphasises the importance of high entry costs into export networks, and there is evidence firms able to bear the costs of export entry are likely to increase their demand for skilled labour and pay relatively high wages as a result (Bernard and Jensen 1997).[2] However, none of these studies address the question of whether differences between exporters and non-exporters have differential effects on MNEs and local plants, and thus MNE–local wage differentials. The purpose of this study is thus to investigate whether MNE–local wage differentials differ between exporting plants and non-exporters.

The paper proceeds to review the existing literature in Section 7.2, and describe the data used and patterns revealed by key descriptive statistics, including unconditional MNE–local wage differentials in Section 7.3. Section 7.4 then reviews the evidence emerging from estimates of earnings equations, focusing on patterns of conditional MNE–local wage

---

2 Bernard et al. (2007) and Greenaway and Kneller (2007) summarise this literature and Sjöholm (2003) analyses exporting networks in Indonesian plants in 1994–1997.

differentials. Finally, Section 7.5 concludes and offers suggestions for further research.

7.2   LITERATURE REVIEW AND METHODOLOGY

As described in the introduction, when large samples of all manufacturing plants are used, previous studies have found that MNEs paid significantly higher wages than local, private plants in Indonesia in 1996 and 2006 (Lipsey and Sjöholm 2004a; Ramstetter and Narjoko 2013) and local (private and state-owned) plants in Malaysia in 2000–2004 (Ramstetter 2012a, 2013). These studies are distinguished from other studies of MNE-wage differentials by the important fact that they account for the educational background and sex of a plant's workers, in addition to plant size, and a plant's capital intensity or a proxy.[3] The Malaysian studies also account for worker occupation, though this indicator is not available for Indonesia. The recent studies also analysed up to 17 industry-level samples, finding significant differentials in most of the samples for Indonesia in 1996 and Malaysia, but insignificant differentials for most Indonesian industries in 2006. Ramstetter and Phan (2007) also found positive wage differentials between MNEs and local, private firms in Vietnam in 2000, 2002, and 2004, after accounting for firm's size, factor intensity, shares of technical workers, and female shares, both in the aggregate and in most industry group samples. In contrast, results from Lee and Nagaraj's (1995) sample of workers in the Klang Valley of Malaysia in 1991 suggest that foreign ownership of a plant had no significant effects on wages of either male or female workers, after several aspects of labour quality and other variables were accounted for.[4]

Other studies of Malaysia (Lim 1977), Thailand (Movshuk and Matsuoka-Movshuk 2006; Ramstetter 2004), and Venezuela and Mexico (Aitken, Harrison, and Lipsey 1996) have found that MNE–local wage differentials tended to persist after accounting for numerous plant- or firm-level characteristics, but were unable to account for labour force quality. There are also numerous studies of individuals that reveal significant returns to human capital, when measured by worker education,

---

3   Material inputs per worker and/or energy per worker are common proxies for capital intensity because the coverage of Indonesia's capital data is poor. For example, 28–33 percent of sample plants in 12 large energy consuming industries did not have data on fixed assets in 1996 and 43–48 percent lacked these data for 2006 (Ramstetter and Narjoko 2012).

4   Worker quality variables were education, experience, occupation, and training. Other variables were union membership, marital status, migration status, total hours worked, plant size, and plant export-orientation.

training, and experience, for example.[5] Still other studies focus on the gender wage gap, usually finding that females earn less than males, even after accounting for education, experience, and other determinants of earnings.[6]

There is thus substantial previous evidence that both plant ownership and worker quality have important influences on worker earnings. It is clear that relatively well-educated, experienced, and well-trained workers generally expect relatively high returns to their work efforts. Firms or plants hiring high-quality workers usually expect relatively high productivity and offer commensurate compensation. Correspondingly, the primary reason that MNEs pay higher wages than local plants is probably the well-documented tendency for MNEs to be relatively technology- or skill-intensive compared to non-MNEs (Caves 2007; Dunning 1993; Markusen 2002). However, even relatively sophisticated studies like Lipsey and Sjöholm (2004a) fail to fully account for MNE–local differences in labour quality. For example, in addition to differences in worker education, there may be important differences in worker occupation, training, background, and experience, which are often accounted for in studies of wage determination among individuals, but are not measured in plant-level data. In this study of Indonesia and Malaysia, for example, it is possible to account for differences in worker education and sex in both economies and worker occupation in Malaysia, but there is no information on worker background (e.g. race, nationality), experience, or training.

Other reasons for MNE–local differentials are perhaps less clear, but there are at least three important possibilities. First, there is substantial evidence that MNEs often find it difficult to identify and retain suitably qualified workers. For example, in 1998, securing adequate quantity and quality of labour was the third most common of 27 possible problems for Japanese affiliates operating in the ASEAN-4 (the four largest developing economies in the Association of Southeast Asian Nations: Indonesia, Malaysia, the Philippines, and Thailand), this problem being cited by 8.5 percent of these MNEs (Japanese Ministry of Economy, Trade and Investment 2001, 536–537).[7] Other surveys also indicated that securing labour

---

5 See Purnastuti et al. (2013) and Sohn (2013) for recent evidence on Indonesia and Ismail and Zin (2003) for analysis of Malaysia.
6 In addition to the study of plant-level data from Lipsey and Sjöholm (2004a), studies of individuals also provide evidence of a substantial gender pay gap in Indonesia (Feridhanusetyawan, Aswicahyono, and Perdana 2001; Pirmana 2006). For evidence on Malaysia, see Chapman and Harding (1985), Lee and Nagaraj (1995), Milanovic (2006), and Schafgans (2000).
7 The most commonly cited problems were (1) competition for local product markets (11.2 percent) and (2) political instability (8.6 percent).

supply was the third most frequently cited of 14 investment motives of Japanese affiliates in Indonesia and Malaysia.[8] Correspondingly, many of the aforementioned studies suggest that MNEs may pay relatively high wages to secure or retain labour.

Second, workers in host economies are often relatively familiar with management practices in local firms and may, therefore, be relatively reluctant to work for MNEs that often use less familiar management styles. This may lead them to demand a premium for working in the relatively unfamiliar MNE environment. Unfortunately, there is relatively little empirical evidence on this point, though many studies mention it and there have been well-documented cases where prominent MNEs from Japan (Guerin 2002) and Korea (Hwan 2011), for example, have been accused of labour rights violations in Indonesia. Correspondingly, one gets the impression that related bad press may have made some Indonesian workers reluctant to work for MNEs. On the other hand, recent surveys of university graduates suggest that MNEs are actually among the more popular employers for educated workers in Malaysia.[9]

Third, MNEs are often hypothesised to have important firm-specific assets in relatively large amounts compared to non-MNEs.[10] These firm-specific assets are generally intangible, and many of them are related to worker quality. However, even when an MNE's firm-specific assets are not directly related to worker skills, they may facilitate higher worker productivity by improving a firm's marketing and management, for example. In other words, the MNE's possession of firm-specific assets has the potential to make workers more productive in MNEs than in non-MNEs, even if labour quality is identical in MNEs and non-MNEs.

---

8   Securing labour supply was cited by 16 percent of replying firms operating in Indonesia in 1996 and 13 percent in 2006, as well as 11–13 percent of replying firms operating in Malaysia during 2000–2004 (Toyo Keizai, various years). The most commonly cited motives were (1) development of local markets (25 percent of Indonesian affiliates in 1996 and 24 percent in 2006; 21–31 percent of Malaysian affiliates in 2000–2004) and (2) strengthening of international competitiveness (19 percent of Indonesian affiliates in 1996 and 34 percent in 2006; 21–31 percent of Malaysian affiliates in 2000–2004).

9   For example, seven of the top 10 employers in 2008 were foreign companies in Malaysia (http://malaysias100.com/media/foreign-firms-the-favorite).

10   Some theorists (especially Dunning) view the possession of firm-specific assets or ownership advantages as a key necessary condition for a firm to become an MNE (in addition to internalisation and location advantages). Other theorists (Buckley and Casson 1992; Casson 1987; Rugman 1980, 1985) dispute this view, choosing instead to emphasise the role of internalisation as the key distinguishing characteristic between MNEs compared to non-MNEs. However, the important point is that all agree that MNCs tend to possess these kinds of firm-specific assets in relatively large amounts.

In such cases, MNEs may find it profitable to pay relatively high wages to compensate for their relatively high productivity, especially when the ability to utilise firm-specific assets is related to workers' firm-specific experience or motivation, for example.

Partially reflecting differences in firm-specific assets, MNE–local wage differentials are thought to result from differences in other plant-level characteristics that might affect labour productivity and/or wages. For example, much of the literature reviewed above suggests that firms or plants that are relatively large or capital- (or input-) intensive often pay relatively high wages and have relatively high labour productivity. In addition, location and industry affiliation are also found to have important influences on the wage levels in firms or plants.

As indicated in the introduction, the literature also suggests that exporters have to incur sunk costs related to the creation of export networks and related firm-specific assets, which are similar to the firm-specific assets possessed by MNEs (Bernard and Jensen 1997; Bernard et al. 2007; Greenaway and Kneller 2007). Sjöholm (2003) provides evidence on this point for Indonesian exporters. However, distinguishing the effects of foreign ownership and exporting on wages is not straightforward because the possession of similar sets of firm-specific assets means that MNEs have a strong tendency to be exporters and vice versa.

7.3 DATA, UNCONDITIONAL WAGE DIFFERENTIALS, AND DIFFERENCES IN WORKER EDUCATION

This analysis is based on plant-level data underlying Indonesia's industrial censuses of medium–large plants (20 or more employees) in 1996 and 2006 as well as Malaysia's census of manufacturing plant activity in 2000 (Malaysian Department of Statistics 2002) and smaller surveys of stratified samples for 2001–2004 (Malaysian Department of Statistics, various years). Indonesia also conducts annual surveys, but they are less comprehensive than the censuses with particularly large differences in coverage for years surrounding 2006. Annual surveys also exclude key data on worker education. Consistent with definitions in the Malaysian data, MNEs are defined as plants with foreign ownership shares of 50 percent or larger.[11]

---

11 The Malaysian data identify three types of firms: those with foreign shares above 50 percent, below 50 percent, and exactly equal to 50 percent. 50/50 joint ventures are usually controlled by the foreign partner and are therefore considered to be majority-foreign plants. This cutoff is higher than the standard one for defining MNEs (foreign shares of 10 percent or more). Previous analysis of Indonesia has also distinguished state-owned enterprises (SOEs)

Small plants with fewer than 20 paid workers are dropped from the Malaysian samples mainly because it is more meaningful to limit analyses of MNE–local wage differentials to medium–large plants than to include small, predominately local plants, in such comparisons. Dropping small plants also has the important advantages of making samples from the census and annual surveys consistent and eliminating most outliers (Ramstetter 2013, 7). For Indonesia, plants with fewer than 20 paid workers and low values of output per worker or value-added per worker (suggesting large, negative profits and/or wage levels well below the minimum wage) were dropped from the samples.[12] The exclusion of these plants removes most outliers and simplifies the interpretation of MNE–local differentials because, as in Malaysia, MNEs were generally large, whereas excluded plants were predominately small, local, private plants (Ramstetter and Narjoko 2013, 9).

For Malaysia and Indonesia in 2006, industry definitions use revision 3 of the International Standard Industrial Classification (ISIC), but 1996 definitions for Indonesia in 1996 use revision 2. Thus, caution is necessary when interpreting industry-level trends in Indonesia.[13] The analysis also excludes five relatively small industries with few MNEs, heterogeneous definitions, and/or heavy government regulation.[14] In order to insure sufficient samples of both exporters and non-exporters, and to include competing plants in the same industry, 9 of the 11 sample industries are defined at the 2-digit level of revision 3 of the ISIC or as combinations of 2-digit categories. Rubber and plastics are defined at the 3-digit level because they are relatively large industries in both economies. The 11 sample industries accounted for 95 percent of paid employ-

---

and local, private plants, but this paper compares MNEs with all local plants because SOEs are not identified in the Malaysian data. In Indonesia, SOEs usually paid higher wages than private plants and MNE–local wage differentials were smaller than MNE–private differentials.

12 The value-added per worker cutoff was 7.9 percent of the national average (including small plants) (ADB 2013) but only 4.5 percent of the published average for medium–large plants (BPS, various years) in 1996. In 2006 these ratios were 6.5 percent and 4.5 percent, respectively, but excluded plants accounted for a larger share of the overall total in 2006 (19 percent) than in 1996 (15 percent).

13 It is impossible to construct a precise correspondence between the two revisions, because several detailed categories (i.e. at the 5- or 4-digit level) in one classification are split among detailed categories in the other classification; see Ramstetter 2014, Appendix Table 5 for the detailed definitions.

14 Four industries (tobacco, printing and publishing, petroleum products, and recycling) had relatively few MNEs in one or both economies while miscellaneous manufacturing is heterogeneously defined. Printing and publishing have also been closely regulated.

ees in all Malaysian manufacturing plants meeting sample criteria and 90–91 percent in Indonesia (Table 7.1). This measure of sample coverage was slightly higher for exporters than non-exporters.

In the 11 sample industries, paid employment in exporters exceeded paid employment in non-exporters in Malaysia and in Indonesia in 1996, but this pattern was reversed in Indonesia in 2006 (Table 7.1). In Malaysia, the largest employers were exporters in electronics-related machinery (23 percent of the total for sample industries), followed distantly by non-exporters in the same industry, exporters in the wood group, non-exporters in wood, non-exporters in the food group, and exporters in the textile group; shares of other groups were all 4 percent of the total or less. In Indonesia, exporters and non-exporters in the textiles group were the largest employers in both years (23 and 12 percent of the sample total, respectively, in 1996; 18 and 15 percent, respectively, in 2006). In 1996, these groups were followed by exporters in wood, non-exporters in food, exporters in food, and non-exporters in wood; no other group accounted for more than 3 percent of the total. In 2006, non-exporters in food, exporters in wood, exporters in food, and non-exporters in wood followed, and again no other group had a share over 3 percent. In other words, food, textiles, and wood were relatively large employers in both economies and electronics-related machinery was very large in Malaysia, but not in Indonesia. Both exporters and non-exporters tended to be large in most of these industries but exporters in food and non-exporters textiles were exceptions in Malaysia.

MNE shares of paid employment were substantially higher for exporters than non-exporters in both economies (53 vs 25 percent in Malaysia and 21 or 34 percent vs 8 or 14 percent in Indonesia; Table 7.1). This reflects the aforementioned tendency for MNEs to be exporters and vice versa. MNEs and exports accounted for larger shares of manufacturing in Malaysia than in Indonesia or most other Asian economies since the 1970s (Ramstetter 1998, 2012b), partially because Malaysia has actively promoted exports and MNE investment, and because Malaysia has always been a relatively small, open economy.

Although Indonesia also encouraged investment by MNEs, it has depended far less on trade and MNEs in manufacturing, partially because it is much larger (especially in terms of population) and because trade policy emphasised import substitution through the mid-1980s. The shift to export promotion after 1985 contributed to substantial, subsequent increases in exports and MNE shares through the mid-1990s (Hill 2000, Chs 5, 6, 8; Takii and Ramstetter 2005). The financial crisis that broke in late 1997 led to a large contraction in 1998 and created severe financial distress for many local companies. As a result, many local partners were forced to sell their stakes in joint ventures with MNEs. Declines in

Table 7.1   Number of paid workers in all plants with viable data (thousand) and MNE shares (%) by export status[a]

Industry	Malaysia, 2000–04 (average)				Indonesia, 1996				Indonesia, 2006			
	Non-exporters		Exporters		Non-exporters		Exporters		Non-exporters		Exporters	
	Total	Share	Total	Share	Total	Share	Total	Share	Total	Share	Total	Share
Manufacturing	630	24	816	53	1,782	7	2,173	21	2,277	14	1,981	33
11 sample industries	583	25	793	53	1,578	8	2,042	21	1,987	15	1,872	34
Food & beverages	79	6	40	26	329	4	196	12	427	9	238	26
Textiles, apparel, leather, footwear	47	27	70	51	448	10	820	25	570	14	682	35
Wood, paper, furniture	92	11	121	20	171	5	465	8	227	5	366	17
Chemicals	22	28	25	50	98	13	85	19	110	15	89	24
Rubber products	23	30	47	42	34	9	81	17	55	26	80	30
Plastics	46	17	49	37	95	4	67	15	119	12	66	24
Non-metallic mineral products	29	15	26	33	106	1	63	12	100	12	61	18
Metals & metal products	57	14	44	40	120	9	89	32	124	14	50	41
Non-electric machinery	23	28	23	60	35	8	9	60	51	47	54	51
Electronics-related machinery	123	62	322	78	65	17	113	68	100	41	133	81
Transportation machinery	42	8	26	21	77	14	53	12	103	31	53	63
Excluded industries	47	8	23	45	204	5	131	17	290	2	109	25

a   Plants with viable data are those with positive paid workers, output, and worker compensation; excluded industries are tobacco, printing & publishing, petroleum products, miscellaneous manufacturing and recycling.

Source: Author's compilations from micro data underlying BPS (various years); Malaysian Department of Statistics (2002, various years).

asset prices and the value of the rupiah created a fire sale, which also encouraged new investments by foreign MNEs. In addition, relaxed restrictions on foreign ownership shares instituted in the mid-1990s were implemented more effectively after the crisis. As a result, MNEs with large foreign ownership shares expanded rapidly during 1996–2006.[15] The growth of paid employment was particularly rapid in MNE non-exporters (149 percent for the 11 sample industries) compared to MNE exporters (46 percent) or local plants (16 percent for non-exporters, –23 percent for exporters; Table 7.1 calculations).

Although MNEs have accounted for larger shares of Malaysian man-ufacturing than non-MNEs, unconditional MNE–local wage differentials were smaller in Malaysia than in Indonesia (Table 7.2). Differentials also declined in Indonesia during 1996–2006, both for exporters and for non-exporters. When all 11 sample industries are combined, MNE–local wage differentials were also smaller for exporters than non-exporters, and the gap between the two groups was relatively small for Indonesia in 2006 (58 vs 74 percent) and Malaysia (31 vs 44 percent) compared to Indonesia in 1996 (89 vs 220 percent). This pattern is also observed at the industry level with MNE–local wage differentials being smaller than correspond-ing differentials for non-exporters in 10 of the 11 Indonesian industries in both years (rubber in 1996 and chemicals in 2006 were exceptions). In Malaysia, differentials were smaller in exporters in eight of the 11 indus-tries (wood, chemicals, and transportation machinery were exceptions), but the gap between exporter and non-exporters was small in another two (textiles and electronics-related manufacturing).

In 1996, MNE–local wage differentials were 33 percent or higher in all 11 industries for Indonesia's non-exporters and in 10 industries for Indonesia's exporters, wage differentials exceeded this level in only seven industries for non-exporters and five for exporters in 2006 (Table 7.2). In Malaysia, similarly large wage differentials were observed in six industries for non-exporters but only four for exporters. In other words, unconditional wage differentials were often smaller at the industry level than when all 11 industries were combined. On the other hand, uncon-ditional wage differentials were never negative for either exporters or non-exporters in these 11 industries.

Table 7.2 also illustrates the strong correlation between MNE–local wage differentials and corresponding differentials in the shares of work-ers with tertiary education among the 11 sample industries. Correlations were 0.84 or higher for both exporters and non-exporters in Malaysia

---

15 MNEs with foreign ownership shares of 90 percent or more accounted for only 6.1 of paid employment in all manufacturing plants in 1996, but this share increased sharply to 16 percent in 2006 (Ramstetter and Narjoko 2013, 24).

Table 7.2 Mean MNE–local ratios of wages and shares of paid workers with tertiary education by export status[a]

Industry	Malaysia, 2000–04 (average)				Indonesia, 1996				Indonesia, 2006			
	Non-exporters		Exporters		Non-exporters		Exporters		Non-exporters		Exporters	
	Wages	Shares	Wages	Shares	Wages	Shares	Wages	Shares	Wages	Shares	Wages	Shares
11 sample industries	1.44	1.79	1.31	1.61	3.20	4.05	1.89	2.10	1.74	2.70	1.58	1.78
Food & beverages	1.72	2.22	1.59	1.84	3.31	4.65	1.67	1.69	1.96	3.34	1.49	1.69
Textiles, apparel, leather, footwear	1.17	0.98	1.15	0.93	1.52	2.92	1.32	1.42	1.42	2.51	1.33	1.11
Wood, paper, furniture	1.19	1.46	1.24	1.52	2.14	2.50	1.51	1.86	1.45	2.39	1.33	1.90
Chemicals	1.33	1.48	1.42	1.65	3.84	3.40	2.18	2.06	1.39	1.78	1.54	1.60
Rubber products	1.41	1.21	1.22	1.16	1.44	0.37	1.62	1.37	1.22	0.78	1.16	0.69
Plastics	1.22	1.38	1.19	1.46	2.66	3.65	1.72	1.96	1.42	1.87	1.05	1.21
Non-metallic mineral products	1.66	2.15	1.49	2.24	2.21	1.94	1.37	1.81	2.05	3.03	1.66	1.31
Metals & metal products	1.36	1.56	1.12	1.21	2.65	2.24	1.47	1.45	1.50	1.42	1.12	0.98
Non-electric machinery	1.59	2.31	1.21	1.55	1.86	2.22	1.76	1.95	1.32	1.28	1.30	0.90
Electronics-related machinery	1.10	1.04	1.05	0.98	1.89	1.16	1.43	1.05	1.19	1.31	1.09	1.14
Transportation machinery	1.23	1.03	1.36	1.45	2.22	1.88	1.41	0.88	1.32	1.29	1.06	1.14
Correlation of means for 11 industries	0.90		0.84		0.71		0.62		0.86		0.51	

a Sample plants are those with 20 or more paid workers, as well as positive output and worker compensation; exluded industries are tobacco, printing & publishing, petroleum products, miscellaneous manufacturing and recycling; wages include all compensation (including overtime, bonuses and social security payments, paid in cash or in kind).

Source: Author's compilations from micro data underlying BPS (various years); Malaysian Department of Statistics (2002, various years).

122

and for non-exporters in Indonesia in 2006. The correlation was also relatively strong for non-exporters in Indonesia in 1996 (0.71), but weaker for Indonesian exporters in 1996 (0.62) and 2006 (0.51). As MNE theory suggests, shares of workers with tertiary education tends to be higher in MNEs, but there are a few industries in which they are higher in local plants. Thus, when examining MNE–local wage differentials, it is clearly important to account for how worker education and other plant characteristics affect wages.

7.4   RESULTS OF ESTIMATING EARNINGS EQUATIONS

In order to determine whether MNE–local wage differentials can be explained by differences in worker education and other plant characteristics, and whether remaining conditional differentials vary between exporters and non-exporters, this paper estimates earnings equations similar to those in Lipsey and Sjöholm (2004a) separately for exporters and non-exporters. The equations account for the influences of worker education (and occupation for Malaysia) and sex, plant size, capital (Malaysia), or energy (Indonesia) per worker, location, and industry affiliation, as well as MNE ownership.

$$LCE = a0 + a1(LKE) + a2(LO) + a3(SH) + a4(S4) + a5(S3)$$
$$+ a6(S2) + a7(SF) + a8(DF) \qquad (7.1)$$

where

LCE = log of compensation per employee (value)
LKE = log of fixed assets (Malaysia) or energy (Indonesia) per employee (value)
LO = plant size, measured as the log of output (value)
SH = share of paid workers in highly paid occupations (percent; Malaysia only)
$S4$ = share of workers with some level of tertiary education (percent; includes unpaid workers for Malaysia)
$S3$ = share of workers completing secondary education (percent includes unpaid workers for Malaysia)
$S2$ = share of paid workers with junior high school education (percent, Indonesia only)[16]

---

16 Because workers with junior high school education are relatively unskilled, this variable is omitted for Malaysia. Previous analysis for Indonesia (Lipsey and Sjöholm 2004a; Ramstetter 2013) also included the share of workers not finishing elementary school, but coefficients on this variable were often insignificant at the industry level and in 2006 so it is omitted here.

124   *Eric D. Ramstetter*

SF = share of paid workers that are female (percent)
DF = dummy variable identifying MNE plants (= 1 if MNE, 0 otherwise)

As in Table 7.2, the dependent variable is defined to include all labour compensation including bonuses, payments in kind, social insurance payments, and other compensation.[17] Reflecting the previous discussion, plants that are relatively capital-intensive, energy-intensive, or have relatively high-quality workforces are expected to pay relatively high wages. Thus, the coefficients *a1*, *a2*, *a3*, *a4*, *a5*, and *a6* are expected to be positive. The coefficient *a7* is expected to be negative because females generally earn less than their male counterparts. To the extent that there are MNE–local differences in shares of foreign workers, worker experience and training, data on which are unavailable, estimates of equation (7.1) may face an omitted variable problem. Finally, the coefficient *a8* is the conditional MNE–local wage differential that remains after accounting for capital or energy intensity, size, as well as worker occupation (Malaysia only), education, and sex, and can be compared to the unconditional differentials in Table 7.2.

Estimates of Equation (7.1) use robust standard errors to account for heteroskedasticity and include region and industry dummies to account for industry-specific and region-specific factors affecting plant wages.[18]

---

17 For Malaysia, nominal wages are converted to real values with the consumer price index, while capital intensity and output are converted to real values using GDP deflators for 24 industries, which were generally defined at the 2- or 3-digit level (Malaysian Department of Statistics 2011). This is reasonable for wages and output, but not very accurate for capital because changes in asset prices are not reflected, but I know of no deflators for fixed assets in Malaysia. Indonesian values are measured in current rupiah.

18 Indonesia dummies are generally defined at the 3-digit level of ISIC revision 2 for Indonesia in 1996 and revision 3 for Indonesia in 2006 and for Malaysia, though a few categories had to be combined to avoid collinearity with DF (351 and 352 for Indonesia in 2006, 242 and 243 for Malaysia); because revision 2 is less detailed, especially in the machinery industries, there are relatively few dummies for Indonesia in 1996. Industry dummies are omitted from industry-level estimates when industries are defined at the 3-digit level. In Indonesia, region dummies identify plants in West Java, Central Java (including Yogyakarta), East Java, and outside of Java (including Sumatra, Nusa Tenggara, Kalimantan, Sulawesi, Maluku, and Irian Jaya), using Jakarta as the reference region. For Malaysia, there are usually nine region dummies using Kuala Lumpur as the reference region. Most are defined at the state level, but states with relatively few plants, similar population densities, and nearby locations were combined (Perlis and Kedah, Kelantan, Terengganu, and Pahang, and finally Sabah, Sarawak, and Labuan). See Ramstetter 2014, Appendix Tables 3 and 4 for the exact number of industry and region dummies in each estimate.

In addition to using industry dummies, estimates are also performed separately for 11 industry groups because allowing both intercepts and slopes, including the MNE-local differential, to vary among industries has an important impact on the results.

For Malaysia, plant-level panels are compiled and year dummies use the first year in as the base in samples for 2000–2004 and 2001–2004. Alternative samples are used to examine sensitivity of the results to inclusion of the census year and facilitate comparisons of a contemporaneous specification with a lagged specification, where all independent variables are lagged one year. Although simultaneity is probably not a large problem because wage levels are not likely to be an important determinant of the independent variables, the lagged specification is less likely to be affected by simultaneity issues and provides an important robustness check.[19] Results of pooled ordinary least squares (OLS) and random effects panel estimates are also compared to evaluate the robustness of the results to alternative econometric assumptions.[20] It is also possible to panelise the Indonesian data, but combining 1996 and 2006 in a single sample is not economically meaningful because there were large changes in many plants (e.g. changes in ownership as discussed above) after the financial crisis. Correspondingly, Indonesian estimates are performed in cross sections only.

Almost all estimates for all 11 industries combined yielded expected results for both countries (Tables 7.3 and 7.4). Coefficients on capital or energy intensity, size, tertiary shares, and secondary shares were positive and highly significant at the 1 percent level with one exception; the coefficient on secondary shares in random effects estimates of the contemporaneous specification for 2000–2004 for Malaysia. Reflecting the tendency for wages to increase with worker education levels, coefficients on tertiary shares were substantially larger than coefficients on secondary shares in both countries and both of these coefficients were larger

---

19 Ramstetter (2012a) also estimates an alternative, contemporaneous specification (see note above) for 2000–2002 and 2002–2004, in addition to 2000–2004. Results for the subperiods suggest that significant, MNE-local wage differentials were more common in the earlier period. This paper focuses on longer panels because they are thought to be relatively reliable and facilitate more meaningful estimates of the lagged specification.

20 Results of the Breusch-Pagan test indicate that the null of no random effects can always be rejected at the 1 percent level or better, but I am primarily interested in checking the robustness of the key results to alternative econometric assumptions. It is also common to test if fixed effects estimates are econometrically preferable to random effects estimates, but if fixed effects estimates are used, the coefficient a8 measures the effects of changes in plant ownership on wages, not the MNE-local wage differential which is the focus of this analysis.

Table 7.3   Estimates of conditional multinational–local wage differentials in Indonesia from Equation (7.1), other slope coefficents and equation indicators; p-values based on robust standard errors (clustered by plant for random effects), 11 industries combined[a]

Independent variable, indicator	1996		2006	
	Non-exporters	Exporters	Non-exporters	Exporters
LKE	0.0583***	0.0594***	0.0503***	0.0556***
LO	0.1248***	0.1083***	0.1099***	0.1010***
S5	0.0087***	0.0141***	0.0076***	0.0060***
S4	0.0024***	0.0023***	0.0046***	0.0027***
S3	0.0012***	0.0009**	0.0031***	0.0020***
SF	−0.0028***	−0.0043***	−0.0024***	−0.0039***
DF	0.3180***	0.2410***	0.0578***	0.1195***
Observations	13,941	3,901	17,006	4,343
R^2	0.48	0.47	0.48	0.44

*** = significant at the 1% level; ** = significant at the 5% level.
a Estimates include 5 regional dummies and 24 (1996), 55 (2006 non-exporters), or 52 (2006 exporters) industry dummies (see the text for definitions); full results including constants and all dummy coefficients are available from the authors.

than the coefficient on junior high shares in Indonesia. Coefficients on shares of highly paid workers in Malaysia and workers with junior high education in Indonesia were also positive and highly significant, while coefficients on female share were negative and highly significant. The MNE–local differential was also positive and highly significant in all estimates, similar to results in previous studies discussed above. R^2 ranged between 0.44–0.48 for Indonesia and 0.50–0.63 for Malaysia, indicating that the models described the variation in plant-level wages reasonably well.

Results indicated substantial differences in several slope coefficients for exporters and non-exporters in both countries (Tables 7.3 and 7.4). Most importantly, the MNE–local differential was somewhat larger among exporting plants in Malaysia (8.9–9.2 vs 6.2–7.5 percent if pooled OLS estimates are used; 7.2–7.8 vs 4.7–6.7 percent if random effects estimates are used) and in Indonesia in 2006 (12 vs 5.8 percent). MNE–local differentials were larger for Indonesia in 1996, but the differential was smaller for exporters (24 vs 32 percent). In short, results from these large samples suggest that MNE–local wage differentials tended to be larger

Table 7.4 Estimates of conditional multinational–local wage differentials in Malaysia from Equation (7.1), other slope coefficents and equation indicators; p-values based on robust standard errors (clustered by plant for random effects), 11 industries combined[a]

Slope coefficient variable, indicator	Pooled OLS			Random effects		
	Lagged	Contemporaneous		Lagged	Contemporaneous	
	2001–04	2001–04	2000–04	2001–04	2001–04	2000–04
Non-exporters						
LKE = capital intensity	0.0214***	0.0300***	0.0312***	0.0155***	0.0335***	0.0340***
LO = output scale	0.1325***	0.1379***	0.1398***	0.1154***	0.1373***	0.1408***
SH = highly paid share of paid workers	0.0061***	0.0059***	0.0074***	0.0034***	0.0055***	0.0071***
S3 = highly educated share of all workers	0.0055***	0.0067***	0.0052***	0.0041***	0.0060***	0.0044***
S2 = moderately educated share of all workers	0.0011***	0.0013***	0.0004***	0.0005***	0.0011***	0.0001
SF = female share of paid workers	−0.0041***	−0.0034***	−0.0035***	−0.0035***	−0.0027***	−0.0026***
DF = MNE-local differential (ratio less 1)	0.0733***	0.0619***	0.0751***	0.0665***	0.0470***	0.0623***
R^2	0.5072	0.5398	0.5241	0.4978	0.5363	0.5202
Observations	11,393	18,003	22,945	11,393	18,003	22,945
Breusch–Pagan Test	–	–	–	3,509***	5,316***	6,823***
Exporters						
LKE = capital intensity	0.0251***	0.0344***	0.0347***	0.0226***	0.0401***	0.0431***
LO = output scale	0.0842***	0.0895***	0.0883***	0.0871***	0.0907***	0.0920***
SH = highly paid share of paid workers	0.0080***	0.0092***	0.0095***	0.0050***	0.0076***	0.0079***
S3 = highly educated share of all workers	0.0069***	0.0071***	0.0066***	0.0051***	0.0072***	0.0064***
S2 = moderately educated share of all workers	0.0012***	0.0009***	0.0009***	0.0009***	0.0005***	0.0008***
SF = female share of paid workers	−0.0036***	−0.0032***	−0.0033***	−0.0037***	−0.0027***	−0.0026***
DF = MNE-local differential (ratio less 1)	0.0899***	0.0888***	0.0918***	0.0724***	0.0775***	0.0721***
R^2	0.6184	0.6287	0.6251	0.6279	0.6263	0.6220
Observations	6,788	9,546	12,421	6,788	9,546	12,421
Breusch–Pagan Test	–	–	–	2,230***	3,536***	5,546***

*** = significant at the 1% level.
a   Full results including constants and coefficients on year, industry and region dummies are available from the author.

for exporters than non-exporters in Malaysia and Indonesia in 2006, but that this pattern was reversed for Indonesia in 1996.

There were also differences in other coefficients for exporters and non-exporters. For example, for Indonesian exporters, the coefficient on the tertiary share was 1.6 times larger than for non-exporters in 1996, but only 0.8 times as large in 2006 (Table 7.3). Corresponding Malaysian results resemble those for Indonesia in 1996, with coefficients for exporters being 1.3–1.6 times larger for exporters in pooled OLS estimates and 1.1–1.5 times larger in random effects estimates (Table 7.4). The coefficient on the secondary share was also relatively low for Indonesian exporters in 2006 compared to 1996 (0.6 vs 1.0 times non-exporter levels), but corresponding Malaysian coefficients were 1.1–1.4 times larger for exporters. On the other hand, the negative coefficient on the female share was always much larger in absolute value for exporters than non-exporters in Indonesia, but of similar magnitude for exporters and non-exporters in Malaysia.

Estimates of equation (7.1) for each of the 11 sample industries also yielded generally expected results for Malaysia, but results were weaker and more varied for Indonesia, especially in 2006 (see Ramstetter 2014, Appendix Tables 3 and 4 for details). For Indonesia, samples were under 100 for exporters in non-electric machinery (37 in 1996, 79 in 2006) and transportation machinery (66 in 1996, 98 in 2006). The minimum R^2 was 0.18, and R^2 was under 0.30 in 2006 for exporters in four industries (rubber, plastics, metals, non-electric machinery) and non-exporters in plastics. The coefficient on size was the only one that was significant at the standard 5 percent level with the expected sign in most estimates for both exporters and non-exporters in both years. Most estimates of coefficients on energy intensity and secondary shares were also significant in 10 or 11 of the industries for non-exporters, but only in a minority of industries for exporters. In contrast, coefficients on tertiary shares were significant in under half of the estimates. Coefficients on female shares were significant in most industries in 1996, but in only about half 2006.

For Malaysia, the minimum sample size was 191 (transportation machinery, exporters), the minimum R^2 was 0.22, and R^2 was less than 0.40 in only two samples (exporters in textiles and non-exporters in chemicals). Moreover, coefficients on size, capital intensity, shares of highly paid workers, tertiary shares, and female shares were significant with the expected signs in three quarters or more of the 132 estimates.

Thus, the industry-level results paint a picture that often differs substantially from aggregate results, and this contrast is also seen in estimates of MNE–local differentials for both countries. For Indonesia, the most striking result is the relative lack of significant MNE–local differentials in 2006, which are observed in only two of the 11 industries, textiles,

Table 7.5   Estimates of conditional multinational–local wage differentials
            in Indonesia by industry from Equation (7.1), p-values based
            on robust standard errors (clustered by plant for random
            effects)[a]

Independent variable, indicator	1996		2006	
	Non-exporters	Exporters	Non-exporters	Exporters
Food & beverages	0.2969***	0.1985***	0.0471	0.0863
Textiles, apparel, leather, footwear	0.0893	0.1378***	0.0745**	0.1622***
Wood, paper, furniture	0.1843	0.1526***	0.0729	0.0647
Chemicals	0.5330***	0.4272***	–0.0325	0.1740*
Rubber products	0.1203	0.2891***	0.1711*	0.1640
Plastics	0.5362***	0.2310**	0.0815	0.0676
Non-metallic mineral products	0.1926*	0.2678	0.0709	0.1828
Metals & metal products	0.3813***	0.2232**	0.1242**	0.2026**
Non-electric machinery	0.1338	0.3285	0.0759	0.1979
Electronics-related machinery	0.2843**	0.2219***	–0.0409	–0.1135
Transportation machinery	0.0908	0.2282	–0.0650	0.0785

*** = significant at the 1% level; ** = significant at the 5% level; * = significant at the 10% level.
a   Other slope coefficients and equation statistics are presented in Ramstetter (2014), Appendix Table 3; full results including constants and coefficients on year, industry and region dummies are available from the author.

and metals (Table 7.5). MNE–local differentials in these industries were substantially larger for exporters than non-exporters (16 vs 7.5 percent and 20 versus 12 percent, respectively) and all of these differentials were larger than corresponding differentials observed when all 11 industries are combined. In other words, the results for all industries combined appear to have been dominated by plants in these two industries in 2006.

In 1996, industry-level, MNE–local differentials were more often significant (Table 7.5). There were five industries where differentials were significant for both exporters and non-exporters (food and beverages, chemicals, plastics, metals, and electronics related machinery). In all five of these industries, differentials were larger for non-exporters than for exporters, with the largest gap observed in plastics (54 vs 23 percent) and smallest in chemicals (53 vs 43 percent). On the other hand, there were three industries in which MNE–local differentials were significant for exporters (textiles, wood, and rubber) but insignificant for local plants.

In short, the results for Indonesia suggest substantial variation of MNE-local differentials among industries and over time, as well as between exporting and non-exporting plants.

MNE–local wage differentials in Malaysia also varied substantially among industries and industry-level results were more sensitive to the lagging of independent variables or the choice between pooled OLS and random effects estimation than aggregate results (Table 7.6). For example, MNE–local differentials were significant in all six estimates for only three of 22 groups, exporters in wood and rubber, and non-exporters in rubber. Moreover, in rubber, random effects estimates of the lagged specification suggest slightly larger MNE–local differentials for exporters, but all other estimates suggest substantially lower differentials for exporters. Wood was the only other industry where all estimates tell a similar qualitative story, suggesting positive and significant differentials for exporters of 5.8 to 8.7 percent and insignificant differentials for non-exporters. Estimates of the contemporaneous specification are similar in textiles suggesting positive differentials for exporters but insignificant or negative differentials for non-exporters, but estimates of the lagged specification indicate differentials were insignificant for both exporters and non-exporters. In contrast, estimates of the contemporaneous specification for chemicals, metals, and non-electric machinery indicate relatively large differences for non-exporters, but estimates of the lagged specification are again inconsistent. In short, as in Indonesia, there is substantial variation of MNE–local wage differentials among industries in Malaysia, and no clear tendency for MNE–local wage differentials to differ among exporters and non-exporters at the industry level.

7.5   CONCLUSIONS AND FUTURE RESEARCH

This chapter first explained previous evidence that MNEs tend to pay higher wages and to hire relatively well-educated workers than non-MNEs, and that positive MNE–local wage differentials remain even after accounting for differences in worker education and sex, as well as plant size and capital or input intensity. On the other hand, there is no known evidence as to whether MNE–local wage differentials differ between exporters, who are more exposed to competition in world markets, and non-exporters, who lack such exposure. Simultaneously sorting out differences between MNEs and non-MNEs and between exporters and non-exporters is complicated because a firm's decision to become an MNE or an exporter (or both) are related to sunk costs incurred in the creation of exporting networks, production technology, and other firm-specific, generally intangible assets.

Table 7.6   Estimates of conditional multinational–local wage differentials in Malaysia by industry from Equation (7.1), p-values based on robust standard errors (clustered by plant for random effects)[a]

Industry	Pooled OLS			Random effects		
	Lagged	Contemporaneous		Lagged	Contemporaneous	
	2001–04	2001–04	2000–04	2001–04	2001–04	2000–04
Food & beverages						
Non-exporters	0.0840*	0.0967***	0.0948***	0.0619	0.1075**	0.0783*
Exporters	0.0564*	0.0819***	0.0937***	0.0731**	0.1158**	0.1105***
Textiles, etc.						
Non-exporters	-0.0024	-0.0656	-0.0196	-0.0645	-0.0800**	-0.0037
Exporters	0.0516*	0.0916***	0.0707***	0.0790*	0.1162***	0.0855***
Wood, etc.						
Non-exporters	0.0208	0.0239	0.0349	0.0437	0.0091	0.0236
Exporters	0.0675***	0.0779***	0.0760***	0.0589**	0.0869***	0.0730***
Chemicals						
Non-exporters	0.0639	0.0839***	0.1021***	0.0671	0.1026**	0.1179***
Exporters	0.0984***	0.0721***	0.0756***	0.0667*	0.0691**	0.0678**
Rubber products						
Non-exporters	0.2639***	0.2318***	0.2497***	0.1592**	0.1866***	0.1662***
Exporters	0.2084***	0.1816***	0.1830***	0.1616***	0.1354***	0.1145***
Plastics						
Non-exporters	0.0971***	0.0522*	0.0791***	0.0797*	0.0005	0.0103
Exporters	0.0871***	0.0919***	0.0953***	0.0672*	0.0546*	0.0700***
Non-metallic mineral products						
Non-exporters	0.1136*	0.0915**	0.0910**	0.0949	-0.0182	0.0308
Exporters	0.0584	0.0266	0.0652	0.0726	0.1023	0.0903
Metals & metal products						
Non-exporters	0.0500*	0.0594***	0.0845***	0.0629	0.0748**	0.0957***
Exporters	0.0591**	0.0586***	0.0714***	0.0429	0.0520	0.0683**
Non-electric machinery						
Non-exporters	0.1464*	0.1422***	0.1229***	0.1585	0.2070***	0.2030***
Exporters	0.0654	0.0380	0.0548	0.0010	-0.0019	0.0273
Electrical machinery						
Non-exporters	0.1072***	0.0636***	0.0528**	0.0795**	0.0493	0.0218
Exporters	0.0299	0.0395**	0.0419***	0.0165	0.0272	0.0304
Transportation machinery						
Non-exporters	0.1142	0.1109*	0.1196**	0.0942	0.1271	0.1674**
Exporters	0.1206*	0.1282**	0.1368**	0.0786	0.0283	0.0674

*** = significant at the 1% level; ** = significant at the 5% level; * = significant at the 10% level.
a   Results of the Breusch–Pagan Test indicate the null of no random effects is always rejected at the 1% level; other slope coefficients and equation statistics are presented in Ramstetter (2014), Appendix Table 4; full results including constants and coefficients on year, industry and region dummies are available from the author.

In large samples of plants in 11 manufacturing industries, mean, unconditional MNE–local wage differentials tended to be somewhat smaller for exporters than for non-exporters of Malaysia in 2000–2004 (31 vs 44 percent) and Indonesia in 2006 (58 vs 74 percent), and the gap was particularly conspicuous for Indonesia in 1996 (89 vs 220 percent). Shares of workers with tertiary education were also smaller for exporters than non-exporters. Conditional MNE–local wage differentials that account for the influences of worker education and sex, as well as plant size and capital or energy intensity, on plant-level wages were much smaller than unconditional differentials, but were always positive and highly significant statistically. In other words, worker education and sex, and other plant characteristics explain much of the unconditional MNE–local differentials, but MNEs tended to pay higher wages than local plants even after accounting for these other determinants of wages. Like unconditional differentials, conditional differentials were smaller for exporters Indonesia in 1996 (24 vs 32 percent). In contrast, conditional differentials were larger for exporters in Indonesia in 2006 (12 vs 5.7 percent) and Malaysia in 2000–2004 (8.8–9.2 vs 6.2–7.5 percent in pooled OLS estimates and 7.2–7.8 vs 4.7–6.7 percent in random effects estimates).

When 11 sample industries are examined separately, the tendency for unconditional MNE–local wage differentials to be smaller in exporters is also observed. However, there is substantial variation in the size of MNE–local differentials and gaps in these differentials between exporters and non-exporters among industries. Moreover, when conditional MNE–local differentials and other slope coefficients are allowed to differ among industries, differentials were often insignificant, especially for Indonesia in 2006. Most importantly, there is no clear tendency for differentials to be related to export status in the industry-level samples. Rather differences among industries appear to dominate differences between exporters and non-exporters, and there are indications that results for all industries combined are driven by results in a relatively few number of industries.

Because this is perhaps the first study to compare MNE–local wage differentials between exporters and non-exporters, there is a long agenda for future research. For example, this study has focused on the differences between exporters and non-exporters because the discrete decision to export is likely to be closely related to the similarly discrete decision to become an MNE. However, it is also potentially interesting to examine differences between importers and non-importers, or between plants with varying degrees of export or import dependence. Similarly, it may be interesting to distinguish among MNEs with differing degrees of foreign ownership, though this is not possible for Malaysia and previous evidence suggests this distinction is not very important to wage determination in Indonesia (Ramstetter and Narjoko 2013). It would also be interesting to examine other host economies, though lack of data on worker education is a key constraint. Finally, as in Lipsey and Sjöholm (2004b, 2005, 2006) and Sjöholm and Lipsey (2006), one could also investigate how takeovers or changes in ownership affect both wages and employment, or the effect of MNE presence on wages in local plants (i.e. wage spillovers). All of these analyses require some degree of data panelisation, which is particularly difficult in Indonesia because annual surveys lack data on worker education, and sample sizes vary greatly between the 2006 census and surrounding years, for example. However, using the panels constructed for Malaysia, it should be possible to do similar analysis for 2000–2004 and maybe subsequent years if data can be obtained.

8 Indonesia: returns to occupation, education, and ability during a resource export boom

Ian Coxhead*

This chapter examines the effects of the recent resources boom and the government policy response on the structure of employment and incentives for human capital investments in the Indonesian economy. The key focus of the chapter is on the slow manufacturing growth and its implications for the demand for labour and, in particular, human capital development in the economy. It is argued that, in the absence of countervailing policies to mitigate the Dutch disease effects on the manufacturing sector, the resource export boom will tend to reduce growth of 'good' (i.e. skilled) jobs and will lower returns to education, especially at more advanced levels. In the long term the economy may, therefore, be less well positioned to make a transition to growth based on skills and innovation, but avoiding the 'middle-income trap'.

The chapter begins with an overview of structural changes in the economy from a historical perspective, with a focus on how the resource export boom and government policy response impacts on manufacturing performance and the theoretical underpinnings of the postulated relationship between manufacturing performance and return to education. The next section provides an analytical narrative of the changing structure of employment and real wages in Indonesia. The following section reports the results of an econometric analysis of the impact of changes in the structure of labour-demand earnings, job security, returns

---

* Parts of this paper are drawn from Coxhead (2014). The author thanks Rashesh Shrestha for excellent research assistance.

to skills, and other factors likely to influence long-term economic well-being. The final section presents a summary of the key findings and policy implications.

8.1   INDONESIAN GROWTH AND STRUCTURAL CHANGE IN THE 2000s

In the 1980s and 1990s, the share of manufacturing in Indonesian GDP and merchandise exports increased continuously.[1] At their peak in 2000, manufactures accounted for 29 percent of GDP and 57 percent of merchandise exports. In the subsequent decade, there has been a notable decline in these shares, falling to 24 percent of GDP and 34 percent of exports by 2012 – the same as their 1993–94 levels.

The time pattern of manufacturing's share of GDP is generally expected to be non-linear as, with rising wealth, skill-intensive services become increasingly important sources of comparative advantage and income. Thus, the timing, pace, and extent of the decline in Indonesia appears unusual. This is evident in Figure 8.1, which plots manufacturing's share of GDP against the log of per capita income for a comparable group of East and Southeast Asian economies. Indonesia (shown in solid black) underwent a dramatic increase, and then an equally dramatic decline.

Since we lack a counterfactual argument against which to evaluate these trends, it is important to try to see them in context. One comparison is with Indonesia itself, in the decade prior to the crisis. Another reference point is the data from comparable neighbouring economies such as Thailand, Malaysia, and the Philippines (e.g. Aswicahyono, Hill, and Narjoko 2011a). Indonesia's GDP growth rate has been roughly similar, and its industrial slowdown has been approximately matched by Thailand. But Indonesia's manufacturing industries *never* achieved a comparable share of GDP and employment, or the levels of productivity or technical sophistication seen in neighbouring economies (Coxhead and Li 2008), and its average per capita income remains well below theirs.

Slow growth in manufacturing relative to overall GDP appears to have more than one cause. It is likely to be due in part to the after-effects of a large and sustained drop in investment during the Asian financial crisis of 1997–98. During 1970–96, the stock of machinery and equipment grew at around 8 percent per year and investment averaged about 30 percent of GDP. Investment fell to 21 percent of GDP during 1997–2001

---

1   Data cited in this paragraph are from World Bank, World Development Indicators Online (http://databank.worldbank.org/data/home.aspx, accessed 1 March 2014).

Figure 8.1   Per capita income and manufacturing share of GDP, East and Southeast Asia (%)[a]

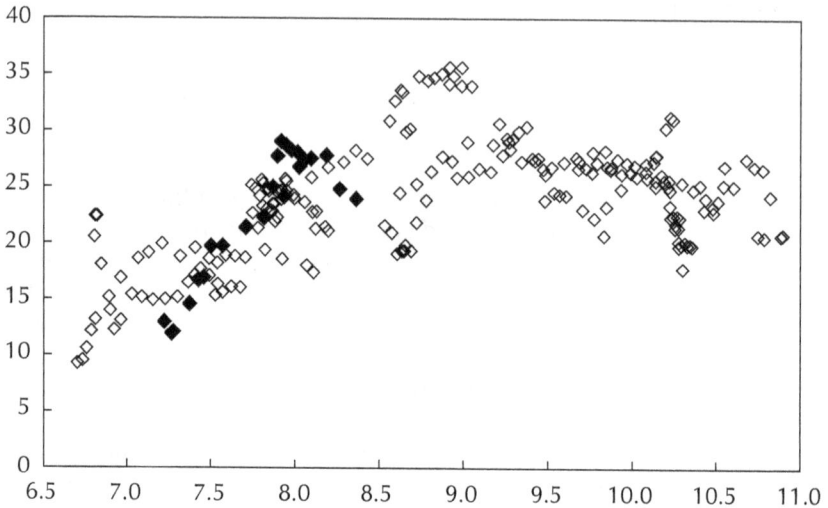

a   Log of per capita income, 1980–2012 (PPP$, constant 2005 prices). Countries: Cambodia, Indonesia (in solid black), Japan, South Korea, Malaysia, the Philippines, Singapore, Thailand and Vietnam.

Source: WDI Online.

and did not regain the pre-crisis rate until 2007. Moreover, growth of total capital stock in the 2000s was led by construction, particularly non-residential construction, rather than by manufacturing (van der Eng 2009, Figure 4). Public investments in infrastructure also fell far behind the pace required to maintain an efficient economy. Inefficient and unreliable ports, roads and traffic management, and electricity supply all now have a large impact on manufacturing sector costs. Thus over the decade 1998–2007, growth of physical capital per worker (excluding construction) was very low, or even negative.

Other flaws in economic management have arguably contributed to diminished employment and wage growth. In the post-democratisation era, momentum in economic reform, including liberalisation of trade and foreign investment policies, has been lost (Wihardja 2013). There has been backsliding and ambivalence on foreign direct investment (FDI) regulations, and even on trade policy – including a recent decision to impose export taxes on unprocessed natural resource products. Labour market regulations – already very restrictive by regional standards (World Bank 2013a) – have been tightened, including moves to raise minimum wages in organised sectors and to impose controls that make hiring and firing more costly. On social policy, spending has increased, most especially on education, but empirical studies do not find evidence that increased spending is mapping into improved educational outcomes (e.g. Suryadarma and Jones 2013; Newhouse and Suryadarma 2011). Nor is public spending on education high by regional standards (Phan and Coxhead 2014).

Finally, Indonesia has without doubt suffered in the 2000s from Dutch disease (Thee 2011). A resource boom in a small, trade-dependent economy, while increasing income, is expected to reduce profits, activity levels, and employment in non-resource tradable sectors such as manufacturing, and increase them in non-tradable sectors (broadly, services). The prices of the former industries will also fall relative to those of the latter. The factor-market implications of Dutch disease are not unambiguous, but theory postulates that real returns to factors used intensively in non-booming sectors will fall, while returns to more mobile factors (commonly, unskilled labour) may rise or fall depending on the extent of real appreciation.

A brief consideration of theory also indicates that many of the effects of these three putative causes of manufacturing decline are correlated. A resource export boom, an investment collapse, and the tightening of labour market and other industrial regulations should all reduce profits, activity levels, and employment in manufacturing sectors. If physical and human capital are complements in production (e.g. Griliches 1969) then a diminished rate of manufacturing-sector investment also reduces growth in demand for skilled workers. Of course, an important contrast between an export boom and an investment collapse or increased level of distortion in the labour market is that the former raises total income, whereas the latter two reduce it. It is therefore clear that among these three influences on Indonesia's manufacturing growth, the resource export boom has been dominant.

If the slowdown in manufacturing growth is more than temporary, does it matter? One reason that it might be is because manufacturing, more than most economic activities, is characterised by technological dynamism, learning by doing, information spillovers, and other sources of externalities that promote economic growth by making capital and other factors more productive (Hanson 2012). Because most manufacturing is tradable and thus highly competitive, and because technologies quickly transfer across national borders, there is much greater scope for productivity growth than exists in industries that are sheltered from international competition, whether through intrinsic factors such as low value-to-weight ratios or extrinsic factors such as trade policy. Finally, the fastest-growing part of global and East Asian trade in the 2000s is in parts and components for final assembly in large assembly hubs within global production networks like China's Pearl River delta. A dynamic

manufacturing industry has many opportunities to further raise productivity through participation in such specialised and fast-moving regional
trade networks. For all of these reasons, international data reveal robust
evidence of unconditional cross-country convergence in manufacturing
growth rates, but not in growth rates of other sectors or in aggregate
income (Rodrik 2013).

A second way in which slow manufacturing growth affects the aggregate economy is through its effects on the demand for labour, and specifically the demand for human capital. The 'lagging' sectors in a Dutch
disease-affected economy are those where profitability (and thus investment incentives) becomes trapped between rising domestic costs and
output prices that are fixed in world markets. Some agricultural subsectors are vulnerable in this way, and so is much of manufacturing, the
most skill-intensive and technologically dynamic sector. In the absence
of countervailing policies, therefore, a sustained resource export boom
will tend to reduce growth of 'good' (i.e. skilled) jobs and will lower
returns to education, especially at more advanced levels. This in turn
exerts downward pressure on enrolment, retention, and graduation
rates at upper secondary school and tertiary levels, especially as rising
labour demand in low-skill industries increases the opportunity cost of
schooling. In the long term, the economy may be less well positioned to
make the transition to growth based on skills and innovation – that is, to
transition into and through middle income, since this has been shown
to depend greatly on improving educational attainment at secondary
and tertiary levels (Eichengreen, Park, and Shin 2013). And finally, since
education is the most important pathway to economic mobility, lower
returns to schooling are associated with rising income inequality, another
striking feature of Indonesia's economy since 2001 (Yusuf 2013). In Indonesia, the gradient of schooling attainment rates from lowest to highest income quintile is steep by comparison with neighbouring countries
such as Thailand and Vietnam (Phan and Coxhead 2014).

In the past decade Indonesia has invested heavily in increasing access
to education. But low rates of educational upgrading may not be due
to supply constraints alone. Changes in the country's international
trading position and in the structure of domestic final demand may be
contributing to diminished *demand* for education as well. In particular,
China's emergence as 'factory to the world' in the 1990s changed the
terms of trade for other developing-country manufacturers, especially
those based in economies (such as Indonesia) with low initial resources
of skills and high initial endowments of natural resources (Eichengreen
and Tong 2006; Coxhead 2007). Longer-term, the loss of trade-based
growth opportunities in manufacturing industries, accompanied by a
boom in resource exports and in non-traded industries, may have inhib-

Figure 8.2 *Distribution of employment by sector, Indonesia, 1997, 2000 and 2007 (%)*

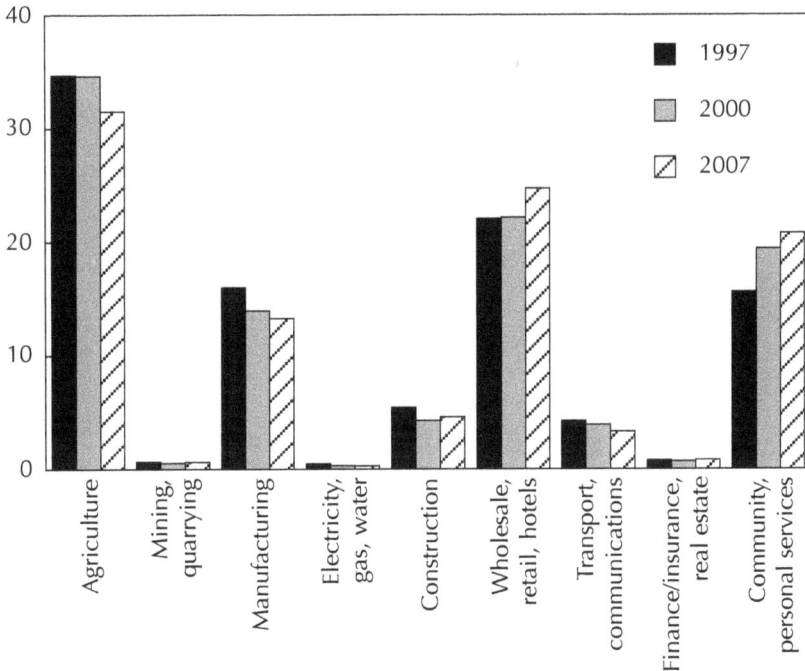

Source: IFLS data.

ited Indonesia's potential to take advantage of the trend toward globally distributed manufacturing (or 'fragmentation'). The risk is now high that electronics, machinery, and other products that are 'made in the world' may not be made in Indonesia (Coxhead and Li 2008; Coxhead and Jayasuriya 2010). The loss of momentum in manufacturing, the most technologically dynamic and skill-intensive sector that is accessible by most workers, may in turn be linked to declining rates of return to educational investments.

8.2 CHANGING STRUCTURE OF EMPLOYMENT AND REAL WAGES: A LOOK AT THE DATA

As with manufacturing output, Indonesia's patterns of non-farm employment growth have begun to diverge from the typical developing country case. Figure 8.2 summarises the sectoral structure of employment for all workers, calculated from the Indonesia Family Life Survey (IFLS) rounds

Figure 8.3   Distribution of youth employment by sector, Indonesia, 1997, 2000 and 2007 (%)

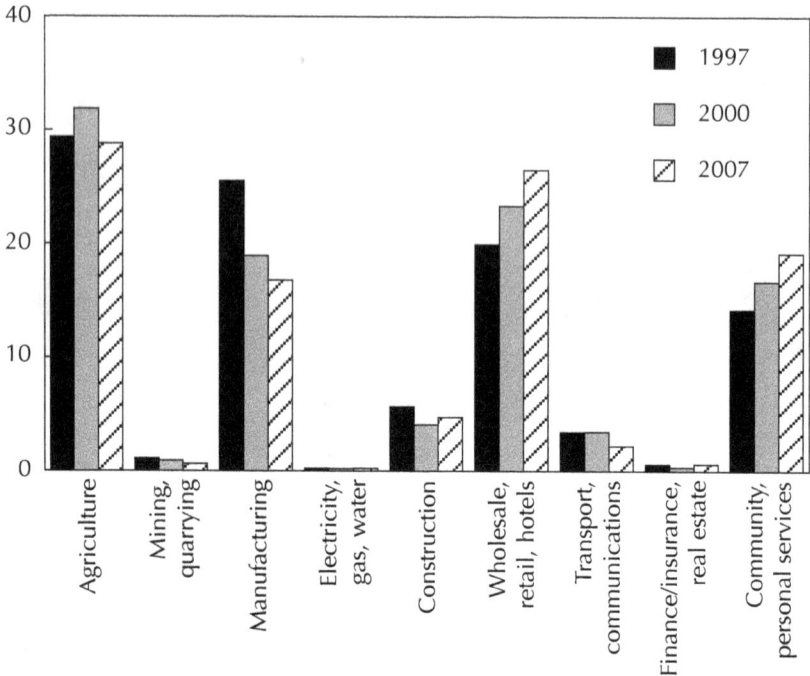

Source: IFLS data.

of 1993, 1998, 2000, and 2007 (we discuss ILFS in more detail below). These data reveal that agricultural employment has fallen slightly as a share of total employment. The share of employment growth in manufacturing has declined more sharply. Meanwhile in services, and especially in low-skill subsectors, there has been substantial growth.[2]

These trends are much more strongly pronounced if we look only at the distribution of employment among new labour market entrants, that is, among workers aged 15–24 in each survey year (Figure 8.3). Before the Asian financial crisis, 25 percent of new job market entrants in Indonesia found employment in manufacturing. By 2007, only 17 percent did so — a drop of one-third. Meanwhile, the share of young workers finding

---

2 The IFLS is based on a large but not nationally representative sample. By comparison, data from Sakernas, the national labour force survey, show for all workers that the share of manufacturing has risen very slightly (from 12 percent to 13 percent of workers), while blue-collar services plus construction have risen from 42 percent to 48 percent of total employment.

Figure 8.4   Average real wage trends, 2000–2010 (Rp thousand/month, in constant 2000 prices)

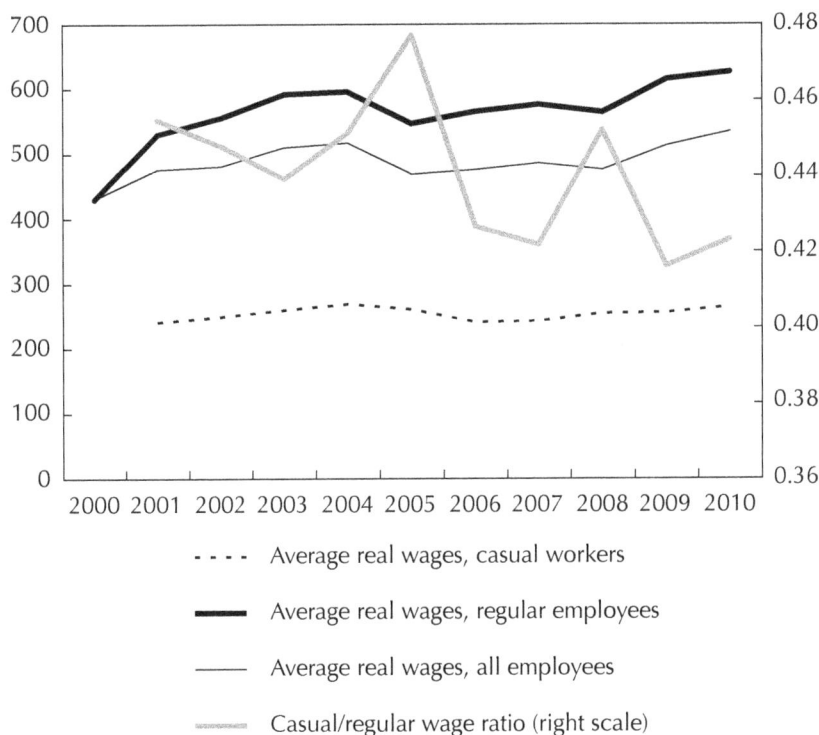

- - - -   Average real wages, casual workers

━━━━   Average real wages, regular employees

──────   Average real wages, all employees

═══════   Casual/regular wage ratio (right scale)

Source: ILO (2011).

employment in wholesale/retail trade and personal services rose from 20 percent to 26 percent, and in government/community services from 14 percent to 17 percent. These trends in employment shares correspond with data pointing to diminished profitability and output growth in manufacturing.

In addition, post-crisis real wages in Indonesia have been essentially flat. ILO data show real wages of regular (formal) employees rising slightly in the 2000s; however, real wages for casual workers remained constant at about Rp250,000 (US$28) per month throughout the decade (ILO 2011; see also Figure 8.4), even as average real per capita income increased at a healthy rate of 4–5 percent per year. Youth unemployment in Indonesia, at around 20 percent, is also much higher than in regional neighbours (ILO 2013a).

Trends in the sectoral composition of employment and real wages may be linked. Informal employment arrangements are prevalent in

Table 8.1   Median earnings per worker in wholesale/retail/personal services, relative to manufacturing wages

	1997	2000	2007
Private employment	0.88	0.85	0.85
Self-employed without employees	0.80	0.70	0.53

Source: IFLS data.

Indonesia, but less so in manufacturing than in agriculture or services. Expansion of service sector jobs thus means more workers in informal employment — other things equal. While it is possible that some workers opt for informal employment (and especially self-employment) as a means to build a business or a more flexible career, it is more typically true that jobs in informal services provide a 'sink' for workers who would otherwise be recorded as unemployed or underemployed. There are some indications that this is the case during the 2000s. From 1997 to 2007, median earnings of workers in private wage employment in domestic trade and personal services remained roughly constant relative to those in manufacturing, while the relative earnings of self-employed workers fell sharply (Table 8.1). The fall in relative returns to self-employment is inconsistent with positive selection of workers into self-employment in order to advance their careers.

Third, in spite of public commitments to educational reform and a new constitution that committed government to spend not less than 20 percent of its budget on education, there has been comparatively little progress on educational infrastructure or the quality of schooling (Suryadarma and Jones 2013). Indonesia's labour force is poor by international standards: the country is close to the bottom of many global comparisons of educational achievement.[3] The recent resource export boom era has resulted in no discernible catch-up relative to slower-growing economies.

Fourth, economic returns to education in Indonesia are low and, unusually among Asian developing countries, have actually declined since the pre-crisis era (Purnastuti, Miller, and Salim 2013; Coxhead 2014). This trend, also, is inconsistent with the typical experience of low- and middle-income countries. We explore the dimensions and reasons for this phenomenon in more detail in the next section.

---

3 Indonesia continues to underperform on international comparisons of educational achievement, most recently in the OECD's 2012 PISA scores (www.oecd.org/pisa).

8.3   STRUCTURAL CHANGE IN LABOUR MARKETS: EMPIRICAL ANALYSIS

As discussed, Indonesia's post-boom job growth has been strong in services and weak in manufacturing and other tradables. What does it mean to a worker to take up employment in one of these industries instead of another? In this section we ask how changes in the structure of labour demand are affecting earnings, job security, returns to skills, and other factors likely to influence long-term economic wellbeing.

Data and definitions of key variables

We use data from recent rounds of the IFLS.[4] The IFLS is a longitudinal socio-economic and health survey based on a sample of households representing about 83 percent of the Indonesian population living in 13 of the 26 provinces that existed at the time of the first survey wave, 1993. The survey collects data on individual respondents, families, households, and communities on a wide array of health and education resources and outcomes. The first wave (IFLS1) was administered to individuals living in 7224 households. The second wave (IFLS2) was fielded to the same respondents in 1997, immediately prior to the Asian crisis. The third wave, IFLS3, was in 2000, and the most recent wave, IFLS4, was administered in late 2007 and early 2008 on the same 1993 households and their split-offs. In that wave, 13,535 households and 44,103 individuals were interviewed.

An important feature of the IFLS methodology is the attention given to minimising attrition. Average attrition (both of original respondents and of split-off households) in IFLS4 is less than 10 percent overall, although the rate is somewhat higher in areas affected by armed conflict and natural disasters, and in the capital city, Jakarta. Strauss et al. (2009) provide complete documentation on sampling, survey instruments, methods and protocols, and supply a breakdown of basic data about respondents.

We use data on men and women of working age (15–65) and only those in the labour force at the time of interview. In 2007 this was 78 percent of men and 42 percent of women surveyed (Table 8.2). Of those not working, 8 percent of men and 7 percent of women were attending school; 3 percent of men and 47 percent of women were engaged in housekeeping, and smaller percentages were searching for a job, retired, invalids, or otherwise out of the labour force.

In order to estimate determinants of earnings, we fit a modified earnings equations (Mincer 1974) to the data. Initially, we restrict attention to

---

4   The following description paraphrases text in Strauss et al. (2009).

Table 8.2   Distribution of primary activities by age group (% of respondents)[a]

	Entire sample		16–25		26–45		45+	
	Male	Female	Male	Female	Male	Female	Male	Female
2007								
Working	78	42	58	32	92	47	78	45
Job search	3	1	7	1	2	0	1	0
Attending school	8	7	24	20	0	0	0	0
Housekeeping	3	47	3	45	3	52	5	45
Retired/invalid/ other non-working	8	3	8	2	3	1	17	9
N	13,839	15,214	3,343	4,017	6,465	6,751	3,672	4,405
1997								
Working	72	40	46	29	93	49	75	41
Job search	8	3	21	9	5	1	2	1
Attending school	11	9	30	26	0	0	0	0
Housekeeping	1	40	1	35	1	49	2	37
Retired/invalid/ other non-working	7	7	3	2	1	1	21	21
N	9,128	10,780	2,399	2,783	3,645	4,577	2,725	2,038

a   The definitions of some categories varied slightly between surveys.
Source: IFLS data (file: IFLS_Tables_03_03_2013).

the most recent data, from IFLS4. This gives us a picture of determinants of variation in earnings in 2007, well after the end of the Asian crisis era and firmly into the resource export boom period. Table 8.3 summarises the main variables used in the estimation.

Earnings are measured as the log of monthly labour income in rupiah. We measure education by the number of years reported.[5] Tenure is the number of years an individual reports having held a specific job. Experience is reported as years in the labour force. In order to allow for diminishing returns, both these variables also enter in quadratic form. We

5   Of course, there are significant markers of educational attainment (such as completion of a schooling stage), so using discrete educational levels rather than years allows for non-linearities in returns. We have also estimated these, but the results add little to the empirical story.

Table 8.3   Summary statistics: working-age individuals with employment information, 2007

	Observa-tions	Mean	Standard deviation	Mini-mum	Maxi-mum
Education (years)	18,133	8.639	4.086	0	18
Urban	19,272	0.515	0.500	0	1
Region					
Sumatra	19,272	0.157	0.363	0	1
Java	19,272	0.438	0.496	0	1
Male	19,272	0.574	0.494	0	1
Hours worked per year (log)	19,223	7.150	1.029	0	9.075
Formal employment	19,272	0.685	0.464	0	1
Height (log)	18,857	5.049	0.122	2.653	5.261
Mother's education (years)	16,219	3.957	3.688	0	17

Source: IFLS4 data.

include dummy variables for urban location, and for Sumatra and other Indonesia (the excluded category is Java). Hours per year are calculated from reported hours in paid work for the reporting period.

Height, parents' education, and household assets are included to control for early childhood wellbeing. A large literature based mainly on wealthy-country datasets finds that early childhood health, nutrition, and family socio-economic status have significant and persistent effects on cognitive and non-cognitive abilities throughout childhood and that these are measurable in labour market outcomes (Currie 2009; Almond and Currie 2011). We assume that the same is true in Indonesia. Following a large and well-established literature, we use adult height (measured in 2007) as an instrument for early childhood conditions (Silventoinen 2003; Case and Paxson 2006; Case, Paxson, and Islam 2009). This literature establishes that childhood health and nutrition is important in determining schooling outcomes. In developing country datasets, these effects are found to persist even after schooling choices are taken into account (Glewwe, Jacoby, and King 2001; Alderman, Hoddinott, and Kinsey 2006; Hoddinott et al. 2008). Thus failure to control for factors determining cognitive and non-cognitive ability result in estimates of returns to education that are upwardly biased.

Another important variable is the indicator of formal-sector employment. Formality is known to be a highly influential determinant of labour productivity and earnings; for discussion of a closely comparable case, that of Mexico, see Hanson (2010). Firms in the informal sector are less intensive in their use of capital and technology, so the marginal value product of human capital and labour is lower than in formal firms. Informal employment contracts typically do not entail training other than 'on the job', and casual employees, for their part, are likely to have fewer incentives to give their all (including creative effort) to employers who offer no long-term commitment. We use a definition of formality based on employment status. We count a worker as formally employed if they receive any benefits (bonus, pension, insurance, training, transportation, or health) as part of their employment, regardless of the enterprise type. This definition allows for informal or casual employment contracts even within formally incorporated enterprises. By this definition, 74 percent of workers in IFLS4 are classified as informally employed (Table 8.4), a figure very similar to those for countries such as Brazil, Mexico, South Africa, India, the Philippines, and Vietnam, which range between 50 percent and 85 percent (ILO 2013b, Table 2.6).

Finally, our earnings function estimation strategy includes both pooled data with controls for sector and occupation, and also separate estimates by occupation. Selection into a particular occupation is partly endogenous, and empirical studies frequently deal with this by pooling data and including occupation controls. In a developing country context, however, there seem to be several complications to this. One is that since occupations are not equally represented among sectors (there are few white-collar jobs in agriculture, for example), the changing sectoral structure of labour demand also implies a changing set of occupational choices. Second, there may be significant barriers to occupational choice—in part because of exogenous factors (to the adult) such as location, ethnicity, and childhood nutrition, health, and socio-economic status. Third, informal employment arrangements, as discussed above, are far more prevalent is some occupations than in others.

As an estimation strategy, fitting earnings functions separately by occupation gives us a quantitative sense of the differences among them and provides a window into determinants of variation in earnings power *within* each occupational group, conditional on selection into that group. This comes at a cost, since estimating earnings separately by occupation imparts a downward bias to the earnings contributions of factors that facilitate entry by some workers into higher-paying occupations while constraining others to less rewarding activities (Case et al. 2009). Construction of a completely integrated model of constrained occupational choice by heterogeneous workers is a more complex task and the subject of ongoing work.

Table 8.4   Subsample sizes in formal and informal employment

	Total (no.)	Informal (%)	Formal (%)
Occupation			
Professional/technical	1,245	29.7	70.3
Administrative/managerial	63	63.5	36.5
Clerical	805	22.6	77.4
Sales	3,787	84.3	15.7
Service	3,078	64.4	35.6
Agriculture/forestry	6,320	95.0	5.0
Production line workers	1,547	60.4	39.6
Semi-skilled production workers	592	43.8	56.3
Blue-collar production workers	2,620	69.4	30.6
Total	**20,057**	**73.7**	**26.3**
Sector			
Agriculture	6,352	94.7	5.3
Manufacturing	2,668	52.5	47.5
Wholesale	4,975	83.9	16.1
Services	4,188	43.9	56.1
Other	1,973	70.1	29.9
Total	**20,156**	**73.5**	**26.5**
Employment type			
Self-employed (no employees)	7,130	100.0	0.0
Self-employed (permanent employees)	343	100.0	0.0
Government	1,421	16.5	83.5
Private	5,942	35.9	64.1
Casual	5,317	93.4	6.6
Total	**20,153**	**73.5**	**26.5**

Source: IFLS4 data.

Employment, earnings, and returns to schooling during the boom

We turn now to estimates of the 2007 earnings functions, using the log of monthly earnings as dependent variable. We obtain these estimates by OLS. This method leaves unaddressed the possibility of estimation bias due to non-random selection into the labour force. In practice, however, prior estimation of earnings and employment functions using IFLS data has revealed no significant differences between estimates obtained from OLS and those obtained from two-stage models accounting for selection into the labour force; see Purnastuti, Miller, and Salim (2013) for a review of these studies. Our regressions control for many exogenous characteristics of individuals in the hope that any remaining variation due to unobserved traits has only random effects on earnings.

Table 8.5 shows results of the earnings regressions. The first column shows estimates for all workers, and subsequent columns show results conditional on occupation (occupational definitions are from IFLS). Results for controls such as experience, tenure, location and sector are suppressed to save space. Most results are strongly intuitive and are broadly consistent with comparable studies. Among the findings, the following are of particular relevance.

First, unconditional earnings (the intercepts of the earnings functions) vary greatly, with services the lowest by a long way. Earnings are appreciably (and in almost all cases significantly) higher for workers in urban areas, and for males. Moreover, formal employment contracts are highly valuable. Across all occupations, formal employment increases earnings by 31.3 percent, and the magnitude of this gain is broadly similar across the individual occupations.

Second, the marginal earnings gain of an additional year of education averages 6.5 percent across all occupations, taking account of occupational and educational choices and controlling for other factors such as region, tenure, experience and sector. This rate of return corresponds with other estimates from Indonesian data (e.g. Purnastuti, Miller, and Salim 2011), though all of these estimates are somewhat lower than those for broader samples of developing countries (Psacharopoulos and Patrinos 2004).[6] Across occupations, however, there is wide variation, with additional schooling worth most to workers who find employment in professional and clerical jobs, and least to those who work in agriculture, services or blue-collar production work. For most Indonesian workers the relevant non-farm occupational choices are between blue-collar or production line work, sales, or services. Among these choices, returns to additional schooling in manufacturing (7.7 percent for production line workers and 8.8 percent for semi-skilled workers) are considerably higher than for the other occupations. Structural changes that increase labour demand in non-tradable activities (services and sales) relative to production work thus lower the expected returns on schooling investments, other things equal. As the probability of employment in sales

---

6   The lower estimate of returns to education was also found in similar data from Vietnam, another resource-dependent low-income Asian economy (Phan and Coxhead 2013).

Table 8.5 Earnings function estimates, 2007 (dependent variable: log of monthly earnings, Rp thousand)

Variable	All	Professional	Clerical	Sales	Service	Agriculture/ forestry	Production line	Semi-skilled	Blue-collar
Education years	0.065***	0.083***	0.114***	0.062***	0.059***	0.051***	0.077***	0.088***	0.051***
	-0.004	-0.015	-0.016	-0.009	-0.008	-0.009	-0.013	-0.016	-0.008
Urban	0.166***	0.332***	0.078	0.200***	0.182***	0.036	0.080	-0.041	0.261***
	-0.023	-0.062	-0.089	-0.055	-0.058	-0.064	-0.073	-0.091	-0.047
Male	0.493***	0.391***	0.259***	0.536***	0.432***	0.529***	0.729***	0.093	0.506***
	-0.023	-0.062	-0.066	-0.047	-0.054	-0.062	-0.068	-0.138	-0.081
Log height	0.212**	0.147	-0.074	-0.006	1.102***	0.186	0.145	-0.279*	0.235
	-0.092	-0.208	-0.183	-0.126	-0.359	-0.183	-0.127	-0.165	-0.190
Formal	0.313***	0.210**	0.349***	0.146**	0.354***	0.282***	0.506***	0.471***	0.279***
	-0.026	-0.085	-0.099	-0.063	-0.052	-0.090	-0.095	-0.094	-0.053
Constant	9.685***	10.32***	11.29***	11.29***	5.251***	9.971***	10.55***	13.02***	9.995***
	-0.497	-1.147	-1.018	-0.666	-1.824	-0.93	-0.711	-0.852	-1.039
Controls									
Tenure & experience	Y	Y	Y	Y	Y	Y	Y	Y	Y
Parents' education	Y	Y	Y	Y	Y	Y	Y	Y	Y
Employment type	Y	Y	Y	Y	Y	Y	Y	Y	Y
Region	Y	Y	Y	Y	Y	Y	Y	Y	Y
Sector	Y	Y	Y	Y	Y	Y	Y	Y	Y
Occupation	Y	N	N	N	N	N	N	N	N
Observations	11,315	967	597	2,213	1,945	2,422	976	432	1,727
R-squared	0.341	0.388	0.37	0.291	0.357	0.166	0.362	0.302	0.270

Robust standard errors are in parentheses. *** p<0.01, ** p<0.05, * p<0.1. The administrative/managerial category has been dropped (36 observations).

or services occupations increases, young adults have less incentive to remain in school or proceed to the next level of education.

Third, adult height is significant and positive in the pooled data: greater cognitive and non-cognitive abilities (for which adult height is an instrument) make a substantial contribution to higher earnings, taking account of their effects on decisions over schooling, sector and occupation. However, most occupations display no significant within-group variation: conditional on occupational choice, unmeasured abilities do not contribute to higher earnings except indirectly, for example through schooling outcomes. The big exception is services, where the effect of height is both very large and highly significant. In this occupational category, each 1 percent increase in height increases earnings by 1.1 percent. Male height in Indonesia averages 162 cm with a standard deviation of 6.5 cm, so a male of height one standard deviation above the mean earns almost 10 percent more than one who is one standard deviation shorter than average. This is true even if they both have the same education, terms of employment, and other conditions — all of which, plus the probability of working in services versus another occupation, are themselves subject to influence from height differences. Thus the 10 percent difference is unambiguously a lower-bound estimate. Early childhood health and nutrition — the key determinants of adult height differentials — remain very strong influences on earnings in the Indonesian labour market.

The foregoing analysis focuses only on a single year of data. In related work, we examine trends across pre- and post-crisis waves of the IFLS, comparing the labour market fortunes by age cohort (Coxhead 2014). That work reveals that returns to education are low not only in certain occupations, but also for younger workers. Low returns are especially evident for workers with informal labour contracts. Returns to education for young workers (15–28 years old in 2007) in informal employment were dismally low at just 1.4–3.9 percent, compared with 3.6–7.0 percent for workers in older cohorts. Finally, returns to schooling declined from rates broadly comparable with other developing counties in 1997, to rates significantly lower by 2007.[7]

Other things equal, lower probability of employment in high-skill industries reduces students' incentives to stay in school beyond the legal minimum age. Moreover, the higher is the probability of informal sector employment, the lower is their expectation of returns on human capital investments. Both of these probabilities appear to have fallen in Indonesia between 1997 and 2007, in spite of sustained and rapid growth of the aggregate economy in the post-crisis years.

---

7 The decline in returns confirms findings of a number of other studies, notably Purnastuti, Miller, and Salim (2011, 2013).

8.4 DISCUSSION AND CONCLUSIONS

The Indonesian economy has grown steadily since 2001. However, its labour markets show a contradictory trend, notably a rising share of employment in industries characterised by low labour productivity and prevalent informality of labour contracts; low and declining returns to education, and in the fastest-growing occupational group, persistently large returns to individual characteristics associated with early childhood health and nutrition. The causes of these changes in labour demand are overdetermined, being consistent with the expected effects of the crisis-era drop in investment, a natural resource export boom, and policies tending to reduce labour market flexibility and increase trade protectionism. The relative contribution of each of these influences is a matter for further research. What is far more important, however, is that these labour market trends are much *less* easily reconciled with those to be expected in an economy making a sustained transition from low income and resource dependence to industrialisation and middle income, with the accompanying rise of industries built on investments in capital, technology and skills.

The history of economic development confirms that rapid economic growth can be sustained in the long run only through technological dynamism and a matching increase in the skills of the labour force. Together, these are forces powerful enough to overcome other deficiencies that undermine growth: 'formal manufacturing industries are natural "escalator" industries that tend to propel an economy forward, even in the presence of bad governance, bad policies and a disadvantageous context' (Rodrik 2013, 27). Manufacturing growth, in those developing economies that pursue their comparative advantage, is also a fast track to higher employment growth and improved labour productivity.

In an analysis of labour market data, we find that the areas of economic activity showing greatest growth are also those in which returns to education and skills are relatively low. Young Indonesians, perceiving a lower probability of employment in sectors or occupations where schooling commands a higher premium, are likely to reduce their planned educational investments as a result. Policies intended to increase enrollments, retention, and graduation rates at secondary and tertiary levels by increasing the supply of schooling thus face the additional obstacle of weaker growth in educational *demand*.

The solution to low incentives to increase education and skills acquisition must rest with a mix of macro, micro and fiscal policies. To the extent that structural change in labour demand reflects the lingering after-effects of the Asian crisis-era investment collapse, there is little to be done but wait. But if low educational demand growth is a long-run consequence of a natural resource export boom, then future Indonesian governments would benefit by carefully considering the optimal combination of sterilisation and investment policies required to re-stimulate growth in manufacturing and other non-resource tradables. Finally, the evidence strongly suggests that it is time for Indonesia's government to radically revise policies on education, training, industrial promotion, trade and foreign investment in order to forestall unintended consequences that may impair long-run growth.

9   Labour market regulation and employment during the Yudhoyono years in Indonesia

*Chris Manning**

Professor Hal Hill has been a tower of strength and inspiration for economic research on the Indonesian economy over almost three decades, both for international as well as Indonesian scholars. This author's academic career spanned much the same time period as Professor Hill's, both as a PhD scholar and a decade later as a researcher for 20 years at the Australian National University (ANU). Our interests have been similar – understanding the diversity and resilience of the Indonesian economy, often against all odds, internationally, and often in spite of the interventions by politicians in Jakarta. The author personally owes a great debt of gratitude for Hal Hill's support and a wonderful friendship, for much of this period, especially during his 20 years as a researcher at the ANU in 1991–2011. *Terima kasih Pak.*

During his career, Professor Hill developed a healthy scepticism of regulated markets in the Indonesian context. Partly, this scepticism reflects changes in the approaches to development policies among mainstream economists since the 1960s and 1970s when he began his career. It also manifests a judgment that successive Indonesian governments have been unable to keep their promise of improving efficiency and erasing inequities through market interventions, partly because of weak legal institutions and poor governance. In this chapter, I take up this theme

---

*   The initial ideas and empirical analysis for this paper were first developed in a policy brief prepared for the Australia Indonesia Partnership for Economic Governance (AIPEG) in Jakarta in 2013. The author would like to thank Bill Wallace, David Neller, and Paul Bartlett for comments on earlier drafts.

by focusing on some of the effects of regulations of Indonesia's labour market in recent times.

One of Indonesia's main development problems is that a high proportion of the workforce—around two-thirds—are employed in low-productivity agriculture and in the informal sector. Mainly, this is related to Indonesia's stage in economic development as a lower middle-income country. The meagre stock of both physical capital per worker and human capital reflects Indonesia's stage of development. Not enough workers have moved into higher productivity jobs especially in manufacturing, and that transfer slowed after the Asian financial crisis of the late 1990s, despite reasonable and improving rates of economic growth in the 2000s (World Bank 2010b).

It has been suggested that both low productivity and high wages in some segments of the economy have contributed to high and rising unit labour costs relative to productivity, compared with neighbouring countries (Nellor 2013).[1] That process has also contributed the poor employment record. Part of the problem relates to the dualistic structure of output in manufacturing, which is related to technology and market orientation. Favours granted to the more capital-intensive, often protected investors producing for the domestic market often give them the edge over more labour-intensive, export-oriented firms that have the potential to create more jobs (Aswicahyono, Hill, and Narjoko 2010, 2011b).

As Hal Hill and his colleagues have pointed out in their work on Indonesian manufacturing, obstacles to improving productivity partly relate to a policy environment that has contributed to a low level of investment in infrastructure, and to barriers to trade and investment in the private sector. They have also highlighted some of the labour-market constraints. Comparing employment–output relationships in Indonesian manufacturing in the period 1996–2006 with those a decade earlier, it has been argued that less flexible labour markets played an important role in limiting job creation in 1996–2006: 'That is, employment was increasingly responsive to wage changes in the first decade [1986–1996] but less so in the second … We would contend that tighter labour market regulation had an adverse impact on traditional labour-intensive sectors, especially textiles, clothing and footwear …' (Aswicahyono, Hill, and Narjoko 2011b, 128–129).

---

1 Unit labour costs (ULCs) measure movements in wages relative to productivity. Rising ULCs indicate that wages are growing faster than productivity, which means that a particular industry or activity is becoming less competitive. For international comparisons, changes in ULCs reflect relative movements in international prices. Depreciations lower unit labour costs relative to those of other countries and appreciations have the opposite effect (Nellor 2013).

This chapter takes up some of these themes. It argues that employment appears to have suffered partly because of regulations and policies towards labour markets. These regulations and policies tend to make labour costs unnecessarily high relative to the supply price in much of the labour market. Slow growth in jobs also relates to a poorly designed minimum wage setting mechanism, which increases uncertainty and allows too much weight to be given to political interests in implementation. Finally, from the labour supply side, Indonesian institutions are not investing enough in skills that meet the demands of the labour market. Also firms do not seem to investing enough in the basic training of their workers and importing skilled foreigners remains under tight control.

The next section deals with indicators of labour market performance, in the context of recent economic and employment changes. The third and fourth sections deal with two sets of regulations—those impacting on recruitment and firing costs and minimum wages—and then skills development and training issues, followed by some concluding remarks.

9.1   GENERAL LABOUR MARKET CONSTRAINTS, STRUCTURE, AND DEVELOPMENTS

Labour market inefficiency and poor quality workers have been highlighted in diagnoses of obstacles to Indonesian development (World Bank 2010b). Nonetheless, Indonesia is not by any means a rank outlier according to indicators compiled by the world competitiveness index (WCI). Table 9.1 presents some of these indicators from the WCI for a sample of comparable Asian countries. It shows the international ranking of various Asian countries on two measures of labour market efficiency (flexibility and efficient use of talent) and three measures of human capital (the quantity and quality of schooling and on-the-job training).

Indonesia is mostly ranked behind higher income countries such as Malaysia, China, and Thailand, especially in labour market efficiency measures, although Indonesia tends to score higher than Asian countries at a lower level of per capita income such as the Philippines, India, and Vietnam. Consistent with Aswicahyono, Hill, and Narjoko's (2011b) observations outlined above, labour flexibility appears to be a major problem; in this case Indonesia's rank is very low internationally (91 out of 144 countries) and low relative to all of the other countries, except the Philippines, as shown in Table 9.1.

It is widely argued that more efficient labour market outcomes can play a significant role in supporting economic growth in the middle-income stages of development, when both job creation and rising productivity are critical to improving living standards. This was the experience

Table 9.1   Ranking of a sample of 144 Asian countries on labour market efficiency and human capital indicators, 2012–2013[a]

Country	GDP per capita, 2011 (US$ PPP)	Labour market efficiency		Selected human capital indicators[b]			Total competitiveness
		Flexibility	Efficient use of talent	Quantity of schooling	Quality of education	On-the-job training	
Malaysia	9,700	45	42	82	25	12	25
China	5,414	73	34	85	47	50	29
Thailand	5,394	77	49	73	66	58	39
Indonesia	**3,509**	**91**	**60**	**90**	**55**	**48**	**50**
Philippines	2,223	96	69	79	64	47	65
India	1,389	64	63	101	43	57	59
Vietnam	1,374	65	61	91	74	121	75

a   The index records the ranks of each country from a sample of 144 for which data are available. The highest rank is 1 and the lowest is 144.
b   These human capital indicators have been taken from a broader category called 'Higher education and training' (5th pillar) in the *Global Competitiveness Report*. On-the-job training is a composite of two indicators: availability of research and training services, and the extent of staff training.
Source: The Global Competitiveness Report 2012–2013.

of the Asian 'newly industrialising economies' or NIEs (Korea, Taiwan, Hong Kong, and Singapore) some decades ago, and China for much of the period of rapid economic growth until regulation began to play a role on wage determination in the modern sector. These policies (the absence of state interventions) supported flexible labour markets; at the same time all these countries invested heavily in the quantity, and increasingly the quality, of skills needed for better jobs and growth (Fields and Wan 1989; Booth 1998; World Bank 2013c). It is this combination of policies that facilitated the deployment of labour into higher productivity jobs and sharply rising labour incomes.

Bearing this policy context in mind, what do the conventional labour market indicators tell us about Indonesia's labour market performance in recent years? The picture is mixed. Certainly there is no evidence of a 'take-off' in employment and wages that became increasingly clear in China towards the end of first decade of the 2000s (Garnaut 2006). Comparatively, Indonesia is still a high-unemployment country. With national unemployment rates at just over six percent in 2013 (and youth unemployment at over double that rate), only the Philippines has recorded similar rates of unemployment among the six Asian comparators shown

Table 9.2   *Working-age population, labour force, employment and unemployment, Indonesia, 2002–2012*

	Number, 2012	Growth (% p.a.)		
		2002–07	2007–12	2002–12
Working-age population (million)	174	2.0	1.2	1.6
Labour force (million)	118	1.7	1.4	1.6
Primary or less	55.9	0.0	–1.1	–0.5
Junior high	21.9	3.7	0.8	2.3
Senior high (general)	19.1	4.5	4.5	4.5
Senior high (vocational)	10.5	0.6	7.3	3.9
Diploma I/II	1.0	8.5	–7.1	0.7
Tertiary	9.5	7.3	10.4	8.9
Employment (million)	110.8	1.7	2.1	1.9
Agriculture	38.9	0.1	–0.6	–0.4
Manufacturing	15.4	0.4	4.3	2.4
Services	17.1	3.0	7.1	5.0
Non-agriculture				
Formal	39.6	2.5	7.1	4.8
Informal	32.3	3.1	0.8	2.0
Unemployment (million)	7.2	1.8	–6.5	–2.3
Real wages (Rp/month, in 2012 prices)				
Agriculture	798,000	0.2	6.4	3.3
Non-agriculture	1,570,000	0.6	2.8	1.7

Source: BPS, National Labour Force Survey (Sakernas), 2002, 2007 and 2012.

in Table 9.1. More importantly, the large informal and agricultural sectors confirm that Indonesia has a major challenge in providing employment for much of the low-productivity workforce.

Some of these employment data are shown in Table 9.2. For a country with a large backlog of labour in low-productivity jobs on heavily popu-lated islands such as Java and Bali, the share of employment in manu-facturing is small: just 13 percent of total employment in August 2013 compared with, for example, Malaysia, South Korea, and Taiwan where manufacturing contributed closer to 25 percent of total employment at similar stages of development (Manning 1999).

While formal-sector employment has been growing strongly in recent years following the doldrums after the Asian financial crisis in 1997–98[2] and unemployment fell somewhat, most new jobs have been created in services. In services, annual growth rates were three times faster than in manufacturing (Table 9.2). All services accounted for just under half of all jobs in 2012, but they made up 80 percent of the increase in non-agricultural jobs from 2002, with manufacturing and mining accounting for a paltry 20 percent. Noteworthy were the contributions of financial services, personal and social services, and construction to the growth of jobs in services. Contract and regular wage jobs, rather than casual work, grew more quickly after the crisis.

Nonetheless, the labour market stories for the first and second half of the 2000s are very different. These seemingly conflicting trends need to be reconciled for a sensible discussion of policy options. Two points are particularly relevant. First, it took around five years for the Indonesian economy to recover from the 1997–98 crisis and for many businesses to adjust to the wide-reaching political and bureaucratic restructuring that accompanied *reformasi*. Labour was one area where the change in the regulatory and institutional environment was striking. The country moved from a centrally controlled, pro-business, environment under Suharto to one where labour was extended broad backed by far-reaching regulatory and legal reform (Hadiz 1997; Manning 2006).

Second, by around 2006–2007, there was significant change in investment and growth that had far-reaching implications for formal sector employment. On the demand side, Indonesia was again considered by business as an alternative to China for labour-intensive investments, as wages began to rise in China.[3] Just as important, investors began to discover Indonesia as a potentially large domestic market for consumer goods. Resource booms and steady service-sector growth (fostered in part by some market-oriented reforms after the crisis) fuelled an unexpected, rapid growth in the size of the middle class. This became a target for multinationals, as well as regional and national investors, looking for places to invest capital during the global recession of 2008–2009 (World Bank 2011a).

---

2 While impressive, the rate of formal sector growth in recent years is almost certainly exaggerated. A small part, perhaps one-third, of the growth in formal sector employment can be accounted for by underestimates of the size of the formal sector workforce in the mid-2000s by Badan Pusat Statistik (BPS), the national statistics agency.

3 Indonesia had been ahead of China as a country with a favourable outlook for labour-intensive exports in the late 1980s and early 1990s, but that situation was reversed when Indonesia went through the Asian financial crisis in 1997–98. Several multinationals, including Sony and Reebok, moved most of their investments to China and Vietnam.

Figure 9.1   Share of the workforce by level of schooling, 2002–2012 (%)

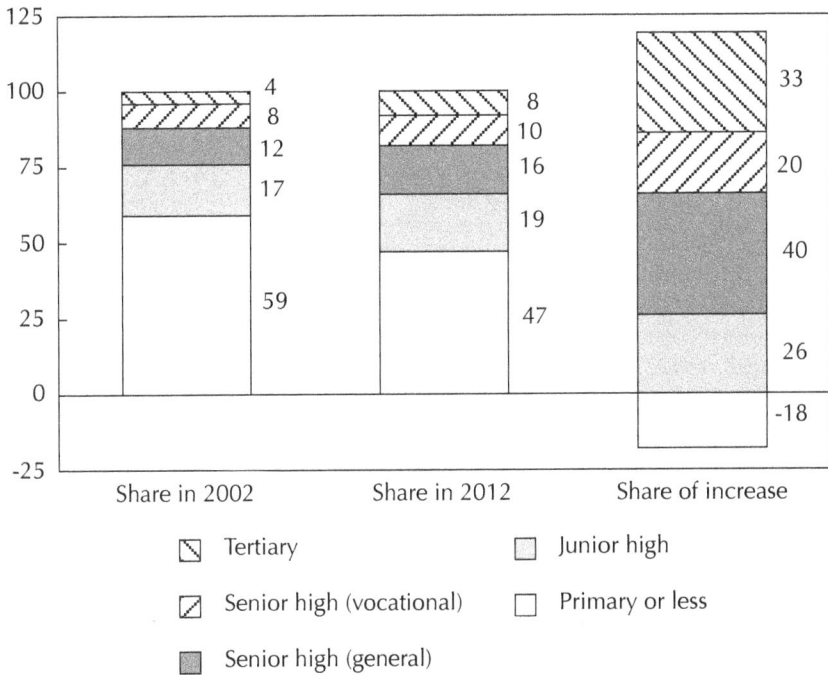

Source: BPS, National Labour Force Surveys (Sakernas), August round, 2002 and 2012.

On the supply side, the educated workforce has expanded dramatically at senior high and tertiary levels accounting for over half of the growth in the labour force from 2007–2012 (see Figure 9.1). While there were significant problems with the quality of the skilled workforce, Indonesia now boasts a core of well-educated workers ready to support new investments.

Finally, a note of caution is in order. While the labour market has shown some improving trends, the most recent developments are not so bright. Unemployment rose, albeit slightly, in August 2013 for the first time in seven years as Indonesia began to feel the impact of both the slowdown in world commodity demand and seemingly ad hoc restrictions on international trade and into 2013 (Allford and Soejachmoen 2013). Manufacturing employment also fell after growing more strongly for several years.[4]

---

4 Unemployment rose by 0.1 percent and manufacturing employment fell by around 3 percent according to the National Labour Force Survey (August 2012 and August 2013).

It is against this background of mixed experience in labour outcomes that we discuss labour market regulations, policies and institutional changes that many claim have inhibited investment. Some have been part of the regulatory framework for a long time while others were introduced after the 1997–98 Asian financial crisis and regime change.

9.2   THE MAIN REGULATORY CONSTRAINTS TO LABOUR MARKET EFFICIENCY

The international comparisons shown in Table 9.1 above indicate that labour market flexibility was an issue in Indonesia. The data suggested that reform of this dimension of labour markets is more pressing than issues related to the quantity and quality of schooling and training.

Table 9.3 provides more detail on indicators that contribute to labour market flexibility and the mobilisation of talent, the two subcomponents of the WCI labour market efficiency index. Indonesia ranks lowest among the sample of seven countries by quite a large margin on the overall index of labour market efficiency (Indonesia's rank is 120 overall of the 144 countries ranked) as well as on redundancy costs on which Indonesia was close to the bottom (130 out of 144 countries ranked). Indonesia also ranks low on flexibility in wage determination and low among the sample of Asian countries on cooperation in industrial relations, (although Indonesia was not low compared with all other countries on this score). For women in the labour force, the one gender-related indicator in regard to labour market efficiency, Indonesia also records a low rank internationally (113), far below China and Vietnam.

These main constraints to labour efficiency are discussed below. The discussion starts with labour redundancy costs and their relationship to labour outsourcing, and then turns to wage determination. We examine both the regulatory environment and bureaucratic practices and capacity.

Redundancy costs, and the spread and regulation of outsourcing

Several clauses of Indonesia's Labour Law of 2003 (No. 13) have been a continuing source of contention between employers and unions, with the government caught in the middle and, when pressed, unwilling to oppose the unions on issues of reform. Two major attempts by the central government to revise the law in 2006 and again in 2010–2011 failed in the face of strong trade union opposition, backed by civil society groups.

The Indonesian Labour Law of 2013 codified a plethora of national regulations into one package. Many provisions were already in place but often ignored in the private sector, while others were new. In some cases,

Table 9.3   *Ranking of a sample of 144 Asian countries on selected labour efficiency indicators of the Global Competitiveness Index, 2012–2013*

Country	Indicators of labour market flexibility				Selected indicators of the efficient use of talent[a]		Total labour efficiency	Global Competitiveness Index
	Cooperation in industrial relations	Flexibility in wage determination	Hiring & firing	Redundancy costs	Women in the labour force	Pay & productivity		
Malaysia	15	22	34	108	119	3	24	25
China	57	77	42	117	34	16	41	29
Thailand	41	97	41	130	62	27	76	39
Indonesia	**61**	**114**	**52**	**137**	**113**	**34**	**120**	**50**
India	50	61	71	73	133	57	82	59
Philippines	38	117	108	120	109	43	103	65
Vietnam	53	45	57	104	19	18	51	75

a The total refers to the Labour Market Efficiency Index, which encompasses both the labour market flexibility and efficient use of talent subcategories in the Global Competitiveness Index. The labour efficiency indicators contribute a total of 17% to the efficiency-enhancing group, which in turn accounts for around one-third of the total competitiveness index (depending on stage of development).

Source: World Economic Forum, *The Global Competitiveness Report, 2012–2013.*

benefits that were already in place were also extended, although basic provisions such hours worked, overtime and annual leave remained basically the same.

At the heart of business objections to the new labour law was the very high level of redundancy payments mandated in the law which meant firms were reluctant to take on new regular workers; employers were particularly worried about the potential size of payments if they were forced to lay off a significant number workers. The labour law extended what were already very high levels of redundancy according to existing regulations. Thus, a redundant worker with 5–10 years experience could expect to receive between a minimum of 8–15 months salary in severance (together with long-service benefits). These provisions are more generous by far than any redundancy payments required in the labour laws of neighbouring countries.

Indonesia was not alone in requiring firms to pay severance to laid-off workers. Because few lower middle-income countries in Asia have comprehensive unemployment benefits, many countries mandate quite high levels of severance as a substitute (Holzmann and Vodopivec 2013). The costs are mostly borne entirely by the employer. Thus, six out of seven of the Asian countries in our sample were ranked above 100 out of 144 countries on redundancy costs (see Table 9.3). This rank is in contrast to more favourable rankings on other indicators of labour market efficiency compared with other developing countries.[5] Indonesia's ranking was lowest (137 out of 144 countries) among the seven countries for which we have compiled comparator data. Indonesia's actual score of 58 weeks was over 60 percent higher than the next nearest country's score of 36 months (for Thailand). Figure 9.2 highlights how much an outlier Indonesia is on this score.[6]

The high rates of severance encourage employers to look at alternative employment contracts that do not require payment of severance to laid-off workers. Outsourcing the recruitment of labour has been one alternative. These arrangements are made between firms and specialist recruiting companies. The latter typically employ workers on short-term contracts that do not necessitate the payment of severance (Tjandraningsih 2010; SEADI 2013). Further, these recruiting companies are more likely to fall under radar of labour inspectors and are rarely unionised.

---

5 According to the GCI measure, redundancy costs (measured in weeks) monthly wages comprise the average value of notice requirements, severance payments and penalties due when terminating a redundant worker.

6 It is also possible that the outcry about severance pay in Indonesia is partly because the government is more serious than several neighbouring countries about implementing severance pay among modern-sector firms.

Figure 9.2   Rank and score on redundancy costs, selected Asian countries, 2012–2013[a]

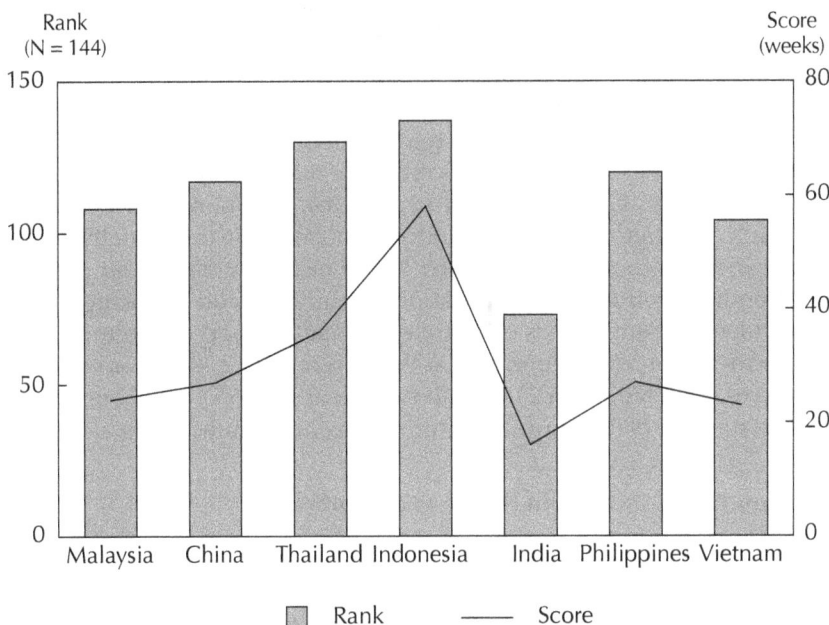

a Refers to the cost of lay-offs. Cost equals weeks of salary payable to employees (standard duration of employment).
Source: World Economic Forum, *The Global Competitiveness Report 2012–2013.*

It appears these strategies have been used more widely since the labour law was introduced in 2003.

Such arrangements create other labour market distortions that adversely affect productivity. Firms are less likely to invest in the training of workers and less likely to seek strategies for upgrading skills needed to move up the value chain. Secondly, high rates of severance have contributed to further regulation, industrial unrest, and uncertainty. Throughout 2012, unions caused significant disruption by demonstrating for tighter controls of outsourcing which led to a government ban in all except five ancillary activities (such as catering, transport of workers, and security) introduced in November 2012.[7] Not only is the outsourcing of labour recruitment banned, all outsourcing arrangements have to be registered by the Ministry of Manpower and Transmigration (MOMT), adding to bureaucratic red tape. Classifying and registering

---

7 See Ministerial Regulation No. 19, 2012. Firms were given 12 months to adjust labour contracts and to register with the ministry.

all service arrangements in the economy is a huge task and it is assumed that the process will contribute to increased rent-seeking on the part of bureaucrats in a ministry where governance problems have been major issues in the past.

Another major issue is implementation of these high rates of severance, as well as other articles of the labour law. Firm compliance is low, estimated at around 30 percent in the case of severance pay (World Bank 2010b).[8] It is widely reported that even if the matter is taken to the industrial-civil courts that rule on labour disputes, the rulings of the courts are rarely implemented and the individual complainants usually strike a deal with the company concerned.[9] One major issue in labour administration has been the decentralisation of functions and financing to the district level where there is often little financial support or incentives for labour inspectors. It is reported that there were only 2,300 labour inspectors across the country in 2012, with the talk of supervising labour standards in some 25,000 large and medium firms in manufacturing alone.

Minimum wage setting in theory and in practice

Besides its poor ranking on redundancy, Indonesia also ranks low in regard to flexibility in wage setting. As shown in Table 9.3, Indonesia's ranking for this variable was 114 out of 144, which, together with the Philippines, was well below all other Asian countries covered in the table.

Minimum wage policy contrasts with most labour protection policies in that standards are adjusted annually and they are done so at a regional level. While broad principles are laid down by in the labour law by the central government, annual adjustments are made on the recommendation of the district head (*bupati*) to the governor of the province, based on advice from wage councils at the district level. Wage councils are made up of employers, unions and government (ratio of members 1:1:2 respectively), with the provision for inclusion of independent representatives if required. The national and provincial councils provide oversight and broad policy guidelines.

District councils collect data on workers' costs of living each month as inputs for revisions of the level of the Kebutuhan Hidup Layak (KHL) or the Decent Standard of Living Index.[10] In 2013, it is estimated that

---

8   These very high figures include very low levels of compliance among small firms.

9   This point was made to the author strongly by a former labour leader and active researcher in Jakarta in an interview in October 2013.

10   The KHL is based on the price of 60 items regarded as essential for the basic standard of living for a single worker (Ministerial Regulation No. 13, 2012).

the minimum wage was, on average, 89 percent of the KHL, although it exceeded the KHL in several cities and districts, especially in the Greater Jakarta region. Other criteria such as changes in labour productivity and general economic conditions are, in theory, also applied to determine annual adjustments, although there are no guidelines as to how these criteria should be applied.

As with many legal-bureaucratic arrangements in Indonesia, the mechanisms for implementing this policy appear functional. However, there are flaws in the design and in implementation. First, the KHL is a negotiated value between employers and employees and, in many cases, unions carry the greatest weight in negotiations. Thus, increases in the KHL tend to exceed the cost-of-living index, sometimes by a large margin. Over time, they bear little relationship to increases in the CPI in various provinces (SEADI 2012).[11] More generally, the wages councils are, in practice, bodies for bilateral negotiation between unions and employers with the MOMT representatives as umpires, rather than forums acting in the public interest.

Second, for a large part of the modern sector, government minimum wages are oriented towards setting entry wages for most new employees. Thus they do not seek to provide a social safety net for the lowest paid workers, which is the traditional role of minimum wages as they evolved in most countries. In most regions of Indonesia, minimum wages are close to the average (median) wage, and hence are not targeting support for those at the bottom end of the wage distribution. Rather, they push wages up in the middle to upper end of the wage distribution for blue-collar workers and have an independent affect on average wages.[12]

Third, the recommendations of the wage councils are frequently overridden by the district head or the governor, as union groups exert political pressure on local leaders to grant higher wages. This happened in several cities close to Jakarta in 2013 as a result of a concerted and successful union campaign, which ultimately succeeded in raising wages by around 50 percent across the region, far above the estimated cost-of-living increases.

---

11 In 2013, the president's office drafted an instruction (INPRES) that sought to engage the BPS as an independent expert body to collect cost-of-living data for the wage councils. However, the INPRES was dropped due to lack of political support.

12 For example, in Jakarta in 2012 the median wage was approximately Rp1.9 million and the minimum wage was Rp1.5 million or some 80 percent of the median. In many other regions, the minimum wage was above the median wage.

In short, minimum wage regulations and their implementation are in need of reform in order for them to assume their conventional role of setting a social safety net for low-wage workers.[13]

9.3   IMPROVING THE SKILLS OF THE WORKFORCE

International comparisons based on the *Global Competitive Index* do not suggest Indonesia is an outlier in regard to the quality of schooling or on-the-job training.[14] However, other research suggests that Indonesia can greatly improve the kind and quality of skills required by the private sector, besides educating more students in higher quality, formal schooling (Di Gropello 2013). Vocational training and on-the-job training are two areas that have been highlighted in recent years and both need attention. Another issue is mobilising talents through the recruitment of foreign workers. We deal briefly with vocation training centres and on-the-job training, before turning to the issue of employing foreign workers.

Several general propositions on education expansion in Indonesia in recent years are presented as a backdrop to the discussion:[15]

- As noted above, Indonesian enrolments have risen very fast for secondary (both academic and vocational) and tertiary levels in recent years.
- According to student scores on several international tests of academic performance, Indonesia's ranking in terms of the quality of secondary schooling is low; although it is on a par with the Philippines, it ranks slightly behind Thailand and is a long way behind Malaysia (Al-Samarrai and Cerdan-Infantes 2013, 117 and 119).
- Return to schooling at all levels have not increased much in recent years suggesting that supply is keeping up with demand; however, falling educated unemployment rates imply improved demand for senior secondary and tertiary graduates, and a rising skill premium.
- Vocationally educated students are regarded as less valuable to employers than students in academic streams at both secondary and

---

13 The introduction of social security legislation to protect all citizens in 2014–15, beginning with health and later covering pensions, may provide an opportunity for the government to rethink this all-embracing approach to minimum wages.

14 Interestingly the GCI scores in Table 9.1 suggest that Indonesia has a bigger problem with the quantity than the quality of formal schooling, while other international studies have focused on the latter in particular in recent years (e.g. Jones and Suryadarma 2013).

15 See especially Di Gropello, Kruse, and Tandon (2011), Al-Samarrai and Cerdan-Infantes (2013), and Suharti (2013).

tertiary level because of less developed life-learning and academic abilities; however, vocational graduates are more appreciated for their technical skills.
• High-quality generic and life-learning skills (English language, computing, thinking skills and behavioural skills) are at least as much (if not more) in demand as technical and professional skills.

The government has made efforts in recent years to improve the labour market for skilled labour. Major efforts to extend certification of skills in collaboration with business have been one major initiative to increase access and mobility of skilled workers. Nonetheless, while Indonesia is not a long way out of line compared with its neighbours in terms of formal training initiatives, there appears to be significant under-investment in training both through public institutions and in the work place. One example is vocational training centres (Balai Latihan Kerja, or BLK) that are run by the central, provincial and district levels, in order of size and generally of quality of staff, equipment and courses. A survey of training centres in 2008 found a number of fundamental problems: incomplete application of competency based training, a severe shortage of instructors, out-dated equipment, limited budgets and insufficient support from the private sector (World Bank 2011b). The centres at district level were particularly badly affected. The report recommended greater cooperation between institutions to 'reinforce their comparative advantage' (p. 7) and a major revamp to improve the quality of institutions at all levels.

A second example of insufficient training conducted by the private sector comes from the enterprise surveys conducted by the World Bank in 2009. Large and medium-scale firms provide, on average, half the training in Indonesia to that provided by firms in other East Asia and Pacific countries; only a small fraction of small firms provide training in Indonesia compared with other countries. Exporters and foreign firms do not fare much better (see Figure 9.3).

Why do Indonesian firms underinvest in training? While not entirely satisfactory given the recorded gap between Indonesia and other countries, two explanations have been put forward. One simple explanation is that the government does not offer generous tax relief for investment in training, unlike in many other countries, including some of the East Asian success stories such as Korea, Taiwan, and Malaysia.[16] Another explanation might relate to the high proportion of firms that recruit blue-

16 For example, besides providing generous tax incentives to investors in education, the Malaysian government also allows for deductions for a range of pre-employment and post-employment training expenses.

*Figure 9.3   Share of large and medium firms providing on-the-job training
in Indonesia and in the Asian region (%)*

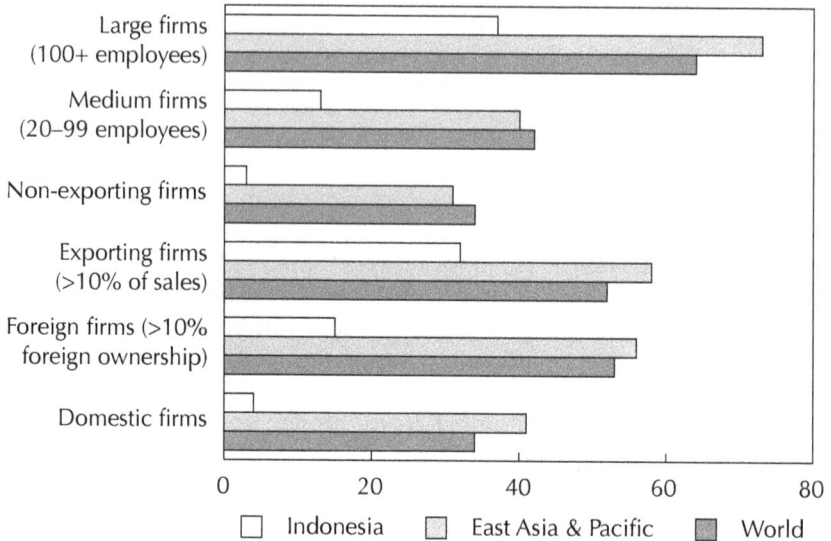

Source: World Bank, Jakarta, based on Enterprise Surveys 2009.

collar workers on temporary contracts or through outsourcing companies, partly in response to the high costs of redundancy.

Employment of foreign workers[17]

One final dimension of improving skills relates to importing foreign talents. Indonesia has adopted a conservative approach to the employment
of foreign workers. In many respects, policies are similar to those in the
Philippines, and contrast with more open policies towards foreign workers adopted by the Singaporean and Malaysian governments, although
both countries are adopting tighter restrictions in regard to the employment of foreigners. Both Singapore and Malaysia have regarded foreign
workers as an essential component for industrial and technological
upgrading, increasing the supply of 'creative talents'. Closely monitored,
including minimum salaries for professionals and managers, foreign
workers are viewed as complementary to nationals, adding value and
facilitating the creation of more jobs through the temporary deployment
of foreign talent.

---

17 This subsection rests heavily on Manning and Aswicahyono (2012).

The main principles in the Labour Law of 2003 assert that foreign workers should only be employed if there is evidence that no Indonesians are available to take up positions.[18] A list drawn up in 1995, and periodically updated, provides a long list of occupations mostly closed to foreigners. This tight policy with regard to foreign workers seems to contradict several assessments of the labour market that point to bottlenecks related to shortages of skilled workers, especially managers and professionals (Di Gropello, Kruse, and Tandon 2011).

In 2012, the MOMT officially gave worker permits to 57,800 foreigners, down from a peak of 77,100 in 2011.[19] This is a very small number of foreign workers for a country of Indonesia's size: in relative terms it is equal to around 0.5 percent of all white-collar workers in Indonesia in 2010.[20] Many of these foreign workers were tertiary educated and were employed in foreign-owned businesses on transfer arrangements, or as technical and professional staff, and most worked in the services sector (see Figure 9.4).

Most of the foreign workers in 2011 were from Northeast Asian, mostly Chinese, many of whom were engaged on construction projects. Indians and Filipinos are now also significant groups among the expatriate workforce, replacing Americans and Australians that dominated in earlier years. Quite a large share (around 20 percent) of work outside Java is in natural resource industries (Bank Indonesia 2010) although the majority of expatriates are still concentrated in the capital Jakarta (amounting to just under 30,000 in 2009).

In bilateral and regional agreements, the government has tended to pursue a policy of concluding bilateral swaps, or commitments with other neighbouring countries. Thus, in contrast to Singapore and Malaysia, this policy muddles the issue of national need for skilled workers with opportunities for Indonesian skilled labour abroad.

---

18 Employers should obtain a permit from the MOMT justifying the appointment of foreigners, and nominate and undertake training of potential replacements. They also pay a modest foreign worker fee of $100 per month. Foreigners should also have a least five-years experience in the relevant field and be fluent in the Indonesian language. See Ministerial Regulation, Ministry of Manpower (Number Per.02/Men/III/2008).

19 There is some contradiction in the the numbers from various sources. Based on a Bank Indonesia report, Manning and Aswicahyono (2012, 34) cited a figure of 57,000 for all foreign workers in 2011. It is likely that the Bank Indonesia data do not cover the entire year.

20 This compares with closer to 10–20 percent of all professionals and managers comprising foreign employees in Singapore, and a slightly smaller proportion in Malaysia.

Figure 9.4   Selected characteristics of foreign workers in Indonesia, 2011 (%)

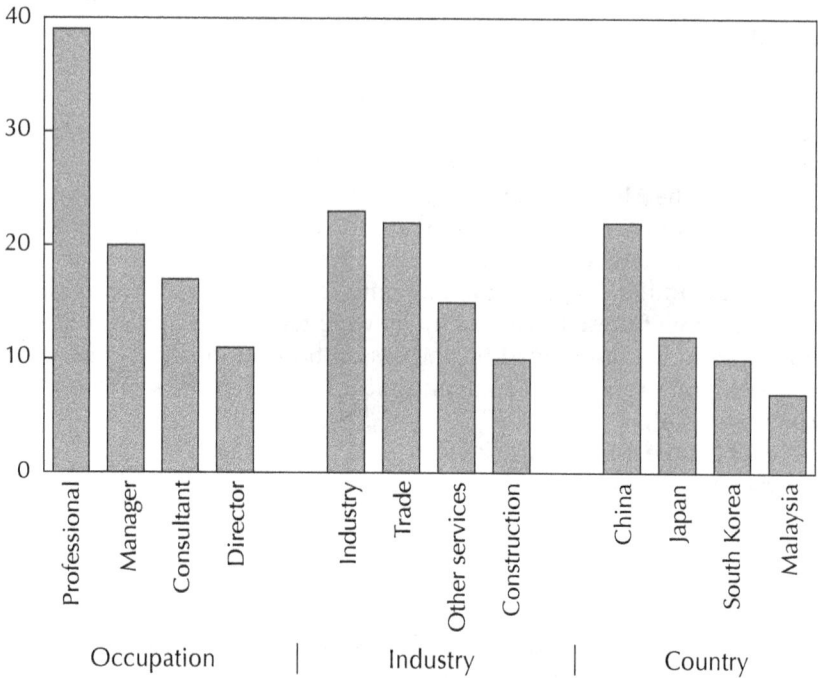

Source: Bank Indonesia, 'Survey of Indonesian overseas workers, 2011' (unpublished), cited in Manning and Aswicahyono (2012).

Of the four main groups of skilled labour (business visitors, traders and investors, inter-corporate transfers and movement of professionals abroad), the movement of the professionals abroad is the most difficult. While the movement of the first three categories of skilled labour is reasonably fluid in relation to trade and investment relationships, movement of professionals depends on mutual recognition agreements for skills or mutual recognition agreements (MRAs). These agreements are much more complicated between the sending and receiving countries for a range of reasons, including difficulties of assessing overseas competencies and countering the protectionist regulations of professional organisations.[21] Nevertheless, although it is moderately restrictive, Indonesia

---

21 Thus in the seventh round of the ASEAN Framework Agreement on Services (AFAS) negotiations completed in 2009, none of the ten priority sectors were affirmed as completely open to temporary labour migration of professionals into Indonesia (Nurridzki and Raharja 2010, 10).

does not stand out in the ASEAN context in this regard, especially since many of the cross-border problems encountered with MRAs are generic.

In summary, while difficult in a more nationalistic environment in the post-Yudhoyono years from October 2014, a concerted campaign seems needed to convince government and non-government players of the need to employ a larger number of foreign workers to assist with Indonesian industrial restructuring.

9.4   CONCLUSION

This chapter has focused on some issues related to labour market regulation in Indonesia from an international perspective. The government faces some major problems in regard to labour market efficiency and flexibility, although Indonesia is not alone within Asia in terms of constraints to competitiveness in the labour area. The chapter also detailed policy developments. It has been argued that, despite ambitious employment targets, the Yudhoyono government made little progress towards a more flexible labour market. When combined with the evidence of under-investment in training and skills development, this area of policy will need more attention to create better jobs and raise general living standards.

What are the prospects of reform that would give job creation a stronger place in the national policy agenda? An active minimum wage policy is likely to remain a key issue in labour policy, especially given the impact that it is perceived to have on equity, at a time when there is growing concern about income distribution trends in Indonesia. One source of worsening income distribution has been through the labour market (Lee and Wie 2013; World Bank 2014). Revisions of the labour law in regard to severance pay are badly needed to deal with high, quasi-fixed costs that impact on competitiveness. But despite general awareness of this problem, reform has been steadfastly opposed by a stronger, more vocal and politically influential union movement.

But at the same time, there is some hope of policy reform. The far-reaching labour law reforms of the early 2000s are now a decade old and there is likely to be less resistance to revisions than there was when the Yudhoyono government came into power in 2004. A new government and a new president in Jakarta from October 2014 offer prospects for new initiatives. Reforms in politically sensitive areas like labour are often more easily achieved by a more populist government that seems likely to hold sway in Jakarta for the next five years. In addition, there is now a growing awareness that Indonesia needs to improve its skills base and labour productivity if it is to compete with neighbouring countries after

2015. Freer trade, investment, and labour mobility are likely to be introduced as part of the ASEAN Economic Community reforms that are to be introduced at the end of 2015.

Like other areas of economic policy reform, Indonesia often surprises, as Professor Hal Hill has taught us through his careful and innovative empirical research on Indonesia and Southeast Asia over several decades.

10   Vietnam: trapped on the trail of the tigers?

James Riedel and Thi Thu Tra Pham

Twenty years ago it seemed likely that Vietnam would follow the trail of the East Asian Tigers, emulating their success under the export-oriented industrialisation strategy. Conditions in Vietnam in the early 1990s were comparable to the initial conditions in Taiwan in the 1960s, Thailand in the 1970s, and China in the 1980s, when each successfully launched an export-oriented industrialisation strategy (Riedel 1993). Like those countries, Vietnam was modestly endowed with natural resources and amply endowed with human resources, with massive under- and unemployed labour in its densely populated rural sector. Like those countries at the outset of export-oriented industrialisation (EOI), industry was largely capital-intensive and state-owned. The level of industrial development in Vietnam was lower than that in the comparator countries when they launched the EOI strategy, but this could be judged an advantage for Vietnam since industrialisation under the import-substitution strategy that preceded EOI was generally inefficient. Vietnam's only disadvantage vis-à-vis its comparators was its relatively weak, practically non-existent private enterprise sector, but that was something other countries had demonstrated could be developed quickly by establishing a policy environment conducive to private investment that could draw on surplus labour in the countryside. There was no reason to doubt that Vietnam could and likely would follow the trail of its successful neighbors, possibly even surpassing their success.

In the early 1990s, Vietnam did, in fact, adopt many of the policies associated with EOI and subsequently, for about a decade, enjoyed relatively rapid growth, although not quite as rapid as the growth of the comparators during their take-off phase of EOI. Since 2006, however, when Vietnam was at long last about to join the World Trade Organization (WTO), the momentum of export-oriented industrialisation dissipated and the economy entered a prolonged (and still ongoing) period of declining growth and rising macroeconomic instability (Pham and Riedel 2012).

Not surprisingly, many observers proclaim that Vietnam is stuck in the 'middle-income trap'. The middle-income trap is routinely associated with the export-oriented industrialisation strategy which, it has been argued, leads to a dead end where prosperity is limited to the level of productivity of unskilled workers in labour-intensive manufacturing (Ketels et. al. 2010; World Bank 2010a).[1] Calls for a new growth model and a new industrialisation strategy in Vietnam are commonplace.

Before assessing any proposed new strategy, one surely must understand why the EOI strategy did not live up to expectations. Were its limitations due to inherent weaknesses of the strategy itself or were they due to failures on the part of the government in implementing the strategy? If the latter then the best path forward may be backward—back to the old strategy, not on to some new untried strategy. This is the central issue addressed in this chapter—should the government's objective be to revive export-oriented industrialisation in Vietnam or to abandon it in favour of some new strategy?

10.1   COMPARING VIETNAM'S PERFORMANCE UNDER EXPORT-ORIENTED INDUSTRIALISATION

It is useful to begin by comparing Vietnam's growth performance under EOI to that of the three comparator countries—Taiwan, Thailand, and China—during their take-off stage of EOI. As Figure 10.1 indicates, Vietnam's record of economic growth since the mid-1990s is strong, with real GDP growth averaging almost 8 percent per annum from 1994–2006 (excluding 1998 and 1999 when growth was negatively impacted by the Asian financial crisis). As impressive as that is, Vietnam's growth record has, however, fallen short of all three of the other countries during their take-off phase of EOI. Taiwan gets the gold and China the silver medal

---

1 The World Bank seems to believe that most developing countries are in a middle-income trap: 'For decades, many economies in Asia, Latin America, and the Middle East have been stuck in this middle-income trap, where countries are struggling to remain competitive as high-volume, low-cost producers in the face of rising wages costs, but are yet unable to move up the value chain and break into fast-growing markets for knowledge and innovation-based products and services' (World Bank 2010a, 27).

Figure 10.1   *Average annual growth rates in Taiwan, Thailand, China and Vietnam (%)*

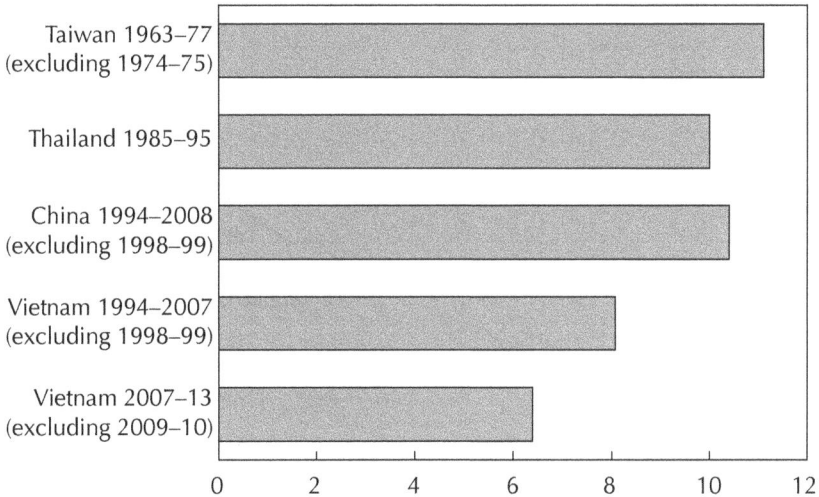

Source: IMF, *International Financial Statistics,* www.imf.org/external/data.htm; Council for Economic Planning and Development, *Taiwan Statistical Data Book,* 1981.

for sustained double-digit growth during the take-off phase.[2] Even Thailand had a period of sustained double-digit growth, an achievement that eluded Vietnam in spite of the relatively low base from which it launched its take-off.

Since the EOI strategy was aimed at capturing the gains from increasing trade orientation, it is useful to compare the level and rate of increase in trade orientation. The standard measure, trade as a percent of GDP ratio, is presented for each country over its take-off period in Figure 10.2. In terms of the increase in the ratio, Taiwan again comes in first, with the ratio rising 3.5 times over the 15-year period; in Thailand and Vietnam the ratio increased 2.5 times over comparable periods and in China 1.8 times. In terms of the level of the trade–GDP ratio, Vietnam comes out on top. It would be a mistake, however, to suggest that this result indicates that Vietnam pursued export-oriented industrialisation more vigorously or more successfully than the other countries, because there are factors other than strategy and policy that determine the level of trade

---

2   The average annual growth rate for Taiwan for the period 1963–1978, excluding 1974 and 1975, when growth was negatively impacted by global recession; for China the period is 1994–2008, excluding 1998 and 1999, when growth was negatively impacted by the Asian financial crisis.

Figure 10.2   Trade (export and import) as a percent of GDP in Taiwan, Thailand, China, and Vietnam during EOI take-off

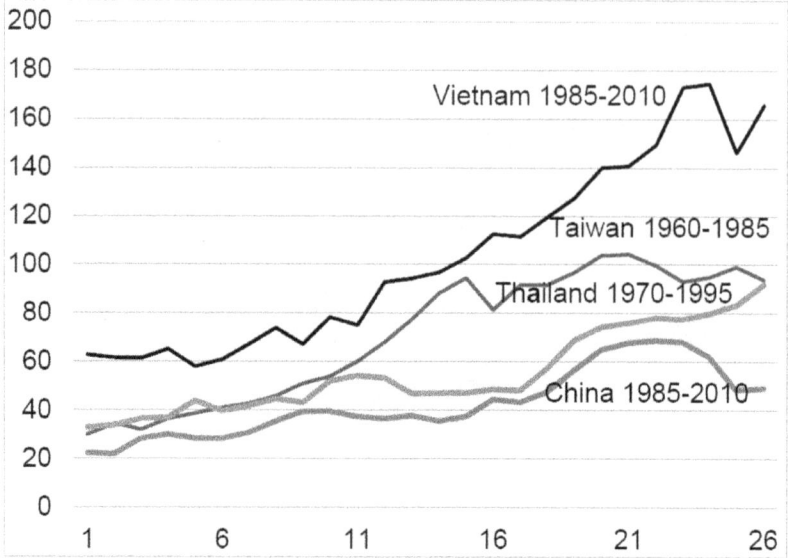

Source: Penn World Tables, version 7.1.

orientation, including importantly country size. Typically, larger countries rely less on trade than smaller ones.

Another problem with the trade–GDP ratio as a measure of trade orientation is that it exaggerates the importance of exports when imported intermediate inputs are used in the production of exports, as they are in Vietnam and the other countries as well. If one cannot determine to what extent the value of gross exports represents domestic value-added (as opposed to the value of the imported inputs), one cannot say much about the relative importance of exports in the economy.

10.2   DOMESTIC VERSUS FOREIGN VALUE-ADDED IN EXPORTS

Input–output tables provide the data required to estimate the relative contributions of domestic and foreign value-added of exports. In order to separate the domestic and foreign value-added of gross exports, however, it is necessary to have input–output tables that differentiate the intermediate input requirement by source, domestically produced or imported. The General Statistics Office of Vietnam (GSO) has provided

Table 10.1   *Direct and total (direct plus indirect) foreign and domestic value-added shares in total and manufactured exports, 2007 (%)*

	Foreign value-added share		Domestic value-added share	
	Direct	Total	Direct	Total
Total exports	25.8	39.5	74.2	60.5
Manufactured exports	31.3	48.2	68.7	51.8

Source: Own calculations using input–output tables, 2007, provided by the GSO.

the authors with the 2007 input–output tables for Vietnam, together with their estimates of domestic and imported intermediate input transactions, albeit with the caveat that they do not consider their estimates to be particularly reliable. Our calculations of domestic value-added content in gross exports for Vietnam, using input–output tables provided by the GSO, must therefore be considered tentative at best.[3]

Table 10.1 presents our preliminary calculations of the direct and total (direct and indirect) imported and domestic value-added as a percent of the gross value of total merchandise exports and manufacturing exports for 2007. These results, taken at face value, suggest that a large share of gross exports, almost 50 percent in the case of manufactures, constitutes the re-export of imported intermediate inputs used directly and indirectly to produce exports.

A major limitation of the calculations reported in Table 10.1 is the implicit assumption that the imported input content varies only by sector, not by market (selling in the domestic market versus exporting) or by type of firm (domestically owned versus foreign-owned) or by location of production (within or outside an export-processing zone where exporters receive tariff and tax privileges that encourage the use of imported inputs). Several recent studies of the import content of Chinese exports have found that failure to take account of the different import intensities of so-called 'normal exports' (those produced outside export-processing zone) and 'processing exports' (those produced inside export processing zones mainly by foreign-owned firms) leads to a significant underestimation of the overall share of foreign value-added in gross exports (Koopman, Wang, and Wei 2012; Dean, Fang, and Wang 2009).

The findings of these studies are summarised in Table 10.2, which presents the direct and total foreign value-added shares for Chinese exports

---

3 The methodology we used is described in the appendix.

Table 10.2   Share of domestic value-added in China's exports, 2002 (%)

	Direct	Total
Total exports: undifferentiated	85.0	74.6
Total exports: differentiated	57.6	53.9
'Normal' exports	95.5	89.2
Processing exports	27.5	25.7
Manufactured exports: differentiated	55.0	51.3
'Normal' exports	95.1	88.4
'Processing' exports	27.0	25.1

Source: Koopman,Wang and Wei (2012); Dean, Fang and Wang (2011).

with and without differentiating the import content of 'normal' versus 'processing' exports. The total foreign value-added share almost doubles (from 25.4 to 45.1 percent) when the different imported input intensities are taken into account. It is found that the share of foreign valued-added of exports produced in export-processing zones is about 90 percent, seven times higher than normal exports.

These findings for China suggest that the domestic value-added share of Vietnamese exports is likely to be much lower than what we have estimated, since the share of processing exports in total exports is likely as high or higher in Vietnam than in China. It could well be, therefore, that the domestic value-added share in gross exports of Vietnam is as low as 20–30 percent.

Unfortunately we do not have data to differentiate processing from normal exports, nor do we have data on exports by firm ownership, so we are unable to replicate the China study for Vietnam. We have, however, obtained the results of a firm survey conducted by the Institute of Labor Science and Social Affairs (ILSSA) of the Ministry of Labour that contains information on the direct domestic and foreign value-added for a sample of firms in four key export industries: textiles, garments, plastic products, and food processing. The findings of the survey are presented in Table 10.3 and confirm that the foreign value-added content of production is significantly higher for firms that are highly export-oriented than for those that mainly sell in the domestic market. It is also found that foreign-owned firms make significantly greater use of imported inputs than their domestically owned counterparts.

Because of data limitations we cannot measure with any precision what role exports play in Vietnam's economy. In all likelihood, the

Table 10.3 *Share of direct value-added, domestic inputs and foreign inputs in total sales for a sample of Vietnamese firms in four sectors*

	No. of firms sampled	As % of total sales			Ratio of imported to domestic inputs
		Value-added	Domestic intermediate inputs	Imported intermediate inputs	
Exports as % of sales greater than 75%					
Textile	13	49.0	14.3	36.7	2.57
Garment	69	58.0	13.7	28.6	2.08
Plastic	9	39.3	19.3	41.3	2.14
Food processing	19	26.0	72.2	1.8	0.02
Exports as % of sales less than 25%					
Textile	4	49.6	46.2	4.2	0.09
Garment	11	65.7	18.6	15.7	0.84
Plastic	52	32.5	33.3	34.2	1.03
Food processing	5	32.5	67.5	0.0	0.00
100% foreign-owned firms					
Textile	14	44.9	22.9	32.2	1.4
Garment	23	55.7	11.2	34.9	3.13
Plastic	7	39.4	11.8	48.8	4.14
Food processing	3	24.7	64	11.3	0.18
Domestically owned firms					
Textile	15	53.5	26.2	18.1	0.69
Garment	71	61.7	15.7	22.4	1.43
Plastic	56	31.0	35.8	32.8	0.92
Food processing	28	28.0	71.6	0.4	0.01

Source: Vietnam Institute of Labor Science and Social Affairs.

domestic value-added of Vietnam's exports is significantly less than half the gross value, but how much less than half we cannot be certain. If domestic value-added is no more than 30 percent, then the ratio of export value-added to GDP is no more than about 20 percent (i.e. 30 percent of 70 percent), which is not particularly high by international standards, given the small size of Vietnam's economy and its skewed resource endowment favouring a strong comparative advantage in labour-intensive manufacturing.

10.3   THE LOGIC OF EXPORT-ORIENTED INDUSTRIALISATION IN EAST ASIA

The reason EOI works as a launching pad for rapid economic growth is because it promotes specialisation in the production of goods in which a country has a comparative advantage in world markets and, in so doing, generates a higher level of income and much more employment than it would otherwise obtain. With a higher income, countries can save and invest more and grow faster and more 'inclusively'. In addition, EOI allows a country to raise productivity by engaging in technology catch-up (importing capital goods that embody new and better technology) and inducing efficiency by forcing domestic producers to compete at the international level (Pham 2013).

The way EOI has worked in East Asia is, however, different in at least one important respect from the way comparative advantage and the gains from specialisation are portrayed in textbooks. In textbooks, the gains from trade liberalisation are illustrated by movement along the production possibility frontier, as labour and capital are drawn out of previously protected capital-intensive, import-competing sectors and into relatively labour-intensive manufacturing sectors in which the country has a comparative advantage. The gains from specialisation following trade liberalisation are greater the more that labour and capital are reallocated.

In East Asia, however, the starting point of EOI was characterised not only by import barriers that distorted production in favour of capital-intensive import-competing goods and against labour-intensive exports, but also by massive unemployment, mainly residing in the rural sector. Because a large stock of surplus labour existed, what was necessary to launch EOI was not a move to free trade or the elimination of subsidies for import-competing enterprises, but instead a more modest (suboptimal) agenda of reforms aimed at removing or offsetting the disincentive in the system that worked against producing for export (Bhagwati 1988; Riedel 1991). The EOI strategy, in the East Asia setting, allowed countries, at least for a time, to have it both ways—create a fast-growing, labour-intensive, export-oriented manufacturing sector and at the same time maintain, and even expand, the favoured, highly protected state-owned, import-competing industries. The difficult political decision to withdraw protection from the largely state-owned, capital-intensive industrial sector could be postponed.

Figures 10.3 and 10.4 illustrate how Taiwan and China were able to have it both ways in the first decade or two after launching EOI. Even though Taiwan did not follow the socialist economic path, state-owned enterprises nonetheless played a major role in the manufacturing sector at the outset of EOI in 1960, accounting for almost 50 percent of industrial output and about 80 percent of fixed investment in manufacturing. Over the following 20 years, from 1960 to 1980, state-owned enterprises continued to grow, with output expanding at an average annual rate of 10 percent, while at the same time their share in manufacturing output dwindled to 12 percent as non-state-owned enterprises, mainly private, small and medium-sized companies, expanded at double the rate of the state-owned enterprises (SOEs). SOEs in Taiwan were marginalised, not privatised.

The same process—marginalisation of state-owned enterprises—occurred two decades later in China when it launched EOI. The SOE industrial sector expanded at a 12 percent per annum rate, but the non-SOE sector expanded twice as fast, increasing its share of industrial output from 25–73 percent by 2003.

Assessing quantitatively the relative contributions to industrial development of the state and non-state sectors in Vietnam is difficult for the same reason that assessing just about every economic issue is difficult—the lack of reliable data. It is well known that many so-called private companies in Vietnam are the spin-offs of state-owned companies and are owned and managed by the executives of SOEs who retain special status in the system. In addition, so-called 'foreign-invested enterprises' constitute a separate classification in the industrial output data, but it is not at all clear to what extent they deserve to be considered private as opposed to state-owned since they are often jointly owned by SOEs.

In spite of these limitations, an attempt is made in Figure 10.5 to measure the extent to which the state-owned sector has been marginalised in Vietnam. As the figure shows, the process of marginalisation is clearly underway in Vietnam, but at a significantly slower pace than that which occurred in either Taiwan or China after launching EOI. In Vietnam, after more than a decade of EOI, the SOE sector, which is mainly engaged in heavy, capital-intensive industry, still accounts for almost 50 percent of domestic industrial production. Indeed, the marginalisation of SOEs appears to have slowed, if not reversed, after 2006.

Figure 10.3   Having it both ways in Taiwan: industrial output, 1960–1980 (NTD billion)

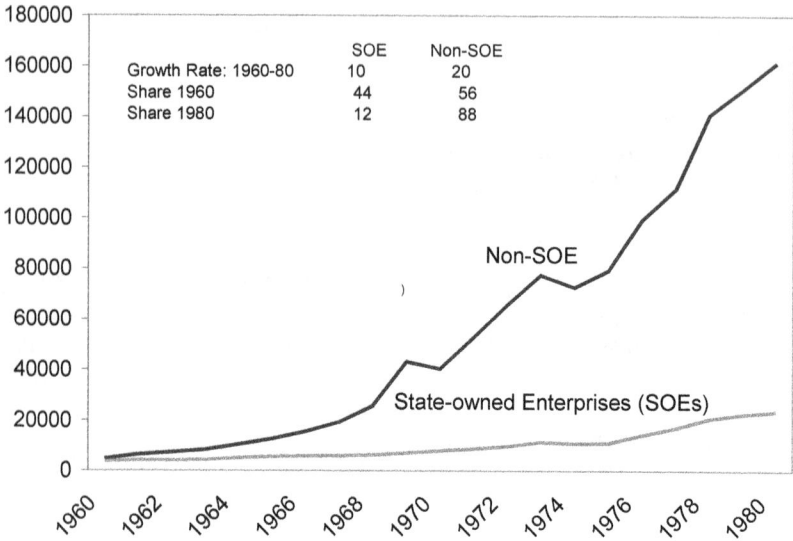

	SOE	Non-SOE
Growth Rate: 1960-80	10	20
Share 1960	44	56
Share 1980	12	88

Source: *Taiwan Statistical Data Book*, 2008.

Figure 10.4   Having it both ways in China: industrial output, 1983–2003 (RMB billion)

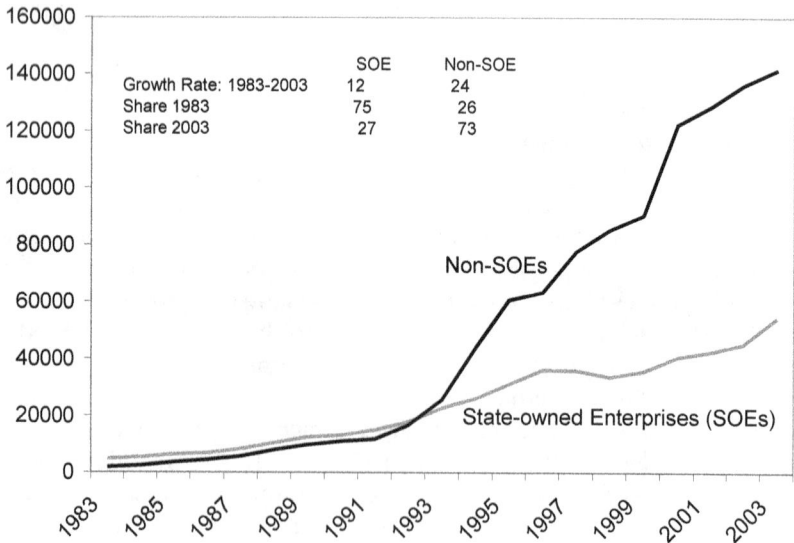

	SOE	Non-SOE
Growth Rate: 1983-2003	12	24
Share 1983	75	26
Share 2003	27	73

Source: *China Statistical Yearbook*, selected issues.

Figure 10.5 *Having it both ways in Vietnam: domestic industrial output, 1995–2010 (VND trillion)*

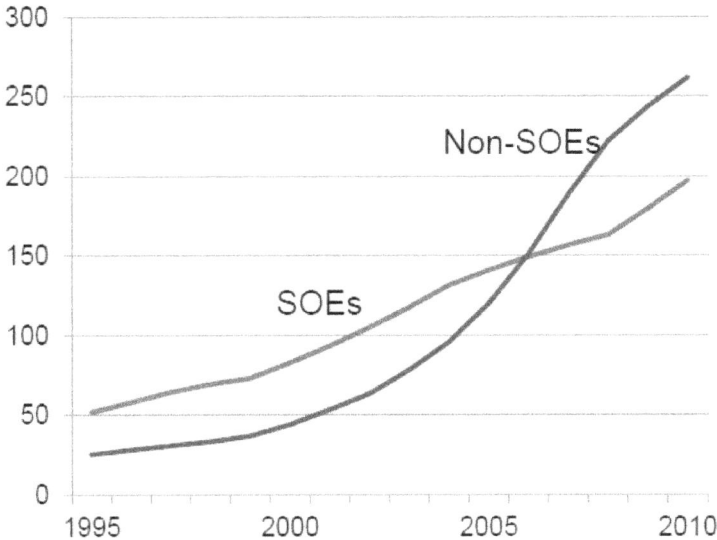

Source: GSO online databank (www.gso.gov.vn).

10.4 EXPORT-ORIENTED INDUSTRIALISATION AND STRUCTURAL CHANGE IN VIETNAM

One would expect that EOI would lead to shifts in the composition of exports in favour of relatively labour-intensive (light) manufactures. As Figure 10.6 illustrates, that is what has happened in Vietnam. The composition of imports, as Figure 10.7 illustrates, has changed very little, which is not surprising since the liberalisation of the import regime was aimed mainly at mitigating the disincentives to exporting.

While the composition of exports has changed in favour of relatively labour-intensive products, the distribution of manufacturing value-added (GDP), capital, and employment has not changed (or changed only marginally) in favour of relatively labour-intensive manufacturing industries. This finding is derived by computing the weighted average capital–labour ratio in manufacturing over the period 2000 to 2008 (the only years for which data are available) using industry shares in total manufacturing value-added, capital stock, and employment as weights. With the industry capital–labour ratios held constant over time, the differences in the weighted average capital–labour ratios reflect differences in the distribution across manufacturing industries of value-added, capital, and employment and the changes in each over time.

Figure 10.6   Composition of non-oil exports (% of total)

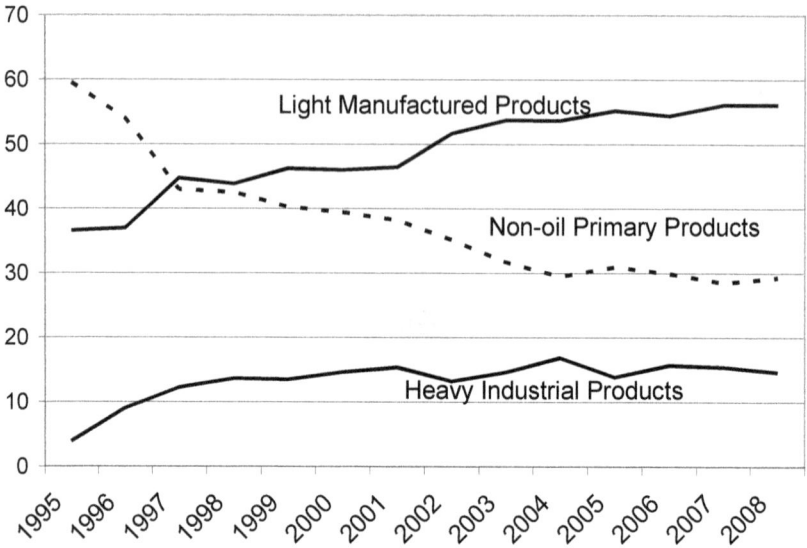

Source: GSO online databank (www.gso.gov.vn).

Figure 10.7   Composition of imports (% of total)

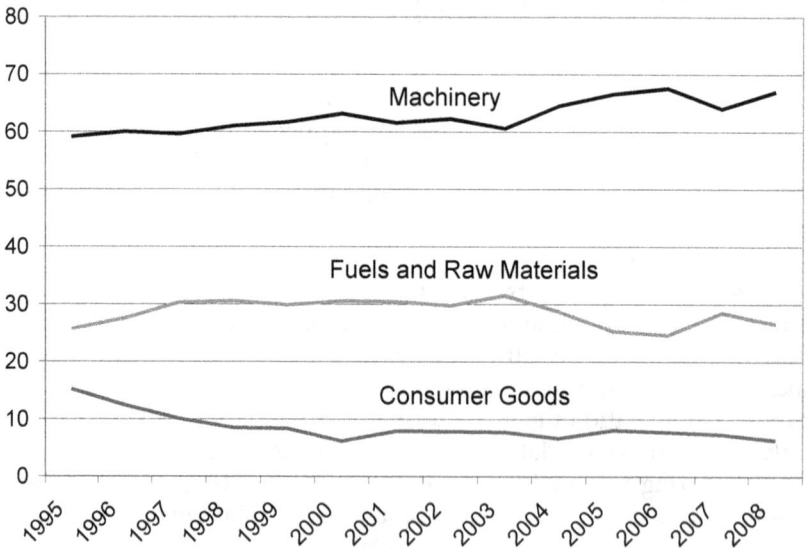

Source: GSO online databank (www.gso.gov.vn).

Figure 10.8   Average capital–labour ratio (VND billion per worker) weighted by sector shares of manufacturing value-added, capital stock and employment[a]

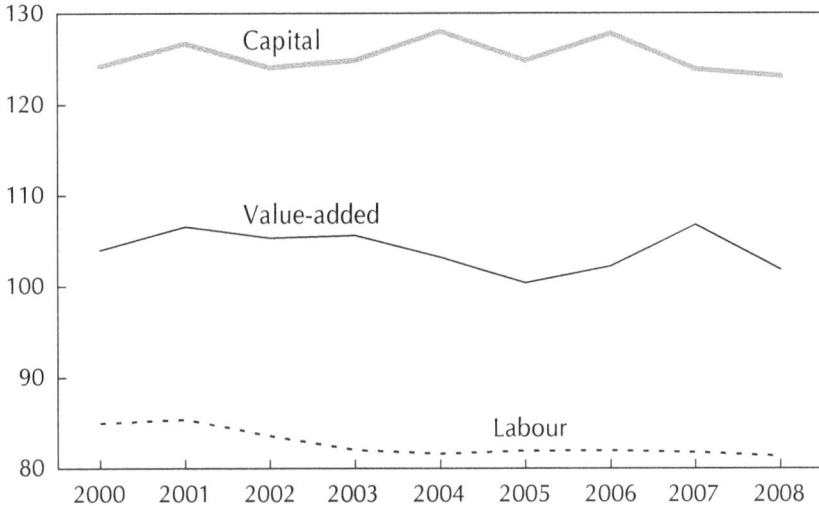

a   The lines indicate the weighted average capital–labour ratio in manufacturing, where the weights are the shares of each industry (at the 2-digit Standard Industrial Classification (SIC) level) in the manufacturing totals of capital (K), labour (L) and value-added (V).

Source: Authors' calculations based on GSO data.

As shown in Figure 10.8, the distribution of capital in the manufacturing sector is weighted much more heavily toward relatively capital-intensive sectors than is labour, which is not surprising. More revealing, however, is the finding that hardly any redistribution of value-added or the capital stock in favour of relatively labour-intensive manufacturing industries occurred over the period 2000–2008.

How should resources in the manufacturing sector be allocated? If the aim is to raise per capita income, then should not resources be moved from industries in which labour productivity is low to those in which labour productivity is high? This sounds right and indeed is it is commonplace to espouse this proposition, even among economists, but it is essentially wrong. The reason is that resources, labour in particular, are not 'moved' from one sector to another like pieces on a chessboard. Jobs must first be created, generally as a result of capital investment, to allow labour to move from one sector to another. This being the case, then should not the rule be that investment should be directed away from sectors where labour productivity is low and toward sectors where labour productivity is high? Sounds right, but again this proposition is wrong. The reason is because in sectors where labour productivity is

Figure 10.9   Scatter plots of capital and labour productivity against capital–labour ratios across manufacturing branches in Vietnam

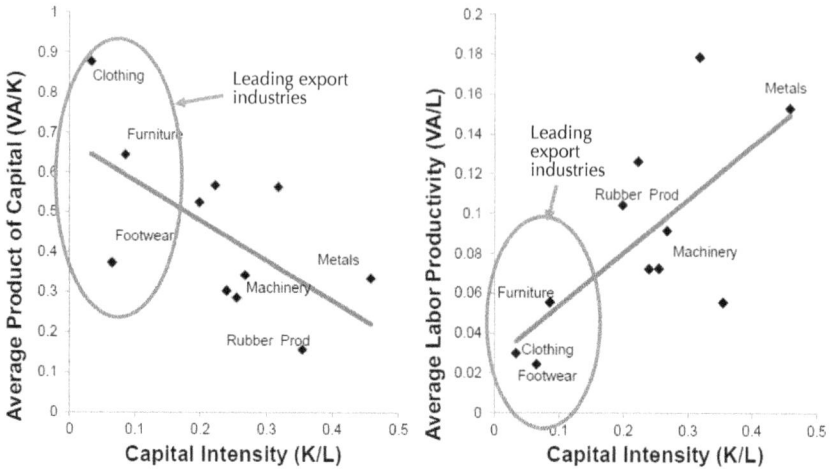

Source: GSO.

high, capital productivity is low (and vice versa), as is illustrated below using industry-level data (Figure 10.9) and firm-level data (Figure 10.10) for Vietnam's manufacturing industry.

As these figures illustrate, investing in capital-intensive industries, where labour productivity is relatively high, yields a return (using value-added per unit capital as a proxy) that is less than half the yield if invested in export-oriented, labour-intensive industries. Moreover, the employment generated from investment in capital-intensive industries is less than a quarter of what it would be if invested in labour-intensive industries. Indeed, if the allocation of investment capital were market determined (allocated according to relative rates of return), the labour-intensive, export-oriented branches of manufacturing would get the lion's share, which they do not get in the existing system where policy trumps other considerations in deciding how the nation's scarce capital resources are allocated.

10.5   THE LIMITS OF EOI

That EOI works as an effective means for launching rapid growth is amply demonstrated by the experience of the Asian Tigers and a number of other countries in the region that followed them, including China

Figure 10.10   Scatter plots of capital and labour productivity against capital–labour ratios across 1,200 manufacturing firms in Vietnam

Capital productivity versus capital intensity

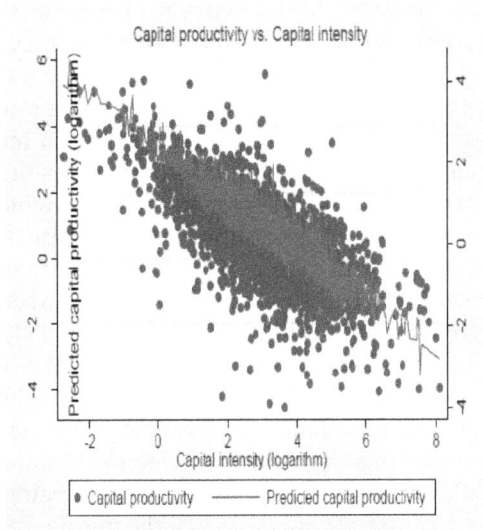

Capital productivity vs. Capital intensity

Labour productivity versus capital intensity

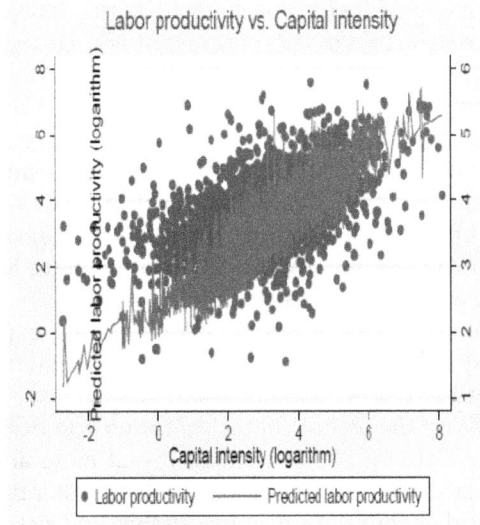

Labor productivity vs. Capital intensity

Source: World Bank Vietnam Enterprise Survey, 2005.

and several in Southeast Asia. As we interpret it, the EOI strategy was largely a matter of government getting out of the way and allowing firms, mostly medium-sized private firms, to exploit the countries' comparative advantage in world markets (Riedel 1988).

Clearly there are limits to a growth strategy that is essentially one of 'just getting out of the way'. It may work for a time to absorb the rural unemployed into productive employment and that may in turn generate relatively high growth rates, but eventually, once surplus labour is absorbed, competition for labour and capital between tradable and non-tradable goods sectors and within tradables between labour-intensive, export-oriented, and capital-intensive import-competing sectors will require that government 'level the playing field' on which firms across sectors compete for resources. In addition as wages rise, the demand for a more skilled workforce will require the government to invest more and invest more efficiently in education and training. If governments do not meet these challenges, then it is likely that growth will slow down.

Perhaps this is what is currently referred to as the 'middle-income trap' into which many observers claim Vietnam has fallen even though the income level of the vast majority of people in Vietnam is below the arbitrary line drawn by the World Bank between low- and middle-income countries (around US$1000). Much has been and is being written about what Vietnam should do to avoid or escape the middle-income trap. The basic premise, as put forward in an influential study that attempted to draw lessons for Vietnam from the experience of East Asia and Southeast Asia, is that 'countries that compete on the basis of cheap labour cannot move beyond lower middle income status' (Dapice 2008).

This sounds reasonable if only because it is a tautology — countries with low wages are by definition low-income countries whose average labour productivity is low relative to other countries. Low wages are, in fact, what make countries with low average labour productivity competitive in world markets. If such countries exploit the advantage of low wages to raise income and invest efficiently, labour demand and real wages will rise, after which a country will no longer be able to compete on the basis of low wages because it will no longer have low wages as its relative resource endowment has changed.

The recommendation currently in vogue among experts, domestic and foreign, especially aid donors and the international financial institutions (IFIs), is for Vietnam to take measures to 'increase domestic value-added' and move up the 'value-chain'. As for how to do that, the World Bank's advice to Vietnam is that it 'must invest more and with greater efficiency in physical and human capital, foster substantially more innovative activity, and encourage entrepreneurship and risk-taking' (World Bank 2010a, 21).

When the World Bank declares that a country must do something, presumably it means that its government must do it. If it is suggested that the government of Vietnam should do a better job of supplying public goods and create a policy environment that encourages individual entrepreneurship and risk-taking, who could object? These are, after all, the fundamental responsibilities of every government in a market economy, no matter what the share of domestic value-added in exports or the country's niche in the international supply chain. If, on the other hand, those who exhort Vietnam to move up the value chain are suggesting that the government should adopt an industrial policy aimed at increasing the domestic value-added share of exports or produce higher-tech, more sophisticated products, then that is something else, something eerily reminiscent of the long-ago discredited industrial policy of 'picking winners' that defy comparative advantage.

The data reported in Figures 10.9 and 10.10 suggest that a shift of capital investment from relatively labour-intensive industries producing final goods for export (clothing, footwear, and furniture) to relatively capital-intensive intermediate input industries. While it may raise domestic value-added in exports, this shift would likely lower domestic value-added in the manufacturing sector as a whole. For example, according to the industrial survey data, textile production requires seven times more capital per worker employed than clothing production, which may explain why clothing firms find it profitable to import textile fabrics than to rely on domestic suppliers. If measures were taken to increase the share of domestic fabric used in clothing manufacture, the share of domestic value-added in clothing exports would likely rise, but aggregate value-added and employment in the manufacturing sector would likely fall.

Surely there are limits to the EOI strategy, but the evidence surveyed above suggests that Vietnam is far from reaching them. Further evidence that Vietnam retains a strong comparative advantage in labour-intensive manufactures is the fact that about 70 percent of the population resides in the rural areas where per capita income is about one-sixth the level in urban areas. In Ho Chi Minh City, the centre of export-oriented manufacturing in Vietnam, real manufacturing wages increased at a rate of only 1.3 percent per year from 2000 to 2009, while over the same period real GDP was growing at about 7 percent per year (Nguyen 2014, 77).

It is useful to compare wage growth in Vietnam to that in China. As Figure 10.11 indicates, real wages in China have been growing rapidly and at an accelerating rate since the mid-2000s, which is interpreted as evidence that China is at, or has passed, the Lewis Turning Point (Cai 2010). Vietnam, which is about 15 years behind China in term of per

Figure 10.11   Level and rate of growth of real wages in China, 2001–2009

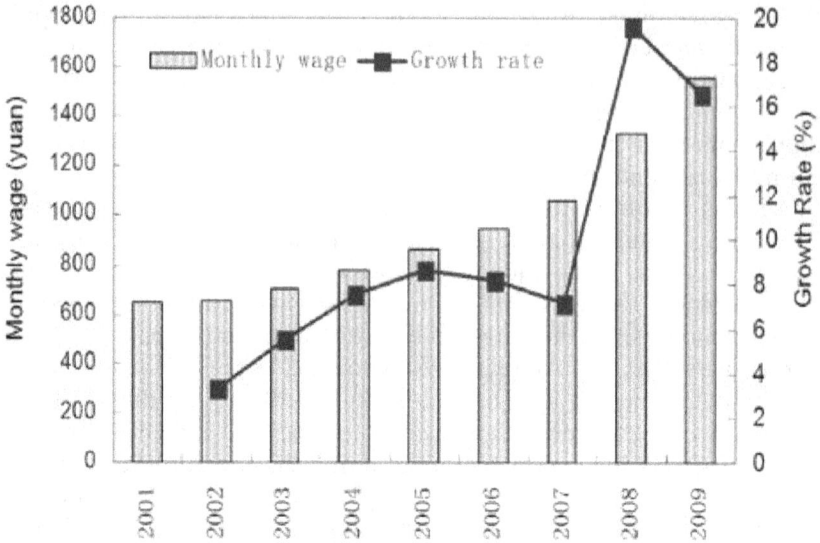

Source: Cai (2010).

capita income, has a considerable distance to go before its reservoir of surplus labour is likely to run out.[4]

10.6   HOW VIETNAM GOT TRAPPED

The global economic crisis that swept down from the north at the end of 2008 dealt a severe blow to export-oriented industrialisation, but it had begun to lose traction in Vietnam several years before the global crisis struck. At the heart of the problem were policy decisions that directly or indirectly, by commission or omission, diverted scarce capital resources away from export-oriented industry. SOEs and SOE conglomerates (general corporations) were given claim to a disproportionate share of investible funds and invested them inefficiently in a wide array of activities outside their core business. Government infrastructure spending both crowds out and crowds in investment in export-oriented manufacturing, the balance between the two depending on the efficiency with which the

---

4   Real purchasing power parity GDP per capita in China (US$7500) is 2.5 times higher than that in Vietnam (US$3100). At a growth rate of 6 percent per year, Vietnam will reach the per capita income level of China in 15 years.

government invests in infrastructure. Unfortunately, government infrastructure spending is widely judged to be 'wasteful and riddled with corruption', which means that the crowding-out effect of government spending is all too likely to outweigh the positive effects of infrastructure investment on business costs and profitability, putting Vietnam's exporters at a disadvantage vis-à-vis its competitors. As an illustration, the World Bank's competitive index reports that the cost of shipping a 20-foot container from Vietnam is twice as high as from China (World Bank 2007).

Macroeconomic circumstances in Vietnam since 2006 have also served to weaken the country's ability to pursue export-oriented industrialisation. The euphoria surrounding Vietnam's accession to WTO led to massive capital inflows and large increases in public and private spending in 2007 and 2008 before a run on the currency occurred in May of that year. With capital inflows in 2007 at a level of 25 percent of GDP, the central bank was obliged to intervene heavily in the foreign exchange market, dramatically increasing money and credit and igniting double-digit inflation and a rise in the trade deficit to 30 percent of GDP (Pham and Riedel 2012).

Accelerating inflation and the consequent real appreciation of the currency naturally weakened EOI. They had, however, quite the opposite effect on asset markets, especially real estate. Foreign capital inflows contributed to soaring prices of stock and bonds, but the price bubbles in financial markets were corrected by market forces unleashed with the run on the currency. The price bubble in real estate proved to be more resilient, defying the logic of market fundamentals, perhaps because property in Vietnam is valued more as an instrument of speculation and a store of wealth than for its intrinsic value. The high cost of land in Vietnam imposes a high cost on those who use land, including the manufacturing industry. Even more detrimental to EOI, however, has been the magnet effect of the property bubble in attracting resources away from manufacturing.

One vivid illustration of the magnet effect of the property bubble on resource allocation is foreign direct investment (FDI). Foreign firms play a large and growth role in Vietnam's economy in general and in its export sector in particular, accounting for about 14 percent of GDP and 47 percent of exports. Until 2006, about 75 percent of FDI in Vietnam was in the manufacturing sector, contributing significantly to overall growth of manufacturing output and exports. Since 2006, however, data on registered FDI, shown in Figure 10.12, indicate that the bulk of FDI in recent years has been directed into the real estate sector, where the potential for employment creation and long-term productivity growth is relatively modest. Moreover, it is reported that a significant share of FDI in real

Figure 10.12   Registered FDI by sector of destination, 2003–2009 (%)

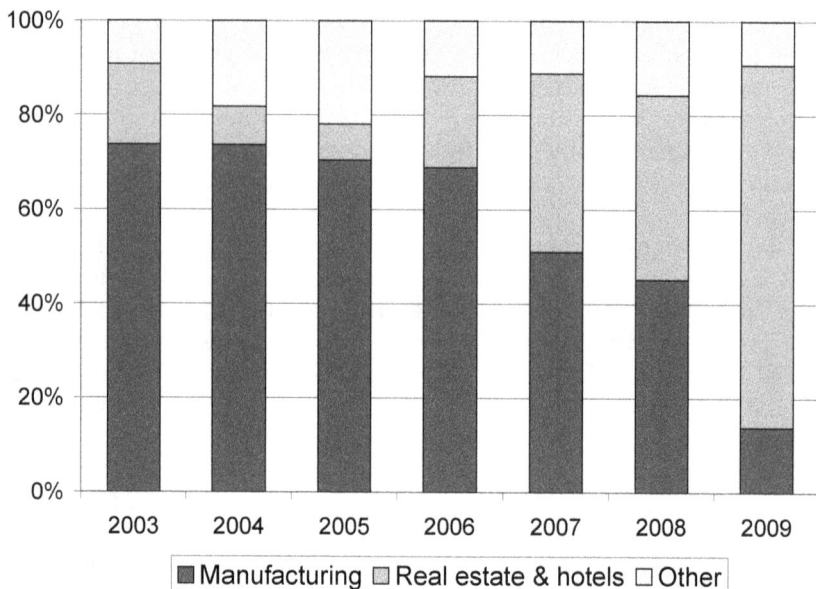

Source: GSO.

estate is financed domestically, potentially crowding out domestic borrowers from the credit market. In addition, FDI in real estate puts a heavy demand on foreign exchange (with which to import building materials for example), again potentially crowding export-oriented manufactures out the foreign exchange market.

10.7   IS VIETNAM TRAPPED ON THE TRAIL OF THE TIGERS?

The answer to this question is affirmative. Vietnam does appear to be trapped on the trail of the tigers, but the trap is one of its own making, as is likely the case of neighbouring countries that are alleged to be stuck in the middle-income trap, since what is usually said to have trapped those countries is their own policies. For example, Woo (2009) argues that too much emphasis on redistribution is what has trapped Malaysia, while Warr (2012) argues that too little emphasis on education and too much emphasis on mega-infrastructure projects that lend themselves to corruption are what have trapped Thailand. What seems to have trapped Vietnam, albeit at a much lower level of per-capita income, is unwillingness on the part of the government to loosen its protective embrace of the relatively inefficient capital-intensive, state-owned enterprise sector or to significantly lessen its discretionary control over the allocation of resources, especially land and capital. In these circumstances, the export-oriented industrialisation strategy does not and would not be expected to function efficiently. Nor, we suspect, would any other strategy that might be proposed as an alternative to export-oriented industrialisation.

Appendix A10.1   Methodology of measuring the relative contribution of domestic and foreign value-added in gross exports

The domestic and foreign value-added content of exports can be estimated using input–output (IO) tables. The standard form of the IO table is:

$$a_{11}X_1 + a_{12}X_2 + \cdots + a_{1n}X_n + Y_1 = X_1$$
$$a_{21}X_1 + a_{22}X_2 + \cdots + a_{2n}X_n + Y_2 = X_2$$
$$\vdots$$
$$a_{n1}X_1 + a_{n2}X_2 + \cdots + a_{nn}X_n + Y_n = X_n$$

where the coefficients (a_{ij}) represent the *direct* per unit input requirements of good i in the production of good j, Y_i is final demand (domestic and foreign) for good i and X_i is the gross output of good i. In matrix notation, the IO system can be written as $AX + Y = X$, where A is an nxn matrix of input coefficients (a_{ij}) and X and Y are vectors of output and final demand, respectively. Solving for X yields $(I - A)^{-1}Y = X$, where $(I - A)^{-1}$ is the nxn Leontief inverse matrix of the *direct and indirect* input requirements (r_{ij}) of good i in the production of one unit of final demand for good j. The column-sums of the $(I - A)^{-1}$ matrix

$$(\bar{r}_j = \sum_i r_{ij})$$

are the *direct and indirect* intermediate input requirement per unit of final demand of good j.

In order to measure the imported value-added per unit of final demand, the A matrix must be decomposed into its two parts: the per unit requirements of domestically produced intermediate inputs (d_{ij}: elements of an nxn matrix D), and the per unit requirements of imported intermediate inputs (m_{ij}: elements of nxn matrix $M = A - D$). Hence, the column-sums of the M matrix

$$(\bar{m}_j = \sum_i m_{ij})$$

are the *direct* imported intermediate input requirement per unit of output. An export (E) weighted average of these coefficients would indicate the direct imported input requirement per unit of the representative export

$$(\bar{m}_E = \sum_j e_j \cdot \bar{m}_j, \text{ where } e_j = \frac{E_j}{\sum_j E_j}).$$

In order to obtain the total (*direct and indirect*) imported input require-ment we must obtain the Leontief inverse of the D matrix $((I - D)^{-1})$ and multiply it by the M matrix, yielding an nxn matrix (M^*) of *direct and indirect* imported inputs per unit final demand $M^* = M \cdot (I - D)^{-1}$. The column sums of the M^* matrix are the direct and indirect imported input requirement per unit final demand of good j

$$(\bar{m}^*_j = \sum_i m^*_{ij}).$$

An export (E)-weighted average of these values

$$(\bar{m}^*_E = \sum_j \bar{m}^*_j \cdot e_j)$$

gives a measure of the direct and indirect imported input requirement per unit of the representative export, or in other words the percentage share (when multiplied by 100) of foreign value-added in gross exports.

PART 3

Political economy

11 Rethinking the role of the state in ASEAN

Peter McCawley

11.1 INTRODUCTION

Our colleague Hal Hill is one of Australia's most well-known economic scholars on growth and development in Asia. He spent much of the first part of his academic career exploring development issues in Asia through the lens of his work on Indonesia. More recently, since the mid-1990s, he has broadened his work on development issues in Asia into numerous studies of economic challenges in other key ASEAN countries. He is now widely recognised internationally as one of the world's leading specialists on ASEAN economic issues. And for those of us who know and work with Hal, he is not only an immensely knowledgeable scholar on development issues in the Southeast Asian region, he is also a warm and generous friend.

On a more personal note, I remember clearly my first contact with Hal. It was in 1975 when I was working as an advisor in Parliament House in Canberra. Entirely out of the blue, an unexpected piece of correspondence arrived amidst the welter of official papers that flowed through the parliamentary office. It was a letter from Hal Hill, who had recently completed a Master's degree at Monash University. He said that he was interested in the possibility of studying for a doctoral degree at the Australian National University (ANU), perhaps specialising on the Indonesian economy. He asked for suggestions. I wrote back encouraging his interest in Indonesian studies. Hal quickly replied (in a letter, of course, because there was no such thing as email in the mid-1970s) saying that he had decided to delay a start on doctoral studies for a year or so, but that he would be in touch again later. I returned to the ANU in early 1976. Before too long, Hal had followed up his earlier enquiries and the head of our department, Professor Heinz Arndt, was very glad to be able to welcome Hal into the department as one of his family of PhD scholars working on the Indonesian economy.

In recognition of Hal's long interest in development issues across Asia, and especially his work on various ASEAN economies, it seems appropriate to discuss some aspects of a key topic in public policy for the region – the capacity of ASEAN states to meet the performance goals expected of them. The main arguments here will be that:

- the capacity of ASEAN states to perform the main functions normally expected of governments varies widely
- in the weaker ASEAN states, the fiscal capacity of governments is very limited; and even in some of the stronger ASEAN states, the fiscal capacity of governments is not strong
- the economic role of governments, including at provincial and subprovincial levels, needs to be reconsidered to recognise the limited capacities of governments in most ASEAN states.

11.2   THE ROLE OF THE STATE

There is a very substantial literature on the role of the state in the developing world. Early thinking in the 1950s about development economics was influenced by events such as the post-war Marshall Plan for Europe (Behrman 2007) and the inclination of post-colonial governments in development countries to favour some form of planning. In the post-war years, there was a tendency across the global development community to accept the idea that the state in developing countries should aim to play a leading role in the promotion of development. Meier (2005, 45) notes that 'Development corporations, national planning boards, and industrial development corporations soon proliferated'. And along with this approach, many policymakers, especially in the developing world, harboured considerable suspicion of pro-market policies. Meier (2005, 46) summarised the prevailing views as follows:

> Criticizing reliance on the price system, desiring social reform along with development, and stressing the pervasiveness of the obstacles to development, the governments of poorer countries became more attracted to central planning than had ever been the case in the historical experience of the now advanced Western nations.

During the 1950s, therefore, ideas about the relationship between the market and the state in developing countries evolved which, in various ways, had a major influence across the global development community.

In the succeeding decades, views about the role of the state and the desirability of relying more on markets in developing countries varied widely. In many developing countries—and especially in the three largest developing countries of China, India, and Indonesia—the strongly held view of many senior policymakers was that the state should have a leading economic role.[1] But during the 1970s and 1980s there was much discussion within the global development community of the benefits of market-oriented, export-oriented industrialisation, especially in Asia (Myint 1972). A number of developing countries, especially in Southeast Asia, adopted an export-oriented industrialisation strategy with considerable success. However, in other developing countries such as Taiwan and the Republic of Korea, state-led industrialisation policies underpinned by considerable government intervention in markets were widely believed to have been quite successful. Thus, the debate between those who favoured considerable state intervention in economic policies and those who were inclined to a more pro-market approach swayed back and forth, partly depending on the politics and economic events of the day, and partly depending on the challenges in particular sectors across different countries.

It should also be noted that much of the public policy debate across Asia about the broad topic of the state and market was—and remains—quite confused. In Indonesia, for example, the discussions about the economic damage caused by 'neo-liberalism', which often flare up in the media, tend to reflect political passion rather than a sound understanding of markets and the price mechanism (Thee 2009). This is perhaps hardly surprising because, for many observers, both the operations of states and markets are often confusing and quite misunderstood. As Wilson and Skinner observed in their survey of *The Market and the State* (1976, v):

> It may indeed be the case that no other great social institution of anything like comparable importance is so imperfectly understood and so inadequately appreciated as is the market.

In many developing countries in Asia in the post-colonial period, support for strong, state-led intervention in the economy, including in key markets, was accepted almost as an article of faith by many political leaders and their supporters. But often, it seems that not much thought was given to the precise goals of policy, or to the most effective forms of state intervention, or to the resources required to support various types of intervention. In short, the costs and benefits of government

---

1 An excellent survey of official views about these matters in Indonesia is contained in Mustopadidjaja et al. (2012).

intervention and regulation were rarely considered in detail, and very rarely quantified.[2]

It was within this context that the World Bank's 1997 World Development Report (WDR), *The State in a Changing World*, focused on the theme of the role of governments and the state in developing countries. The report emphasised that an effective state is vital to support the development process but, at the same time, suggested that there was a need to 'rethink the role of the state' and place an increasing emphasis on state effectiveness. In adopting this approach, the 1997 WDR was reflecting much of the discussion that had been taking place in developed countries during the 1980s and 1990s about the need for new, managerial-oriented approaches to efficiency in the public sector (Schiavo-Campo and Sundaram 2000). To some extent, these discussions tended to focus on administrative issues of control and efficiency within government, but to some extent they touched on more controversial questions about the appropriate role of the state and government.

On one hand, it would hardly seem controversial to suggest that steps should be taken to improve efficiency within government. Across the world, in many countries, there is much dissatisfaction with the effectiveness of government. There are frequent discussions about the need for good governance and the better delivery of public services. But on the other hand, in some key respects, discussions about the role and size of government raise highly controversial issues. Some observers — including many commentators in advanced countries in North America and Europe — argue that as a general rule, most states have become too large and that their role needs to be curbed. Other observers — both in advanced countries and in developing countries — argue that as the World Bank suggested, there is a need to 'rethink the role of the state' with the aim of rebalancing both the size and functions of government in developing countries. This second group of observers argues that while it is true that in some respects the role of government could usefully be reduced, in other respects a larger, stronger, and more effective state is needed in many developing countries. Thus, there are observers who argue for a smaller state, and there are others who argue for a larger state (Streeten 1996, 30). Views about the role of the state in Southeast Asia need to be considered within this context.

---

2 The leading economic planner Widjojo Nitisastro was one policymaker who espoused a more thoughtful approach to the roles of the state and market in Indonesia. In his papers on the experiences of development policy in Indonesia, Widjojo Nitisastro (2010) frequently stresses the need, on the one hand, to find ways of moderating the impact of damaging market forces in Indonesia but, on the other hand, to work with the market to implement policies in such areas as the rice sector, energy, and infrastructure.

11.3 THE STATE IN SOUTHEAST ASIA

Against this background, there are various key issues that arise in considering the role of the state in ASEAN today. Perhaps the most important of these relate to:

- the very marked differences between the capacities of the state in the region
- the goals that should be set for the performance of governments in these very different states
- the steps that might be taken to strengthen the capacity of the states in the region.

It is not easy to measure the capacity of a state. Essentially, the concept is quite closely related to the power that a state can exercise. Power, in turn, can be measured and exercised in various ways — political, coercive (military and police), legal, economic, administrative, and so on. In a useful study, Galbraith (1985) distinguished between three instruments of power (condign, compensatory, and conditioned power) and three sources which underpin these instruments (personality, property and wealth, and organisation). These three sources of power are often evident across the ASEAN states at both the national and subnational levels.

Nevertheless, two important measures of the fiscal capacity of a state are the levels of taxation and expenditure. In discussing state capacity in Southeast Asia, Larsson (2013, 338) suggests that 'the ability to extract resources from society through taxation is one of the defining capabilities of the state'. He supports Slater's view (2010, 35) that 'revenue collection may not be a perfect barometer of state power but it is the next best thing'. This is one view. It is true that revenues raised through taxation are a measure of the capacity of the state to insist that citizens pay for at least part of the services of government. However, in some other aspects, expenditures are a better measure of the capacity of the state because the level of expenditures reflect the capacity of states to respond to the expectations of citizens and to provide the public goods that citizens hope to receive from government.[3]

The statistical data on the fiscal scope of governments in developing Asia are somewhat variable. Different states in Asia report on fiscal matters in different ways. Indeed, considering the importance of the role of government, and considering the substantial attention that the international community has given to discussions about issues such as good

---

3 See Box 2.2, 'Measuring the state — its size, its policies, and its institutional capability' (World Bank 2007, 33).

governance in recent years, the difficulty of obtaining basic data relating to measures of government across Asia is notable. Nevertheless, broad measures of revenue collection (which is not the same thing as the level of taxes) and expenditure are available. Different measures focus on different aspects of governments in the region so it will be useful to consider, separately, several ways of measuring the scope of governments (Table 11.1):

- the total amounts of revenue and expenditure
- revenue and expenditure on a per capita basis
- revenue and expenditure as a share of GDP.

Data for three comparator groups are also provided: for advanced countries in North Asia (Japan and Korea); two OECD countries in the Asia–Pacific region (Australia and New Zealand); and the two major developing countries of the world (China and India).

Several aspects of the overall fiscal picture are notable in the totals for revenue collection and spending for 2012 in ASEAN counties set out in Table 11.1. First, most of the magnitudes—bearing in mind that they relate to the fiscal capacities of nation states—are small. Only Indonesia had budgetary amounts of over US$100 billion. The Republic of Korea, with a population barely one-fifth that of Indonesia, had revenues and expenditures of well over US$200 billion. The Philippines and Vietnam (with populations of around 95 million and 90 million respectively in 2012) supported government expenditure of around US$40 billion. The governments of Myanmar (population: 60 million); Cambodia (population: 15 million); and Laos (population: 7 million) all had very small budgets of less than US$3 billion in 2012. Second, it is notable that despite the demands on all governments to supply increasing amounts of public services, fiscal discipline across the region was strong in the sense that most budget deficits were small; indeed the two small ASEAN states of Brunei and Singapore recorded relatively large surpluses.

These absolute figures are easier to evaluate when set in context: adjustments need to be made both for population size, and for the differing sizes of the regional economies. One useful measure of state capacity is the amount that a government can spend on a per capita basis. Across ASEAN this figure varied dramatically in 2012, from over US$15,000 in Brunei to extraordinarily low figures in Cambodia (around US$190) and in Myanmar (around US$40). In Myanmar, the economic capacity of the state is clearly very limited indeed. Even in stronger states such as the Philippines, Vietnam, and Indonesia, government spending was no more than around US$450–600 per person. By comparison, government spending in China was almost US$1500 per capita and in the Republic of Korea the government spent around US$4700 per person.

Table 11.1   Fiscal indicators, ASEAN and other selected countries, 2012[a]

	Total (US$ billion)			Per capita (US$)		As % of GDP			
	Revenue	Expenditure	Surplus/deficit	Revenue	Expenditure	Revenue	Taxes	Expenditure	Surplus/deficit
ASEAN countries (ranked by per capita expenditure)									
High-spending countries									
Brunei	9.1	6.1	3.0	22,722	15,159	53	n.a.	35	18
Singapore[b]	67.5	41.5	12.2	13,039	8,010	25	14	15	10
Medium-spending countries									
Malaysia	67.9	81.7	–13.7	2,319	2,787	22	16	27	–5
Thailand	69.3	78.5	–9.2	1,076	1,219	18	15	20	–2
Low-spending countries									
Indonesia	133.3	149.0	–15.6	539	603	16	11	18	–2
Vietnam	35.6	40.2	–6.2	401	453	23	21	26	–4
Philippines	37.3	43.2	–5.9	389	451	15	13	17	–2
Laos	2.1	2.3	–0.1	326	346	17	15	25	–1
Cambodia	2.5	2.8	–0.3	166	188	15	12	20	–2
Myanmar[c]	2.1	2.5	–0.3	34	41	23	4	27	–3
Comparator countries									
Australia	353.6	399.6	–23.2	15,577	17,605	23	22	26	–3
New Zealand	57.1	56.4	0.1	12,964	12,815	34	28	33	0
Japan[b]	616.7	1,066.1	–449.4	4,833	8,355	11	10	20	–8
Republic of Korea	290.9	235.6	17.3	5,818	4,712	25	16	23	2
China	1,863.4	1,998.6	–135.1	1,376	1,476	23	19	24	–2
India[d]	166.1	261.2	–71.4	137	215	9	7	14	–5

a   Data are indicative only. Coverage of government sector and
definitions vary considerably between countries.
b   Data are for 2011.
c   Foreign exchange rate used is end-2011.
d   Central government only.

Source: ADB (2013)

These extraordinary differences in per capita spending by governments may be interpreted in different ways. One view is that the different levels are not surprising and, naturally, reflect the different levels of income per capita in the different countries. While this view is doubtless partly true, it is also true that the expectations of ordinary citizens across ASEAN in a globalising world are increasingly influenced by international comparisons. The very marked differences in government capacity, therefore, give rise to sharp differences in expectations of government across the region and of the capacity of government to respond to these differences in expectations.

Another view is that international comparisons of this kind need to be adjusted on a purchasing-power parity (PPP) basis to reflect differences in price levels. But while it is true that notable price level differences exist between countries, PPP measurements often fail to allow for important considerations in making comparisons between countries. For one thing, there are very wide differences in the quality of goods and services between developing countries. In poorer countries where spending per capita is small, prices of goods are relatively low but quality is often low as well. PPP measurements often fail to allow for the fact that the prices of many goods, which governments spend their money on, are set in international markets and do not differ significantly between industrialised countries and developing countries. For example, the world price of (quality-adjusted) infrastructure is often quite similar in different countries. The cost, for example, of constructing a 1000 MW coal power plant does not vary greatly between industrialised and developing countries.

Another useful set of measures to consider is levels of revenue and expenditure as a share of GDP (Table 11.1). Government expenditure as a share of GDP (G/GDP) in OECD welfare states is often well over 30 percent, and depending on the measures of expenditure chosen, can rise to well over 40 percent. In contrast, the average (population-weighted) level of G/GDP in ASEAN countries is notably smaller—around 18 percent. But it is also notable that the ratio of G/GDP varies considerably across ASEAN from as low as 15 percent in Singapore (where significant public-sector activities are carried on by state-owned instrumentalities and are not included in the state budget) to relatively high levels in the outliers of Myanmar (where recorded GDP is very low because much uncounted economic activity is carried on in the informal sector) and Brunei.

ASEAN: overall view

The combination of summary statistics relating to the fiscal capacity of governments in ASEAN (Table 11.1) indicates that there are marked differences across the region. What are the main features that stand out? Taken as a group, the fiscal capacity of governments in ASEAN is quite limited. Total government spending in absolute terms is not large. In the larger ASEAN states, government spending per capita tends to be very modest. Annual government spending of less than US$500 per capita in Vietnam and the Philippines, and around US$600 per capita in Indonesia, suggests that in these countries the resources available to support both the administrative operations of governments as well as the broader delivery of public services is tightly constrained. And not only are levels of spending that the states can support rather low, but the spending of governments in a number of the main states is surprisingly small as a proportion of GDP (around 20 percent or lower in Indonesia, Thailand, the Philippines, and Cambodia).

This picture of limited economic capacity in most of the ASEAN states suggests that it would be useful for governments to reassess strategies of management and of public service delivery. What are the implications for policy and for the delivery of public programs? And more broadly, what should the role of the state be when resources are sharply constrained?

11.4   RETHINKING THE ROLE OF THE STATE

Three main steps would seem to be needed in rethinking the role of the state in ASEAN: a reconsideration of the current generally accepted paradigm of the role of the state in developing countries in Asia; a recognition of the problems that arise when there are excessive expectations about the services that the government and state can provide; and a careful consideration of the best ways that states in developing Asia can be restructured to play an effective role within the very tight budget constraints that they face.

Reconsider role

It will not be easy for leaders and communities across ASEAN to reconsider the role of the state. The current generally accepted paradigm reflects ideas that became widely held in the region during political struggles for independence and in the post-colonial period. There is scant support for notions of slimming down the state or for policies that smack of Anglo-Saxon, pro-market liberalism.

From one point of view, the wide, popular support for some form of strong economic leadership from the state is understandable. Political leaders across the region often emphasise nationalist themes and present themselves as protecting the ordinary populace from the ravages of uncaring, random market forces. And since it is true that markets in developing countries in Asia often seem chaotic and subject to many forms of manipulation, it is not surprising that local communities look to their leaders for protection. But from another point of view, the acceptance of the traditional view across the region of the paternalistic and interventionist role of the state is puzzling. Across developing Asia, there is much scepticism about the role that governments play. Often, governments are seen as corrupt and inefficient, and are frequently regarded as part of the problem rather than part of the solution.

Unrealistic expectations appear to contribute significantly to the ambivalence about the role of governments across developing Asia. It is not unusual for political leaders in ASEAN — as in many other countries — to over-promise and under-deliver. In Indonesia, for example, during his early years in government after his election as president in 2004, Susilo Bambang Yudhoyono (SBY) raised community expectations of a new and 'clean' approach to government by emphasising his determination to combat corruption. It proved very difficult for the president to deliver on his ambitious promises. Now, towards the end of his period in office, which ends in October 2014, disillusionment with the president's performance in improving the processes of government in Indonesia is widespread in the Indonesian media. But arguably, SBY's mistake was not really in underperforming in the herculean task of improving government in Indonesia so much as in raising unrealistic expectations in the first place.

Recognise problems

A second main step towards reconsidering the role of the state, therefore, would be to recognise the problems that arise when there are excessive expectations about the role that the state can play. The data in Table 11.1 indicate that in several of the larger ASEAN states, government spending per capita in 2012 was around US$600 or less. Government spending in OECD countries is generally well over US$10,000 per capita — or around 20 times the level in several of the larger ASEAN states. Clearly, the services that the OECD welfare states can provide, and the economic roles that they can play, are very different to the services and roles that can be expected from ASEAN states and other developing countries in much of Asia.

It is difficult to avoid the impression that in the low-spending ASEAN countries at least, many of the branches of governments are badly overstretched. Put simply, governments are trying to do far too much with far too little. Reports of unsatisfactory performance from government agencies staffed with poorly paid officials abound. Even core agencies such as the courts, police forces, and finance departments are badly under-resourced. Just one of the consequences is that both political leaders and officials are tempted to try to raise revenues through the imposition of unofficial direct charges on members of the public who deal with these agencies (Duncan and McLeod 2007, 79). There are many reports in some ASEAN countries, for example, legal judgements being influenced by payments throughout the judicial system. And when government services are provided on an unapproved fee-for-service basis, governments become marketised and markets develop in parts of the public sector that, in principle, are expected to be non-marketised parts of the economy.

Another worrying problem when budgets become over-stretched and expectations of government are too high is that badly designed social programs and subsidies tend to be introduced into fiscal systems. The evidence that lax, poorly targeted government spending programs often benefit urban, middle-class income groups in developing countries is strong. Examples abound: fuel subsidies in Indonesia and in many other developing countries (Alford and Soejachmoen 2013, 278; IMF 2013c); housing subsidies (World Bank 1997, 59); hospital care in Vietnam (World Bank 1997, 53); and so on. One detailed study of poverty-targeting programs in Indonesia since the 1990s concluded the following (Perdana and Maxwell 2005, 125):

> … the targeting of poverty alleviation programs in Indonesia has been a difficult and frustrating process … Although poor families did benefit to a certain degree, all the programs that we have considered have suffered from two common problems: … undercoverage and leakage, respectively. Undercoverage occurred as many poor households were not reached by the program … there has been a significant amount of leakage, with far too many non-poor households … able to access the benefits.

Summarising the overall results of a survey of poverty targeting in Asia released in 2005, Weiss (2005, 29) observed that:

> In the debates of the 1980s more universal schemes were strongly criticized for their high leakage and their budgetary implications. The more targeted measures of the 1990s … have cost more modest amounts relative to the size of government budgets, but their leakage rates have been disproportionately high, as have their costs per unit of benefit to the poor …

Moreover, the factors that tend to encourage these distortions are in turn partly a result from the extreme pressure that government budgets are under: relatively few administrative resources can be allocated to the proper design and monitoring of expenditure programs, and well-connected lobby groups are able to influence the management of fiscal programs because their political connections, within an underfunded state, are relative strong.

Restructure functions

A third step towards reconsidering the role of the state in developing Asia is to define the role of government carefully. To be effective, an approach of this kind would need to go well beyond the many programs of public management reform, which have been outlined for ASEAN governments in recent years (Government of the Philippines et al. 2003; Asia–Pacific CoP MfDR 2011). Rather, the aim would need to be to design an overall strategy to restructure the role of governments. Appropriate measures to match the functions of governments more closely with resources might include the following:

*   Identify reductions, and strict economies, in the range of services supported by governments with the aim of finding budgetary resources to allow for the strengthened provision of core public services such as improved legal systems, more effective law and order, and improved tax collection and public expenditure programs. As part of this broad approach, it may often be necessary to submit welfare-oriented social programs to strict controls — not because they are not needed but, rather, because budgetary resources to design them properly and support them are so limited.
*   Revise revenue collection programs at all main levels of government (national and subnational), and in main off-budget agencies such as state-owned enterprises. A reasonable mid-term goal might be to lift the total revenues collected to 25 percent of GDP with the aim, in the longer term, of further increasing total official revenues to at least 30 percent of GDP. An important and difficult part of such a program would be measures to curb widespread practices of unofficial revenue collection in public agencies.
*   The systematic simplification of administrative services across government (including those imposed on the private sector and civil society) with the aim of developing a 'lite government' system of administration.[4] The 'good enough governance' approach suggested by Grindle (2002) and others might be considered as a model: this approach outlines 'a condition of minimally acceptable government performance and civil society engagement that does not significantly hinder economic and political development ... and permits poverty reduction initiatives to go forward'.
*   A review of government activities to consider an approach where government agencies 'steer, not row'; that is, where governments move away from the direct provision of services towards, rather, the

---

4   A proposed program of reform for Indonesia is set out in Duncan and McLeod (2007).

regulation of service delivery increasingly provided by the private sector and by civil society.

The last of these measures would need governments to decide on the dividing line between the *direct* provision of services by the government itself or the *indirect* supply of services through reliance on service providers in the private sector or the community. In the case of the former system of direct delivery, the government itself becomes a service provider in the service markets and needs to interact directly with consumers in the delivery of the services. In the case of the latter system, the role of government is quite different: the government becomes a regulator of performance in service markets so government agencies need to develop appropriate regulatory rather than delivery skills. In each case the role of the state is very different.

11.5 THREE SECTORS

Any discussion of a redefinition of the role of governments in developing countries in Asia would need to consider the implications for the way states work with main economic groupings such as the organised private sector, the informal commercial economy, and non-profit community and social groups.

Private sector

The strength of the formal private sector varies considerably across ASEAN. In many parts of ASEAN, especially in rural areas outside of the largest towns, the private sector is weak. Further, the relationship between organised private sector enterprises and local governments is often troubled. One survey of local business conditions in Indonesia described the situation as follows (World Bank 2006):

> The local governance of the investment climate in most districts is poor. In general, local firms face rising capture practices, extensive administrative time requirements, unsatisfactory one-stop licence services, and inadequate tax administration. Overall, district administrations continue to operate on a level that is unsatisfactory to business needs. Most of the reasons for these unsatisfactory business climates are institutional in nature. They can be seen in vague (tax) law enforcement, insufficient legislative oversight and adverse bureaucratic conventions. These issues could be partially addressed by implementing measures to:
> - overcome inefficiency and ineffectiveness
> - build institutional capacities for supervision
> - improve service delivery.

In some areas of economic activity in local economies, the private sector is fragmented and rather disorganised, consisting of a large number of small or medium-sized firms. In other activities, local markets are sometimes dominated by one or two large local firms that may have strong political connections with local political elites. Indeed, various problems arising from the existence of excessively close links between governments and well-connected business players in various countries in ASEAN are well known (Hamilton-Hart 2007). Markets in the formal private sector can therefore be thin and become cartelised with limited competition and restricted choice for consumers. It is difficult for governments to design effective pro-market policies under such circumstances.

Informal economy

The informal commercial economy is often large, even dominant, in many developing countries in Asia. Depending on definitions, over 60 percent of the labour force in Indonesia, for example, is in the informal economy where legal arrangements are lax, contracts are often difficult to enforce, and markets are extremely flexible. Some parts of the informal economy tend to be highly monetised. Other parts, especially in rural areas, operate with many barter arrangements. Governments, burdened down with administrative procedures and red tape, often find it difficult to design effective programs to work with the informal economy or to strengthen the informal economy in the early stages of growth.

Indeed it is not uncommon for some agencies of governments to regard activities in the informal economy as something of a nuisance and to look for ways of restricting the highly entrepreneurial nature of commercial life in this important part of the national economy. But the informal economy is so important that it would be better if effective strategies were developed to support commercial activities in this sector. A useful model of a possible approach was outlined in a recent policy document in Papua New Guinea (Papua New Guinea 2011). Appropriate steps might include the following:

- development of an official development policy towards the informal economy indicating that activities in this part of the national economy are seen as important and will receive support from government agencies
- design of programs for the supply of small-scale basic infrastructure services to supply services to the informal economy such as water, power, transport and communications infrastructure, roads, markets, drainage facilities, and so on
- support for social services such as community health and education

- expansion of microfinance programs (both microcredit and micro-insurance)
- development of appropriate regulatory frameworks and laws for the informal economy so that legal certainty is strengthened for both producers and consumers.

Community and social groups

Local non-profit civil society organisations (CSOs) flourish in developing countries in Asia including in ASEAN states. Yet on a day-to-day basis, they frequently face many of the problems that organisations in the informal economy face. For one thing, their legal status is often uncertain. This does not necessarily affect many of the usual activities of local CSOs because they are accustomed to working in an informal way. But legal uncertainties can often be a significant barrier to access to credit from banks or other official programs. Further, the informal nature of many of the CSOs sometimes means that internal governance and leadership problems can be difficult to resolve. Thus governments can help bring greater certainty to activities carried out in the CSO sector by establishing a firmer legal basis for their work.

Similarly, CSOs can benefit from having clearer relationships with governments in other ways. Governments should bear in mind the needs of CSOs when designing local social and physical infrastructure programs. Arrangements to strengthen the voice of CSOs would be useful as well so that they articulate their needs more effectively (MacLaren et al. 2011). For example in some states in India, Citizens' Charters have been adopted to help make governments more accountable to citizens, including CSOs. Aims of adopting Citizen's Charters include making the administration of governments more accountable, ensuring transparency and the right to information, and adopting a stakeholder approach to the delivery of services. The involvement of CSOs in developing countries in drawing up charters of this kind can help clarify the relationship between governments and civil society.

11.6 WORKING WITH MARKETS

Changes of these kinds to rethink the role of the state in developing Asia are likely to call for a greater willingness on the part of policymakers to tailor policies to support the operations of markets. Paradoxically, changes of this kind would not necessarily call for *less* government intervention in important markets in the region. Rather, what is likely to be needed is a change in the *type* of intervention. If governments could redefine their roles to reduce their activities in the *direct* provision of services, they would have additional resources to strengthen their capacity to carry out their *indirect* support for markets. That is, governments would be better able to 'steer, not row'. Further, policies would often be more effective if they were designed to *improve* the operations of markets rather than to try to *control* market forces.

International thinking about the subject of the state, the market and society in developing countries, including in Asia, has evolved over time. Gunnar Myrdal's sweeping *Asian Drama* study (Myrdal 1968) was an early magisterial survey of the topic. Many other scholars and official reports have considered the issues in the succeeding decades. Following the 1997 WDR on *The State in a Changing World*, the World Bank discussed the place of markets in developing countries in various other reports including in the 2002 WDR on *Building Institutions for Markets*. In the 2002 WDR, four lessons on building effective institutions for markets were set out. Suggestions for improving the supply of effective institutions were (World Bank 2002, 4):

1   designing institutions to complement what exists — with attention to other supporting institutions, human capabilities, and available technologies
2   innovating and experimenting to design institutions that work — and being prepared to drop initiatives that do not

Two further suggestions for strengthening the demand for such institutions were:

3   connecting and linking communities of market players through improved information flows and open trade
4   promoting competition across jurisdictions, firms, and individuals so as to highlight successful institutions and improve the demand for them.

In distilling these lessons, one of the World Bank's conclusions in the 2002 WDR stressed the importance of keeping regulatory systems simple (World Bank 2002, 12):

> For regulatory systems in developing countries to have a realistic chance of success, they need to be simpler, often less information-intensive, and less burdensome on the courts.

More recently, numerous other scholars and studies have discussed these issues as well. Nobel economic prize winner Michael Spence summarised how views have changed over time as follows (Spence 2011, 95):

> The correct insight that markets and market dynamics are of critical importance morphed into the most simplistic view that the problem is government. It has taken more than a decade to correct this mistake. As the report

on the Commission on Growth and Development (May 2008) said, quoting W. Arthur Lewis, 'governments may fail because they do too little, or because they do too much'. Effective governments and markets are both essential ingredients. They are not in competition with each other but rather complementary parts of the process. To be sure, governments *can* be too big and intrusive. But they can also be too small and ineffective.

11.7   CONCLUSION

The summary data relating to the fiscal operations of countries in ASEAN suggest that governments in some of the largest ASEAN states are badly overstretched. Often governments cannot supply the services that have come to be expected of them. A reconsideration of the relationship between the state and markets in the region would be helpful. The task of 'rethinking the role of the state' needs to be undertaken not as a response to Western pro-market liberal ideologies. Rather, a reconsideration of the role of state is needed, quite simply, because governments in the region are trying to do too much with too little and are often failing to perform basic tasks in a satisfactory way. And paradoxically, both government failure *and* market failure is common in many parts of developing Asia. Government failure often exacerbates market failure in the region because overstretched governments cannot perform basic regulatory functions properly. A pragmatic and determined approach to reform is needed to strengthen the operations of *both* governments *and* markets in the ASEAN region.

12 The ill-fated currency board proposal for Indonesia

Ross H. McLeod

In February 1998 Indonesia toyed briefly with the idea of introducing a currency board system as a means of extricating itself from the Asian financial crisis. Although the then president Suharto announced his government's intention to implement such a system, international and domestic opposition was so vociferous that he aborted the plan. In my view, this opposition was ill-informed. Moreover, it was motivated, to a considerable extent, by a desire to use the crisis to force a president widely disliked among the urban intelligentsia to discontinue some of his favoured economic policies – if not to bring about an end to his presidency – rather than giving top priority to dealing with the crisis itself. The nature of the crisis as it played out in Indonesia remains poorly understood, such that an analysis of the currency board proposal provides an opportunity to correct some misunderstandings and dispel some of the myths about this major episode in Indonesia's modern history. In this chapter I argue that in fact Suharto's embrace of the proposal was sensible, and that it was motivated by the desire to restore macro-economic stability – which would have been not only to his own benefit but also that of Indonesia's citizens.

12.1 BACKGROUND

The Asian financial crisis began to engulf Indonesia in July 1997. It had started in Thailand as a consequence of severe mismanagement of the balance of payments in that country. Specifically, Thailand had clung to a pegged exchange rate for many months in spite of rapidly dwindling

Figure 12.1   Indonesia's international reserves (US$ billion)

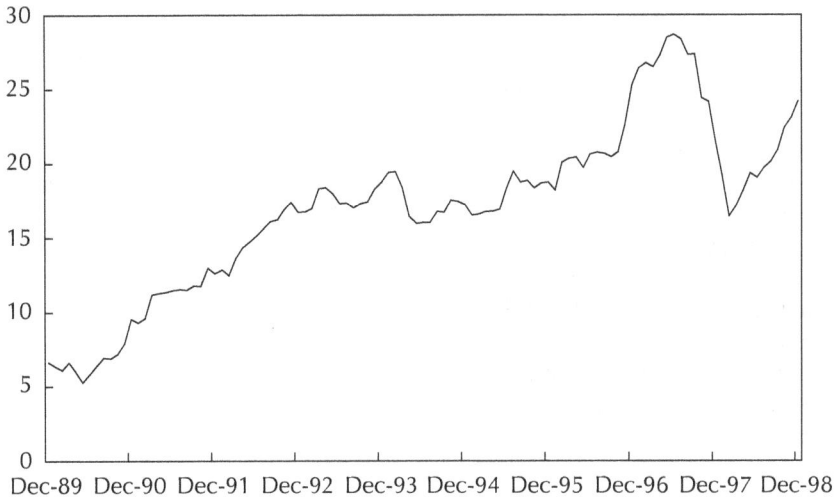

Source: CEIC Asia Database.

foreign exchange reserves, a fact that it managed to hide from public view for some time by selling its reserves forward and failing to disclose this fact (King 2001, 441). When the inevitable could be postponed no longer, Thailand was forced to devalue its currency suddenly and without warning, causing shock and consternation among investors worldwide who, until that time, had regarded the Southeast Asian region as a safe and profitable place in which to lend and invest.

Indonesia was tarred with the same brush, despite the fact that for many months its central bank had been fighting to prevent *ap*preciation of the currency rather than *de*preciation, as a consequence of which it had accumulated very large international reserves (Figure 12.1) – quite the opposite of the Thai case. Moreover, Indonesia had operated its fiscal policy for decades in a highly responsible fashion, always spending broadly within its means. Inflation was running at only about 5 percent annually – a little higher than its neighbours, but at the low end of its usual 5–10 percent band. In short, the key macroeconomic variables in no way suggested the likelihood of imminent devaluation as had occurred in Thailand.

Devaluation of the baht jolted investors out of their complacency. Foreign institutions that had taken on large financial exposures to Indonesia – often without really knowing much about the country – suddenly confronted the worrying prospect that if they had been so ill-informed about Thailand, perhaps the same might be true of Indonesia and other countries in the region. Without the luxury of having the time to undertake a more careful analysis, the prudent response to the threat of sudden devaluation was to withdraw funds as quickly as possible — which, of course, immediately brought about precisely that outcome, given that the authorities had quickly decided to allow the rupiah to float rather than attempt to maintain the pre-existing exchange rate (Lindblad 1997, 5). In such circumstances it is not just foreign entities with an exposure to the country in question that have an incentive to adjust their portfolios. Domestic entities that have borrowed in foreign currency to finance their investments have a similar incentive, because they face the prospect of the local currency value of their borrowings ballooning. To these groups must be added untold numbers who see in the looming crisis the opportunity to make a speculative profit by substituting foreign for domestic assets, or financial assets denominated in foreign rather than local currency, in their portfolios.

The extent of a run on any currency depends, implicitly, on private sector actors' expectations as to the authorities' response to the disturbance that precipitates it. Unfortunately, the track record of Indonesia's central bank, Bank Indonesia (BI), did little to engender confidence: Indonesia had experienced hyperinflation in the 1960s, together with a series of large devaluations (most recently just a decade earlier). In addition, the major decision to float the currency had been taken quickly, without any prior public debate, and with little attempt to reassure the public that this made good policy sense. At least in retrospect, then, it is unsurprising that capital began to flood out of Indonesia, regardless of the prior soundness of the macroeconomic fundamentals.

One important contributor to this panicked reaction was the possibility of regime change. Suharto had been in power for over 30 years, and his regime had dominated economic policy and progress increasingly over that period. Economic performance had been of a very high standard, with growth averaging over 7 percent annually. On the other hand, the president had also abused his power to redistribute income and wealth in myriad ways in favour of his own family and business cronies, who had become fabulously wealthy as a result (McLeod 2000). They were well aware that if he were to fall, their own positions would be in grave danger. Suharto was now well into his seventies, and there were signs his health may be failing (Sadli 1998, 273). These observations, in combination with the sudden loss of the political legitimacy that had accompanied almost uninterrupted economic progress over three decades, suggested to this group that it would be well advised to diversify its assets by shifting funds offshore (Cole and Slade 1998, 65). All the conditions were in place for a perfect financial storm.

12.2   FLOATING THE RUPIAH

In principle there was nothing wrong with the central bank's decision
to float the currency in response to the sudden reversal of capital inflow.
Nevertheless, it is clear in retrospect that there was little understanding
of the further implications of this decision. For many years previously
the *de facto* foundation of Indonesia's monetary policy had been a commitment to a slow and steady rate of depreciation against the US dollar —
although this was never stated explicitly. This policy was itself based on
the misconception of Indonesia as an inherently high-inflation economy.
Whereas other economies had little difficulty keeping inflation down to 1
or 2 percent per annum, the authorities — and even a number of academic
economists in Indonesia — had persuaded themselves that there was
some (never stated) special characteristic of the Indonesian economy that
caused it to experience inflation at more rapid rates. Knowing that if a
country inflates more rapidly than its trading partners its tradable goods
sectors will become increasingly uncompetitive in the world market, this
outcome was to be avoided by steadily depreciating the rupiah, so as to
keep the real exchange rate roughly constant (Nasution 1998, 455). From
September 1986 — the time of the most recent discrete devaluation of the
currency — BI therefore ensured that the exchange rate depreciated steadily at about 3–5 percent per annum.

Although nobody spoke of it in these terms, the 3–5 percent depreciation rate became the implicit nominal anchor for monetary policy and,
rather than being the necessary response to Indonesia's supposed inherently high rate of inflation, it served to ensure that indeed the inflation
rate would always be unnecessarily high. The underlying mechanism
was fairly straightforward. Exchange rate depreciation continued even
though the balance of payments was typically in surplus, as indicated
by the central bank continuously purchasing more and more foreign
exchange in the market, adding steadily to its international reserves. By
purchasing foreign exchange in the market at the artificially high price
implied by the continuous depreciation policy, BI injected more and
more base money into circulation; the rapid growth of the supply of base
money then resulted in elevated levels of inflation. In short, the policy
followed in response to the unfounded belief that Indonesia's inflation
rate was inherently high itself generated the comparatively high levels
of inflation on which that belief was based.

The crucial problem accompanying BI's decision to float the rupiah
was the failure to recognise that this amounted to abandoning what had
served as the nominal anchor for monetary policy for at least the previous decade. In the months that followed there was no such nominal
anchor. Money supply growth ran out of control, inflation and nominal

Figure 12.2   Base money growth and inflation during crisis (Rp trillion, % p.a.)

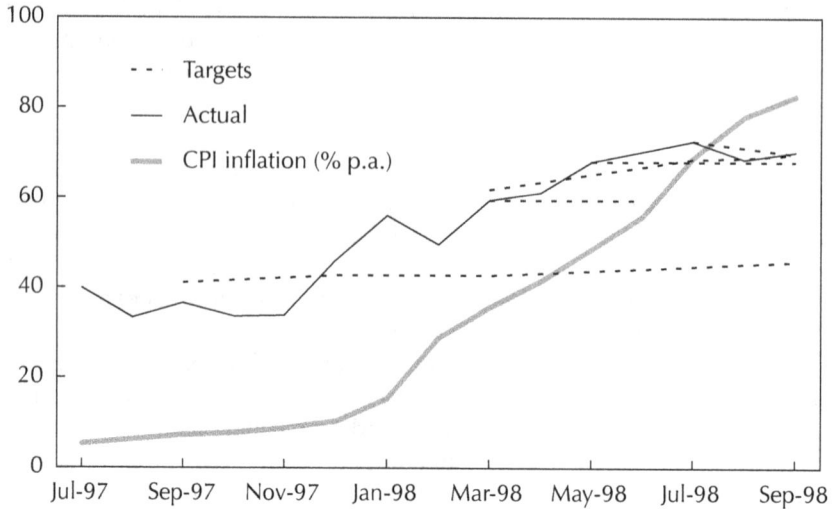

Source: CEIC Asia Database.

interest rates surged, and the exchange rate depreciated beyond observers' wildest expectations.

At least at a superficial level, the reason for loss of control of money supply can be found in the conflict between the central bank's role as monetary policymaker and its role as prudential regulator of, and lender of last resort to, the commercial banks. The initial burst of speculation against the rupiah following devaluation of the Thai baht had significant consequences for many private-sector corporations and their bankers. Many of the outstanding loans from banks to the private sector were denominated in US dollars, which meant that borrowers now faced considerable losses because of the jump in the rupiah value of their liabilities. Failure to repay their borrowings then extended these losses to the banks, many of which had, at best, only a thin margin of capital with which to absorb them. As a consequence, the central bank found itself having to make emergency loans to the banks as lender of last resort, and it did this on such a huge scale that the supply of base money would more than double over the eight months through July 1998 (see Figure 12.2). Accustomed as it was always to find something or someone else to blame for Indonesia's high inflation, rather than seeing this as the predictable consequence of its own policies (McLeod 1993, 122), BI seemed concerned only with its lender of last resort function, oblivious to the monetary impact. The consequences of this extraordinary lapse in the conduct of monetary policy rapidly became apparent.

12.3   ENTER THE IMF

In October 1997 the government had turned to the IMF for assistance. A rescue package was put together, the main feature of which was a large loan in combination with several international standby loans,[1] together with a commitment on the part of the government to change a number of its key economic policies (many of them entirely unrelated to the crisis).[2] One component of this package was a decision to close down 16 small private sector banks[3] that had become insolvent. Despite the government's earlier warnings that it did not guarantee deposits, it now promised that the vast majority of depositors would lose nothing, and that their deposits would be transferred to other banks. Indeed, this process was accomplished with very little difficulty.

The exercise ended in disaster, however. The problem was that although the promise of no losses extended to the vast majority of *depositors*, it did not apply to *deposits* above Rp20 million (around US$5,000 at the time) (Djiwandono 2004, 67). Unfortunately, a very large proportion of total deposits exceeded this ceiling—not only in the banks that were closed, but also in the banking sector more generally. The owners of large deposits held at all the private sector domestic banks therefore suddenly confronted the possibility that banks other than those that had just been closed were in danger of imminent failure (despite the government's reassurances to the contrary), and that they would be unlikely to be compensated by the government if such failures came to pass. Just as private sector entities had pre-emptively withdrawn funds from Indonesia after the Thai currency was devalued, large depositors now began to withdraw funds from Indonesia's private domestic banks. The resulting run on these banks created chaos in the banking system as a whole, and last resort lending by the central bank exploded.

The nature of this run on the banks remains little understood. The stereotypical image of a bank run features long lines of depositors

---

1 The effective size of this IMF rescue package was far less than the amount typically reported: US$43 billion (McLeod 1998a). At its peak the amount actually disbursed by the IMF itself was only about US$11 billion; the loan was fully repaid by October 2006.

2 The first agreement ('Letter of Intent'), for example, required, among other things, the complete divestiture of seven presently unlisted state enterprises within the following 17 months, the reduction of export taxes on logs and sawn timber to 20 percent, submission to Parliament of a draft law on competition to prevent the abuse of dominant position and practices that restrict or distort free competition, and preparation of a mechanism for the regular adjustment of administered food prices.

3 Collectively, these banks accounted for about 3 percent of total commercial bank assets (Djiwandono 2004, 64).

queuing at the teller's window, hoping that they will be able to withdraw their savings before it is too late. Although there was some of this in the early phase of the crisis — particularly at the largest private-sector bank, Bank Central Asia, owned by Suharto's closest business associate, Liem Sioe Liong, and two of Suharto's children (Johnson 1998, 51) — it was no doubt tempered by the fact that the government had just closed some banks and had guaranteed no losses on small deposits. In fact, to a large extent, the supposed bank run was not really a bank run at all, at least in later months. Rather, it was a fierce bout of speculation against the currency, financed by the central bank itself.

In the first step, much of this speculation was financed by domestic banks. Most of the private banks were part of one or other of the conglomerates that dominated the modern sector of Indonesia's economy. Although there were strict rules against banks lending to related entities, these rules were not properly enforced — not least because Suharto's support made them effectively untouchable (Cole and Slade 1998, 65). As the crisis developed, banks rapidly increased their rupiah lending to affiliated firms, which then used these funds to purchase foreign exchange — perhaps in order to pay off their foreign borrowings, or perhaps in order to engage in outright speculation against the currency. This left those same banks with a severe liquidity shortage, exacerbating the shortage that resulted from the shifting of deposits to the state-owned and foreign banks (see Section 12.4). This shifting of deposits enabled the state banks to become part of a similar process, and they increased their lending even more rapidly than the private banks during this period.

In short, at this time of rapidly deepening recession and a deeply uncertain economic and political outlook, the private banks still managed to increase their rupiah-denominated working capital loans at an annualised rate of some 16 percent in just the first quarter of March 1998, while the state-owned banks increased theirs at the extraordinarily rapid rate of 135 percent. It was this astonishing surge in bank lending, made possible by emergency loans from BI (which were to become famous as BLBI: Bantuan Likuiditas Bank Indonesia) (Djiwandono 2004), that explains the precipitous depreciation of the rupiah and the simultaneous surge in inflation around this time.

12.4   INTERPRETING INDONESIA'S CRISIS

Many observers have wrongly interpreted the high inflation in 1998 as a consequence of rapid depreciation of the rupiah. The correct interpretation, as just suggested, is that both depreciation and inflation at that time are readily explained by surging growth of base money. This, in turn, reflected BI's failure to reconcile its responsibility as monetary policymaker with its role as last resort lender, which saw newly created base money injected through last resort lending remaining in circulation rather than being sterilised. The private sector responded to the excess supply of base money by both buying foreign exchange and reducing the supply of goods and services,[4] thus pushing up both the exchange rate and prices.[5]

As just noted, the liquidity problems of private domestic banks at the time were to some extent the consequence of their depositors shifting funds to state-owned and foreign-owned banks, both of which were regarded as safe by virtue of their ownership: it seemed inconceivable that the government would allow its own banks to fail, while the foreign banks were small branches or subsidiaries of much larger institutions with international reputations to protect. This shifting of funds left the private domestic banks short of liquidity, but left the others—especially the state-owned banks—with a surplus. The appropriate response to this would have been to combine last resort lending to the private banks with the issue of a similar amount of central bank certificates (SBIs) to the state-owned banks in order to soak up their surplus funds. The expansionary impact of last resort lending would then have been sterilised (just as the monetary impact of a balance of payments surplus can be sterilised using open market operations). But this was not done. Few seemed to appreciate the crucial importance of having a new nominal anchor—such as the money supply—to take the place of the previously fixed exchange rate.[6]

12.5   FROM CRISIS TO CATACLYSM

The abrupt change in Indonesia's economic circumstances was extraordinary. In mid-1997 its rate of economic growth was very healthy, inflation was lower than it had been for years, international reserves were high and growing, foreign debt was low, and the budget was in good shape. By January 1998 the economy was heading rapidly into a deep recession, the price of foreign exchange had increased more than four-fold, and inflation was spiralling out of control. Drastic action seemed necessary

---

4 If prices rise during a strong recession, this is more because of declining supply than increasing demand.
5 Under a purely floating exchange rate the central bank neither buys nor sells foreign exchange. In fact this was not a pure float: BI was a net seller of foreign exchange from October 1997 through February 1998, but then became a net buyer over the next 12 months (see Figure 12.1).
6 The steady depreciation policy implied a fixed exchange rate on any given day.

in order to save the situation. So it was that the president found himself on 15 January 1998 under the stern gaze of Michel Camdessus, Managing Director of the IMF – like a naughty schoolboy who had been sent to the principal's office – as he put his signature to a new agreement under which many of his favoured economic policies were to be overturned.[7]

Another part of the agreement related to money supply management, with broad money targeted to grow by 16 percent in 1998 through control of base money growth. At least the IMF was conscious of the need for a new nominal anchor, but this aspect attracted virtually no attention whatsoever – not least because the arcane matter of monetary policy had never really been regarded as important in Indonesia. There had long been a commitment to the so-called balanced budget, which really meant ensuring that the government had sufficient funds to finance its expenditures without any resort to borrowing from the central bank – thus removing the most common mechanism for inflationary growth of the money supply. But there had never been any real understanding of the fact that purchases of foreign exchange by the central bank have exactly the same monetary effect as lending to the government (McLeod 1993, 103). Even relatively sophisticated observers had no interest in the money growth targets in each new Letter of Intent from the government to the IMF, much less the journalists reporting on the evolving crisis. It is perhaps unsurprising, therefore, that the central bank itself basically ignored these targets, which would be exceeded by wide margins repeatedly over the next few months (Figure 12.2). Even the IMF seemed unconcerned about this, contenting itself to set out revised base money growth targets in each of several new Letters of Intent, but never putting any appreciable pressure on BI to meet them.

12.6   SUHARTO'S RESPONSE

One can only imagine President Suharto's mood at the time. His regime had recorded outstanding accomplishments over the previous three decades, maintaining an extraordinarily high rate of per capita income growth that resulted in remarkable improvements in living standards for the vast majority of Indonesians. In the main he had been well served (directly or indirectly) by a small team of technocrat ministers and inter-

---

7   This included removing the restrictive trading arrangements relating to wheat and flour, paper and plywood, cloves and cement, and discontinuing a 'National Car' program, all of which had generated enormous rents for members of the first family and Suharto cronies such as Liem Sioe Liong and Bob Hasan.

national advisers, and Indonesia was regarded as one of the great developing country success stories among the World Bank's clients. And yet, in the twinkling of an eye this record of unbroken economic progress had been turned on its head, with nothing those same ministers and advisers recommended coming even close to bringing the crisis to an end. On the contrary: the advisors had succeeded in persuading Suharto to give way on many policy fronts at the expense of his own family and business associates, without any obvious impact on the rapidly worsening crisis. In such circumstances it is understandable that the president would look elsewhere for advice.

Indonesia is not the only country ever to have suffered the collapse of its currency, of course, so it was natural to look for lessons from other countries that have had to deal with this problem. A small number had done so, with considerable success, by replacing their central bank with a currency board. The study of currency boards constitutes a rather esoteric field of economics. Although many countries have had them in the rather distant past, they fell out of fashion (Hanke and Schuler 1994, 3), and most were replaced by central banks, making them a topic for courses in economic history rather than mainstream macroeconomics.

Not every economist took this view, however. In particular, Professor Steve Hanke, from Johns Hopkins University in the US, had had a long-standing interest in currency boards, and had long advocated them as the best way of dealing with collapsing currencies – most recently in expert testimony before the US House of Representatives on 30 January 1998, just before he was to advise Suharto on the issue.[8] The unfashionability of currency boards meant that Hanke was largely unknown to economists in Indonesia and elsewhere. This, combined with the fact that he had been invited to Indonesia at Suharto's own initiative rather than at the behest of the IMF or the central bank, ensured an extraordinarily negative reception for the man and his ideas – notwithstanding his direct involvement in setting up currency board-type arrangements previously in Argentina (1991), Estonia (1992), Lithuania (1994) and, very recently, in Bosnia and Bulgaria (1997). To the shame of the economics profession in Indonesia and its international colleagues, there was a near total failure to consider these ideas objectively on their logical merits and their historical record.

Although we cannot determine which economic policies are sound by taking an opinion poll of economists, it is revealing, nevertheless, that the Indonesian currency board naysayers were able to drown out the

---

8 Hanke's former student, Kurt Schuler, independently suggested the currency board as a potential solution to Indonesia's crisis in a series of articles translated into Indonesian and published in early February 1998 (Schuler 1998).

voices of such luminaries as Gary Becker, Rudiger Dornbusch, Milton Friedman, Merton Miller, Robert Mundell, and Sir Alan Walters (for citations, see Hanke 2002, 216). Walters, in particular, had played a key role in establishing Hong Kong's currency board in 1983.

Hanke would have been immediately able to diagnose Indonesia's economic problems for the president. In simple terms, the central bank had ignored the monetary impact of its lender of last resort activities. Its inability to appreciate the need for a new nominal anchor of monetary policy following its decision to float the currency resulted in chaos in the foreign exchange market, together with surging prices and nominal interest rates. Although it seems unlikely that Hanke explained it in these terms, establishing a currency board system would have had precisely the effect of re-establishing a nominal anchor, this time in the form of a permanently fixed exchange rate rather than the gently but steadily depreciating exchange rate of the pre-crisis years.

From the beginning of his presidency in the mid-1960s, Suharto had shown himself willing to listen to the views of trained economists on economic policy matters—particularly in the field of macroeconomic management. Indeed, he came to power at a time of economic crisis, and relied on these 'technocrats' to formulate and implement the policies needed to restore stability and economic growth. The new crisis of 1997 was quite different from the earlier one (which had been driven by undisciplined *fiscal* policy), and these same technocrats and their successors demonstrably had not been able to come up with a solution to the new problem (which, as just explained, had been driven by undisciplined *monetary* policy in response to an external shock).

Worse still, from Suharto's point of view, the technocrats could be seen to be taking advantage of the crisis—in league with the IMF and the World Bank—to try to force reform of a wide range of microeconomic policies intended to benefit his family and cronies. In these circumstances, the simple and straightforward diagnosis and treatment proposed by Hanke would have seemed vastly preferable to the complex and wide-ranging policy package set out in the Letter of Intent to the IMF that Suharto had signed just two weeks earlier. Implementing the currency board proposal would have relieved Indonesia of any need to beg the international community for assistance, thus obviating the requirement for it to go along with the long list of conditions relating to economic policies that had little or nothing to do with the crisis. In short, implementing the currency board proposal would have allowed Indonesia to solve its own problem, without any need for it to surrender its economic sovereignty or—to put it bluntly—for Suharto to discontinue policies that favoured his family and business cronies at the expense of the general public. By repeatedly inviting Hanke into his own home for ongoing discussions (Torchia 1998), the president signalled clearly that he had lost confidence in his hitherto trusted advisors.

12.7   CURRENCY BOARD ESSENTIALS

A currency board is an alternative to a central bank as the institution responsible for managing countries' monetary affairs. It is helpful to describe it in terms of its very simple balance sheet — dominated on the assets side by foreign exchange reserves, and on the liabilities side by base money, which consists mainly of notes and coin in circulation (but excludes money in the form of bank deposits). By contrast, many central banks have other large assets and liabilities of various kinds (such as loans and borrowings). In particular, a currency board does not lend to either the government or the private sector.

A central feature of the system is that the board stands ready to convert the local currency it has issued to a particular foreign currency (such as the US dollar) at a permanently fixed rate of exchange. Moreover, it is required to maintain a level of foreign exchange reserves at least equal to the value of its base money liabilities (when converted at this fixed rate). Here lies a key difference from central banks: the latter may *promise* to hold their exchange rate fixed, but they do not always maintain sufficient reserves to be able to keep that promise. Thailand in 1997 is an example of this. Unlike a central bank, a currency board cannot run out of foreign exchange reserves: the private sector (including the commercial banks) will necessarily run out of the base money it needs in order to purchase foreign exchange from the board before the board runs out of foreign exchange.

Misunderstanding of this fundamental point is widespread. For example, an editorial in the highly respected *Financial Times* on 12 February 1998 argued — entirely incorrectly — that:

> Optimists blithely assume a currency board would be protected from spec-ulative attack because the central bank's $19bn hard currency reserves are triple the value of rupiah notes and coins at current exchange rates. This is nonsense. Notes and coins are only a tiny fraction of the total money sup-ply. Moreover, the reserves are swamped by the country's US$137bn foreign debt — much of it short term and owed by private companies.

The crucial point that this writer and others at the time and later (e.g. Lakshmanan 1998; Singal 1999, 55) failed to understand was that the major part of the *broad* money supply — bank deposits — cannot be used directly to purchase foreign exchange from the currency board, only *base* money (that is, currency in circulation and deposits of the commercial banks at the currency board). The board's only obligation is to hand over foreign exchange in return for its own monetary liabilities (base money), not the monetary liabilities of the commercial banks. Those who hold bank deposits of any kind must, therefore, first convert them to base money through transactions with some other entity in order to purchase foreign exchange from the board. What this means, in practice, is that when depositors write a cheque on their accounts and use them to purchase foreign exchange from the currency board, their banks' deposits with the currency board — and therefore the supply of base money — will decline by exactly that amount. Since banks' deposits with the currency board are a tiny fraction of the total of their customers' deposits, this process will necessarily come to a halt very quickly. Indeed, contrary to the belief of many, it is basically the value of notes and coins in circulation relative to the amount of reserves that matters.

The currency board relies entirely on the market mechanism to maintain macroeconomic equilibrium. At times when there is a strong demand for it, sales of foreign exchange by the board result in a corresponding reduction in base money in circulation — in simple terms, a reduction in the liquidity of the economy — which raises interest rates. One consequence of this is that borrowing offshore tends to increase because it has now become relatively more attractive. The resulting increase in capital inflow (or decrease in outflow) tends to restore foreign exchange reserves and liquidity.[9] A second consequence is that tightening liquidity reduces the demand for goods, including imports, and encourages the supply of goods, including for export, again tending to restore foreign exchange reserves and liquidity. The bottom line is that monetary conditions are determined by conditions in the foreign exchange market, and thus by international trading conditions, investor sentiment and so on, but not by the authorities.

It is precisely this absence of control of monetary conditions on the part of policymakers that explains the preference of most countries to have a central bank rather than a currency board. Evidently, policymakers prefer to be in control, even though historical evidence suggests that macroeconomic outcomes are generally inferior (Hanke 1998, 297). No country with a currency board has ever experienced hyperinflation, for example, yet many countries with central banks have done so at one time or another. Scores more have experienced uncomfortably high inflation. Indonesia itself experienced hyperinflation in the mid-1960s, and moder-

---

9   In fact, the authorities' initial reaction to the onset of capital flight following the Thai devaluation was to impose a drastic squeeze on base money, by forcing state-owned enterprises to shift their deposits to BI. But this was handled so ineptly that it created chaos in the money markets, resulting in the squeeze being reversed within a couple of weeks (Cole and Slade 1998, 62; McLeod 1998b, 922–3).

ately high inflation in the 1970s (McLeod 1993). Indeed, the chronic lack of success on the part of the central bank in managing monetary policy over several decades has led to the absurd situation described above, in which some observers regard Indonesia as an inherently high inflation economy — a phenomenon unknown in the study of economics.

12.8   RESPONSES TO THE PROPOSAL

The initial market response to the currency board idea — even before it had been officially announced — was strongly positive. After having peaked at Rp13,600/US$ on 26 January 1998 the exchange rate appreciated markedly around the time of Hanke's meetings with Suharto, which were first reported in the international press on Tuesday 3 February 1998 (Solomon and Linebaugh 1998). Indeed, by 11 February the spot exchange rate had strengthened to Rp7,050/US$ — an appreciation of 93 percent in just over two weeks.[10] The forward rate moved in unison with the spot rate, resulting in a dramatic decline in the implied one-year forward interest rate, puncturing the oft-voiced assertion that a currency board would result in soaring interest rates. In retrospect, all this should have been seen as an indicator that the proposal might be capable of extricating Indonesia from its predicament: after all, it was the negative market reaction to the authorities' responses to the initial shock that had provided cause for so much concern. If the market could see merit in this radically different policy approach, at the very least this surely suggested that it was worth considering on its merits. Instead, the response from the policy establishment — the technocrats and their advisors in the IMF and the World Bank — was intensely negative. As a later editorial in the *Far Eastern Economic Review* (2 July 1998) put it:

> The counterattack was swift and massive, leaning more to blackmail and name-calling than reasoned disagreement. Mr Camdessus threatened to pull [the IMF] rescue package. Major news outfits took to referring to Mr Hanke as 'obscure'. It all reached fever pitch when [the high-profile US economist] Paul Krugman attacked Mr Hanke as 'a snake-oil salesman …'.[11]

---

10 The data are difficult to interpret, because the government had also introduced a blanket guarantee of bank liabilities on 26 January (Djiwandono 2005, 122). This new policy was aimed to stop bank runs rather than capital flight, however.

11 At the same time, Krugman is also reported to have said: 'I wish I could say that currency boards are a really stupid thing. They're not. They're just a way of preventing governments from just printing money' (*Dow Jones International News*, 24 March 1998). That, of course, is precisely what Indonesia needed.

Indeed, the IMF's Camdessus, in tandem with US President Bill Clinton, had threatened to urge suspension of its bailout package if Indonesia proceeded with the proposal (*Houston Chronicle*, 14 February 1998). Unfortunately for Indonesia, this bluff succeeded in persuading Suharto to back away.

The obvious question that arises in this context is: was this remarkably strong opposition to the Hanke proposal driven by a fear that it would worsen Indonesia's crisis, or by a fear that it would bring it to an end? Currency boards have been introduced successfully in various countries when poor central bank policymaking has led to a currency collapse, so that the empirical track record speaks in their favour: there was no obvious reason to believe that this approach would be any less successful in Indonesia than it had been elsewhere. Bearing in mind the IMF's position, the latter explanation seems more plausible: successful introduction of a currency board would have meant an enormous loss of face for an institution struggling to persuade the world it still had a useful role to play, despite the fact that the global system of fixed exchange rates that provided its *raison d'être* no longer existed. In this regard, it is revealing that the IMF had supported the introduction of currency boards just months earlier in Bulgaria, and Bosnia and Herzogovina, and later in 1998 and in 1999 would give in-principle support for them in Russia and Brazil, respectively (although the latter two did not proceed) (Hanke 2002, 216).

On his retirement the following year, Camdessus is reported as saying: 'We created the conditions that obliged President Suharto to leave his job … [although that] was not our intention' (Sanger 1999). Former Australian Prime Minister, Paul Keating, went on record to assert that, 'The United States Treasury quite deliberately used the economic collapse as a means of bringing about the ouster of President Suharto' (*Agence France Presse*, 11 November 1999), a view supported by former US Secretary of State Lawrence Eagleberger: 'We were fairly clever in that we supported the IMF as it overthrew [Suharto]' (*Agence France Presse*, 20 June 1998).[12]

Embarrassment for the IMF aside, the mood of the times was that the quasi-dictator Suharto was highly vulnerable for the first time in decades, and that this was a golden opportunity, if not to put an end to his long reign as the virtually unchallengeable leader, then at least to overturn a number of his high-profile policies that operated to the detriment of the Indonesian people. It was natural for the currency board proposal

---

12 Domestically, the replacement of the central bank with a currency board would also have resulted in extensive high-level job losses within the former institution, the threat of which could also be expected to generate significant, strong opposition.

to be seen as the means by which the president might escape with both his position and his policies intact. Alternatively, it was widely imagined that the currency board could be used in the short term to at least protect the immense wealth that had been accumulated by the first family and their business associates, by creating a mechanism with which to move their assets offshore and out of reach of the government. As one commentator (Lakshmanan 1998) put it, some said the currency board proposal was:

> ... a selfish scheme engineered by Suharto's children and friends — who [had] enriched themselves through countless national business projects — to save their fortunes by cashing in rupiah at an inflated exchange rate so they [could] pay off their dollar debts.

This view presumed that the currency board would be established with an unrealistically low exchange rate, and that this elite group would be afforded priority access to the limited international reserves that would be transferred to it from the central bank. In short, the proposal was seen as the means by which Suharto and the conglomerates could make one final raid on the public purse.

12.9 ESTABLISHING A CURRENCY BOARD

This raises the crucial question as to what exchange rate would have been set for the new currency board, were the proposal to be implemented. It appears that Hanke gave little attention to this issue, presumably because he was more concerned to highlight the basic weakness of current policy (that is, the lack of any nominal anchor for monetary policy), and simply to explain the currency board concept, given that it was quite foreign to domestic policymakers and, at best, little understood by their foreign advisors. There were reports that Hanke had recommended a rate of Rp5,000/US$, but this was not the case. In fact he merely stated that: *'on the basis of a back of the envelope calculation'*, '5,000 (rupiah to the dollar) [looked] like a satisfactory number', going on to emphasise that: 'it goes without saying that 5,000 is *not cut in stone*' [emphasis added].[13]

Moreover, it is not plausible that he would have recommended a rate that was unrealistically low, since this would have virtually guaranteed that the currency board would fail, at considerable cost to his professional reputation. Indeed, he was at pains to point out that when:

---

13 Interview with Hanke, 'A case for a currency board', *Asian Wall Street Journal*, 11 February 1998.

… going into one of these arrangements, the thing you can't do is to go with an overvaluation of the currency. You want to feel comfortable that it's priced appropriately and not overvalued or dramatically undervalued.

Nevertheless, many policymakers and commentators argued against establishing a currency board precisely because they thought that the chosen exchange rate would be set artificially low so as to benefit the Suharto group. The crucial weakness in this argument is that the decision about the exchange rate is separate from the decision to establish a currency board. The inability or unwillingness of the policymakers and commentators to see the proposal as anything other than a means of saving Suharto's skin meant that they failed to consider whether it might work if the chosen exchange rate was in fact realistic.

12.10   THE MECHANICS OF DETERMINING THE EXCHANGE RATE

Whereas most commentators simply assumed, first, that the exchange rate would be of the order of Rp5,000–5,500/US\$—and that this was unrealistically low given that the market exchange rate was closer to Rp13,000/US\$ at the time—in fact there was no need for policymakers to determine this rate. As Hanke was to say in an interview in *The New York Times* (20 March 1998):

> I think the best thing to do is announce you are putting in a currency board, let the currency float for 30 days, and then lock in to the exchange rate. *That's exactly what we did in Bulgaria in 1997.* It worked very well, and I think that's probably what they should do in Indonesia [emphasis added].

That is, the best way to proceed is to announce the intention to establish a currency board, and then allow the market to set the rate during a short period of transition (say, one month), with the rate emerging at the end being adopted by the board. This requires that the central bank withdraws entirely from the foreign exchange market, and simultaneously commits to holding the supply of base money constant, during this transition period. In turn, this implies that private sector supply and demand for foreign exchange alone will determine the exchange rate throughout—and at the end of—the transition period.

During the transition, investors will compare the rupiah value of international reserves, converted at the current exchange rate, with the current supply of base money. Anyone who believes that the rupiah price of dollars is lower (higher) than it will be at the end of the transition period—whether because reserves appear too low (high) relative to base money or for some other reason—will have an incentive to buy (sell) foreign exchange now, but the effect will be to push the rate towards this predicted ultimate level. Most of these speculative urges will work themselves out during the transition — indeed, that is precisely the purpose of *having* a period of transition — so that there will be minimal further speculation once the board is operational. In other words, the rate that emerges at the end of the transition could not be 'unrealistic', because it will reflect the market consensus as to the appropriate permanent currency board exchange rate, given the current level of reserves and base money.

12.11   IRONY

If the currency board had been established, and its exchange rate determined in the manner just described, there would have been no possibility of Suharto and those around him looting Indonesia's international reserves, given that BI would have been precluded from selling them off to him or anybody else. The sad irony of Suharto's decision to fold in the face of the Camdessus–Clinton bluff is that this group was able to do so anyway, by different means. BI provided liquidity assistance in huge volumes to the private sector banks — the larger ones all owned by conglomerates, most of which were close to Suharto. The government had then followed up with its blanket guarantee of all bank deposits. The consequence of this was that, directly and indirectly, it became extremely heavily exposed to the private banks — in addition, of course, to its own banks — which then proceeded to collapse. Ultimately, scores of banks were closed, with most of the larger ones — and their accumulated losses — taken over by the government.

The bailout of depositors under the blanket guarantee, and the need for the government to repay the banks' borrowings from BI, eventually cost the Indonesian public something in the order of US$40–50 billion, or about half the value of Indonesia's annual GDP (Fane and McLeod 2002; Frécaut 2004). The main beneficiaries were the conglomerate owners, who had taken enormous loans from their own banks and/or from the state banks, before and during the crisis, which they then failed to repay.[14] The weakness of the legal system (characterised by an incompetent and corrupt legal bureaucracy and judiciary), interfering presidents, and BI's ineffectiveness as supervisor of the banking system, ensured

---

14   Although the owners of private banks lost most or all of their equity when the government took them over, the amounts they owed to these same banks was much greater and, provided they could avoid being forced to repay, they gained on balance. This is the reason why prudential regulations are supposed to ensure that banks lend very little to affiliated entities.

that they could get away with repaying only a very small part of what they had borrowed. One of the most egregious examples is that of Syamsul Nursalim, who was:

> ... arrested and accused of causing the state to suffer losses of US$1.68 billion through the misuse of [BI] loans to his Bank Dagang Nasional Indonesia. However, he was released after one day in detention. ... Investigators estimate that Nursalim [eventually] repaid about 10% of the debt he owed to [the Indonesian Bank Restructuring Agency] (Collins 2007, 110).

Had Suharto followed through with the currency board proposal, both base money supply growth and bank lending to finance speculation against the currency would immediately have been halted, the currency would have strengthened, and firms would have been in a better position to repay their borrowings from banks. BI's loans to the banking system would have been much reduced, and the cost to the government of claims against its deposit guarantee likewise.

According to Hanke, as reported by Blustein (2001, 225), Suharto:

> ... fretted about the inflation that would likely ignite as the result of the rupiah's collapse. ... 'They'll riot in the streets, I'll have to bring in the military, and it could potentially get quite bloody.'

Although the president's predictions would eventually turn out to be entirely accurate, ultimately he chose to stay with the IMF program rather than implement the currency board proposal. This can only be explained by lingering doubts on Suharto's part as to the likely success of the currency board proposal. The IMF loan would not have counted as part of Indonesia's (unencumbered) reserves, so success of the proposal would not have depended on the IMF support package—nor be threatened by its withdrawal. The package was quite small relative to these reserves in any case, and their only real purpose was to persuade the private sector that the rupiah would not devalue further (McLeod 1998a, 40–41). It did 'get bloody'—so much so that in May 1998 Suharto chose to resign (Johnson 1998, 6–9).

At least his detractors had the pleasure of witnessing his demise.

13 What are grain reserves worth? A generalised political economy framework

C. Peter Timmer*

What explains volatility in world food prices? Are the 'fundamentals' of supply and demand the basic factors? Can national or international policies towards food grain reserves help to stabilise food prices? What are food stocks 'worth' if the levels of grain reserves, especially in large countries, affect food trade policies in these countries? This effect would be the reverse of the usual causation where policies can directly affect the levels of both public and private stocks.

There are four basic ways the economics profession thinks about these questions.

The first is second nature to economists, who use basic supply and demand models as the fundamental explanation of price formation. The 'fundamentals' approach uses these models to generate an equilibrium price, where the global level of stocks is an *exogenous* factor that influences the probability of a price spike when there are shocks to supply or demand. A number of well-calibrated models using this structure are used routinely, especially by international research centres such as the Food and Agriculture Organization (FAO), the Food and Agricultural Policy Research Institute (FAPRI), and the International Food Policy Research Institute (IFPRI) to understand the impact of changing trends in supply and demand, and shocks, to food prices.

---

* This chapter was originally prepared for a workshop on the role of food reserves in coping with price volatility, held at FAO Headquarters in Rome, Italy, 30–31 January 2014. Several of the ideas developed in this paper were first presented in Timmer (2009a) and Timmer (2009b).

The second approach explicitly introduces the storability of the commodity into price formation. The supply of the storage model brings in expectations and makes stock levels endogenous with price formation. To be empirically useful, however, reasonably accurate and timely data on levels of stocks held by commercial trade are critical. These models have a long history, but the standard reference remains Williams and Wright (1991). A modern application with important implications for the role of biofuels in food price formation is Roberts and Schlenker (2013).

The third approach recognises that such stock data are often not available for commodities where individuals and small firms hold a major share of stocks between harvest and consumption, a factor that is especially important for the world rice market (Timmer 2009b). To cope with this reality of the industrial organisation of some commodity markets, a behavioural model adds hoarding by individuals, with levels of stocks in the hands of these agents largely unobserved but important for short-run price formation. In this approach, 'non-traditional speculation' in financial and commodities markets can also impact price formation without having a visible impact on *measured* stock levels (Timmer 2012).

The fourth approach is quite new. A political economy model adds the behaviour of policymakers (and other market participants) to explain changes in trade restrictions for grain (especially rice). 'Confidence in trade' is a critical driver of political behaviour and from there to volatility. Domestically held stocks contribute directly to confidence in trade, in a positive manner. In this model, levels of grain stock held domestically are an important factor in explaining price volatility, above and beyond their impact via the supply of storage model.

This chapter reviews each of these approaches in turn. The goal of the paper is to provide new insights into how to answer the question: 'What are grain reserves "worth" in a world where trade restrictions drive food price volatility?'

13.1   A SIMPLE MODEL OF PRICE FORMATION WITH EXOGENOUS STOCKS

Consider the most basic model of commodity price formation that is capable of illuminating our problem (Timmer 2009b):

$$D_t = f(a_t, P_t, sr_d, P_{t-n}, lr_d) = a_t P_t^{sr_d} P_{t-n}^{lr_d}$$

$$S_t = g(b_t, P_t, sr_s, P_{t-n}, lr_s) = b_t P_t^{sr_s} P_{t-n}^{lr_s}$$

where D_t = demand for the commodity during time t; S_t = supply of the commodity during time t; f and g = functional forms for demand and supply functions, respectively; a_t = time-dependent shifters of the demand curve; b_t = time-dependent shifters of the supply curve; P_t = equilibrium market price during time t; P_{t-n} = market price during some previous time period $t-n$; and sr_d, sr_s, lr_d and lr_s = indicators that demand and supply responses will vary depending on whether they are in the short run sr or long run lr. In the specification below, these will be short-run and long-run supply and demand elasticities.

In short-run equilibrium, $D_t = S_t$. For simplicity (and the ability to work directly with supply and demand elasticities), assume the demand and supply functions are Cobb–Douglas. Then

$$\log a_t + sr_d \log P_t + lr_d \log P_{t-n} = \log b_t + sr_s \log P_t + lr_s \log P_{t-n}$$

Solving for the equilibrium price P,

$$\log P_t = [\log b_t - \log a_t] / [sr_d - sr_s] + \log P_{t-n}[lr_s - lr_d]/[sr_d - sr_s]$$

Taking first differences to see the factors that explain a change in price from $t-1$ to t reveals a somewhat complicated result:

$$d \log P_t = \{[\log b_t - \log b_{t-1}] - [\log a_t - \log a_{t-1}]\}/[sr_d - sr_s] +$$
$$[\log P_{t-n} - \log P_{t-(n+1)}][lr_s - lr_d]/[sr_d - sr_s]$$

where $d \log P_t$ = the percentage change in price from time period $t-1$ to time period t (for relatively small changes). This is what we are trying to explain. What 'causes' changes in $d \log P_t$? Why are food prices high or low?

To answer these questions, it helps to simplify the equation. Let SR equal the net short-run supply and demand response $sr_d - sr_s$, which is always negative because $sr_d < 0$ and $sr_s > 0$. Let LR equal the net long-run supply and demand response $lr_s - lr_d$, which is always positive, for similar reasons (note that the demand coefficient is subtracted from the supply coefficient in this case, the opposite from the short-run coefficients above). Let $d \log b_t = \log b_t - \log b_{t-1}$, which for small changes is the percentage change in the supply shifters. Let $d \log a_t = \log a_t - \log a_{t-1}$, which for small changes is the percentage change in the demand shifters. Finally, let $d \log P_{t-n} = \log P_{t-n} - \log P_{t-(n+1)}$, which for small changes is the percentage change in the commodity price for some specified number of time periods in the past, for example, five or ten years (after which the long-run producer and consumer responses to price have been realised).

Combining all of these new definitions, we have a simpler equation explaining percentage changes in commodity prices:

Percent change in P_t = [percent change in b_t – percent change in a_t]/SR + [percent change in P_{t-n}] LR/SR

The 'surprising' result is how simple the answer appears to be. There are four key drivers:

1   the relative size of changes in a_t to b_t – i.e. factors shifting the demand curve relative to factors shifting the supply curve
2   the relative size of short-run supply and demand elasticities (sr_s and sr_d)
3   the relative size of long-run supply and demand elasticities (lr_s and lr_d)
4   how large the price change was in earlier time periods.

A simple numerical example, with plausible parameters, shows the power of this 'explanatory' equation. Assume the following numerical parameters for purposes of illustration:

$$sr_d = -0.10$$
$$sr_s = +0.05$$
$$lr_d = -0.30$$
$$lr_s = +0.50$$

These values imply that $S = -0.15$ and $LR = 0.80$.

The short-run elasticities assumed here are quite low, but realistic for annual responses.[1] Demand responds 1 percent for a 10 percent change in price; supply only responds by half a percent to a similar 10 percent price change (the signs, of course, are negative for demand and positive for supply responses).

The long-run elasticities are also on the low side of econometric estimates, but again, seem realistic for a world facing increasing resource constraints. Although some estimates of long-run supply response are quite high – approaching unity or higher – they were estimated for time periods when acreage expansion was significant and fertiliser usage was just becoming widespread (Peterson 1979).

Assume, as seems to be the case since the early 2000s, that demand drivers have been larger than supply drivers, with demand shifting out by 3.0 percent per year and supply shifting out just 1.5 percent per year. Finally, assume that prices in the past have been 'low'. The change in P_{t-n} is –10.0 percent. What do all these parameters mean for current price change?

Plugging these values into the price change equation yields the following result:

---

[1]   They are also consistent with the estimates by Roberts and Schlenker (2013), although they attribute more of the price response to supply and less to demand.

Percent change in P_t $= [1.5\% - 3.0\%]/-0.15 + [-10.0\%]0.80/-0.15$
$= [10.0\%] + [53.3\%]$
$= 63.3\%\ higher$

This is a very dramatic result. The imbalance between 'current' supply and demand drivers causes the price to rise by 10 percent, but the historically low prices (and 'only' a 10 percent decline in the earlier period) cause current prices to be 53 percent higher, as the long-term, lagged response from producers and consumers to these earlier low prices has a very large quantitative impact. *Much of the slow run-up in food prices from 2003 to 2007 would seem to be caused by producers and consumers gradually responding (i.e. reflecting their 'long-run' responses) to earlier episodes of low prices, especially from the late 1990s until about 2003.* For example, between 1996 and 2001, the real price of rice declined by 14.7 percent per year in world markets!

Over long periods of time, the first driver is obviously the most important — how fast is the demand curve shifting relative to the supply curve? At the level of generality specified in this model, the actual underlying causes of these shifts do not matter. All that matters is the net result. If the demand curve is shifting outward by 3 percent per year, and the supply curve is shifting out by just 1.5 percent per year, the difference of 1.5 percent per year will push prices higher, by an amount determined by net short-run supply and demand elasticities with respect to price. The 'simple' fact is that changes in commodity prices are driven by the net of *aggregate* trends in supply and demand, not their composition.

The analytical model of price formation makes a sharp and important distinction between factors that shift the demand and supply curves (the a_t and b_t coefficients) and the responsiveness of farmers and consumers to changes in the market price (the sr_s and sr_d coefficients), which show up as movements along the supply and demand curve. Analytically, the distinction is very clear, but, empirically, it is often hard to tell the difference. If farmers use more fertiliser in response to higher prices for grain, should this count as part of the supply response or as a supply shifter? If governments and donor agencies restrict their funding of agricultural research because of low prices for grain, is the resulting lower productivity potential a smaller supply shifter a decade later or a long-run response to prices? Whatever the labels, it is important to understand the causes.

In a world modelled by the fundamentals of supply and demand, price volatility is driven by exogenous shocks to either — bad weather on the supply side, for example, or a biofuel mandate to convert corn to ethanol on the demand side. The price response to such shocks then depends on the structural parameters of the model — the short-run and long-run price elasticities of supply and demand — and on the potential for stocks to mitigate shortfalls or surpluses. The size of these stocks, and thus their potential to mitigate price volatility, is exogenous to the model. The next section discusses the potential to bring decisions about stock levels into the supply and demand framework via the supply of storage model.

13.2   THE SUPPLY OF STORAGE MODEL AND SHORT-RUN PRICE BEHAVIOUR

Almost by definition, the role of stocks in commodity price formation is restricted to short-run influences. In the long run, food demand cannot exceed the amount of food supplied. Still, much of the concern about volatile food prices reflects short-run issues. Price spikes, for example, tend to last only a year or two. Food prices can be depressed for decades at a time — from 1985 to 2005, for example, but they are not volatile during these periods because stocks tend to accumulate during periods of low prices. Large stocks and low prices are, of course, linked.

The link between the supply of grain held in storage and prices in both spot and futures markets has long been the subject of analytical attention (Working 1949; Weymar 1968; Williams and Wright 1991). The basic 'supply of storage' model that has emerged from this theoretical and empirical work is the foundation for understanding short-run price behaviour for storable commodities (Houthakker 1987). It stresses the inter-related behaviour of speculators and hedgers as they judge inventory levels in relation to use. *The formation of price expectations is the key to this behaviour.*

The basic supply of storage model is a simple extension of the supply/demand model already used here. The formulation here follows Weymar's presentation, with three behavioural equations and one identity (error terms are omitted for simplicity):

$$C_t = f_c(P_t, P_t^L) \tag{13.1}$$

$$H_t = f_h(P_t, P_t^L) \tag{13.2}$$

$$(P_t^* - P_t) = f_p(I_t) \tag{13.3}$$

$$I_t = I_{t-1} + H_t - C_t \tag{13.4}$$

where C = consumption, P = price, P^L = lagged price, H = production (harvest), I = inventory, and P^* = expected price at some point in the future.

The first two equations, indicating the dependency of consumption and production on current and/or lagged price, reflect traditional micro economic theory. While other variables may appear in these relationships (e.g.

consumer income, government support levels), their exclusion here will not affect the discussion that follows. [The third equation] represents the 'supply of storage' curve ... and reflects the notion that the amount of a commodity that people are willing to carry in inventory depends on their expectations as to future price behaviour. If they feel that the price will increase substantially, they will be willing to carry heavier inventories (supply more storage) than would otherwise be the case. Because the inventory level is in fact determined by the identity expressed in [the fourth equation], the supply of storage function can be used to explain the gap between the current price and price expectations in terms of the current inventory level. [Weymar 1968, 28]

Thus the relationship between current inventories and current price helps explain price expectations, and vice versa. These price expectations can then be expressed in prices on futures markets. The actual working out of this theory empirically requires a close understanding of the behaviour of market participants — farmers, traders, processors, and end users (consumers) — in their role as hedgers or speculators. The current controversy over the role of 'outside' speculators — investors who are not active participants in the commodity system — has many precursors in the history and analysis of commodity price formation on futures markets.

The empirical difficulty in using the supply of storage model to understand short-run price behaviour is having current information on inventory levels. This is not such a severe problem when virtually all the commodity storage is in commercial hands, as with cocoa or wheat, and stock levels for such commodities can be estimated fairly accurately. For a commodity such as rice, however, which is mostly grown by smallholders, is marketed by a dense network of small traders and processors, and is purchased by consumers in a readily storable form (milled rice), stock levels can change at any or all levels of the supply chain, and there are virtually no data available on these inventory levels. To make matters worse, a number of countries (especially China) regard the size of publicly held stocks of grain as a state secret. It is thought that China holds as much rice in storage as the rest of the world combined.

For the purposes here, then, the main advantage of the supply of storage model is its ability to build conceptual links between long-run supply and demand trends, where basic models of producers and consumers provide operational guidelines to decision-making and price formation, and very short-run movements in prices that often seem totally divorced from supply and demand fundamentals. Because long-run trends are gradually built up from short-run observations, these links are essential for understanding price behaviour even in the long run.

The key, then, to making the supply of storage model operational in the short run is to use it to gain insight on formation of price expectations. In the very short run, from day to day or week to week, these expectations seem to be driven by a combination of price behaviour for commodities broadly and the specifics of individual commodities. Broad commodity price trends are captured by the IMF commodity price index, the *Economist* price index, or the Goldman-Sachs commodity price index, for example. Thus, traders operating in any one specific commodity market, such as oil, corn or wheat, will be following closely the broader price movements for all commodities (Irwin, Sanders, and Merrin 2009). These broad price movements seem to be driven by basic macroeconomic forces such as rates of economic growth, the value of international currencies, especially the US dollar, and relative rates of inflation.

But traders are also following closely the specifics of the commodity as well. Here inventories (especially relative to actual use for consumption) are the key to price formation, once the harvest/supply situation for the crop is established. At this point, the analytics of price behaviour for oil or metals begin to look quite different from the analytics of food commodities at this stage, as seasonal production and the inherent need to store the commodity for daily use throughout the year drive inventory behaviour via the supply of storage.

Typically, commodities for which inventory data are reasonably reliable tend to have their prices driven by unexpected supply behaviour. Commodities with poor data on inventories, especially where significant inventories can be in the hands of millions of small agents — farmers, traders, consumers — tend to have their extremes in price behaviour generated by rapidly changing price expectations themselves, and consequent hoarding or dis-hoarding. The short-run price dynamics for rice thus look significantly different from those for wheat or corn, partly because of the different industrial organisation of the respective commodity systems. Gilbert (2012) and Tadesse et al. (2013) reach the same conclusion.

13.3   BEHAVIOURAL DIMENSIONS OF FOOD SECURITY: HERD BEHAVIOUR AND HOARDING

Experience with world rice prices since the middle of the decade illustrates the importance of behavioural factors in short-run price dynamics. The actual production/consumption balance for rice has been relatively favourable since 2005, with rice stocks-to-use ratios improving slightly. This stock build-up was a rationale response to the very low stocks seen at the middle of the decade and to gradually rising rice prices — exactly what the supply of storage model predicts. Short-run substitutions in both production and consumption between rice and other food commodities are limited, and until late 2007 it seemed that the rice market might 'dodge the bullet' of price spikes seen in the wheat, corn and vegetable oil markets. The lack of a deeply traded futures market for rice also made financial speculation less attractive.

But the world rice market is very thin, trading just 6–7 percent of global production.[2] While this is a significant improvement over the 4–5 percent traded in the 1960s and 1970s, it still leaves the global market subject to large price moves from relatively small quantity moves.

The global rice market is also relatively concentrated, with Thailand, Vietnam, India, the US, and Pakistan routinely providing nearly four-fifths of available supplies. Only in the US is rice not a 'political commodity' from a consumer's perspective (although it certainly is a political commodity for producers in the US). All Asian countries show understandable concern over access of their citizens to daily rice supplies. Both importing and exporting countries watch the world market carefully for signals about changing scarcity, while simultaneously trying to keep their domestic rice economy stable.

As concerns grew in 2007 that world food supplies were limited and prices for wheat, corn, and vegetable oils were rising, several Asian countries reconsidered the wisdom of maintaining low domestic stocks for rice.[3] The Philippines, in particular, tried to build up its stocks to protect against shortages going forward. Of course, if every country—or individual consumer—acts the same way, the hoarding causes a panic and extreme shortage in markets, leading to rapidly rising prices. Even US consumers are not immune from this panic, as the 'run' on bags of rice at Costco and Sam's Club in April 2008 indicated. Such price panics have been fairly common over the past 50 years, but the hope was that deeper markets, more open trading regimes, and wealthier consumers able to adjust more flexibly to price changes had made markets more stable. It turns out this was wishful thinking.

After an acceleration started in September 2007 in the gradual price increases seen for half a decade, concern over the impact of higher rice prices in exporting countries, especially India, Vietnam, and Thailand, started to translate into talk, and then action, on export controls.[4]

---

2 The standard early introduction to the distinctiveness of the world rice market is Wickizer and Bennett (1941). The most recent review of the world rice economy, especially the crisis in 2007–2008, is in Dawe (2010).

3 A brief overview of the 'fire' in the world rice market from late 2007 until mid-2008 follows. See Slayton (2009) for a detailed analysis and chronology.

4 It is almost amusing that Indonesia announced a ban on rice exports early in 2008, before its main rice harvest started in March. Historically, Indonesia has been the world's largest rice *importer*, surpassed only recently by the Philippines, and no one in the world rice trade was looking to Indonesia for export supplies. But there was a rationale to the announcement by the Minister of Trade—it signalled that Indonesia would not be needing imports and was thus not vulnerable to the skyrocketing prices in world markets. The calming effect on domestic rice market participants meant that little of the hoarding behaviour seen in Vietnam and the Philippines was evidenced in Indonesia.

Importing countries, especially the Philippines, started to scramble for supplies. Fears of shortages spread and a cumulative price spiral started that fed on the fear itself.

The trigger for the panic was provided by inter-commodity price linkages. In India, the 2007 wheat harvest was damaged by drought and disease — as in so many other parts of the world. Thus, the national food authority had less wheat for public distribution. Importing as much wheat as in 2006 — nearly 7 million metric tons (mmt) — would be too expensive (both economically and politically) because of the high wheat price in world markets, so the food authority announced it needed to retain more rice from domestic production.

Barriers were put on rice exports in September — India is often the second largest rice exporter in the world, 5 mmt in 2007 — and eventually an outright ban on exports of non-Basmati rice from India was announced in February 2008. Other rice exporting countries followed, as rice prices started to spike.

The newly elected populist government in Thailand did not want consumer prices for rice to go up, and the commerce minister openly discussed export restrictions from Thailand — the world's largest rice exporter, 9.5 mmt in 2007. On 28 March 2008, rice prices in Thailand jumped $75 per mt. Prices continued to skyrocket until it cost over $1,100 per mt in April. This is the stuff of panics.

Low and declining rice stocks have been held accountable for the rising prices, with the argument that rice consumption has outpaced rice production for a number of years since 2000 (a mathematical inevitability if rice stocks are falling). Rice stocks in China have come down over the past decade, but that was a sensible response to growing reliance on trade as the buffer, and to lower prices in world markets. There has been little change in rice stocks in the rest of the world — indeed, the stocks-to-use ratio has been rising since 2005. Holding rice stocks in tropical conditions is extraordinarily expensive, so a smoother flow of rice internationally reduces this wasteful stockholding (Dorosh and Rashid 2013; Gouel 2013).

Now that the exporting countries are clearly willing to put bans on rice exports to protect their own consumers, nearly all countries will be forced to resort to domestic stockpiles. That is a real tragedy for poor consumers and for economic growth — capital tied up in funding inventories is not very productive in stimulating productivity growth.

The psychology of hoarding behaviour is important in explaining why rice prices suddenly shot up starting in late 2007. Financial speculation seems to have played only a small role (partly because futures markets for rice are very thinly traded). Instead, decisions by millions of households, farmers, traders, and some governments sparked a sudden surge in demand for rice and changed the gradual increase in rice prices from 2002 to 2007 into an explosion.

A rough calculation of the effect of household hoarding of rice shows the potential. Assume that one billion households consume 1 kilogram of rice a day (for a total consumption of 365 mmt, for the year, which is the right magnitude).

Assume they keep a one-week supply in their pantry, or 7 kilograms per household, which is 7 mmt of household stocks in total. This quantity probably varies by income class, with the very poor buying hand to mouth, and better off households storing more just for convenience. When prices start to rise, or the newspapers or TV start talking about shortages of rice, each household, *acting independently*, decides to double its own storage, thus buying an additional 7 kilograms per household. This means the world rice market needs to supply an additional 7 mmt of rice over a short period (a few weeks). This quantity is about one quarter of total annual international trade in rice (recent levels have been 27–30 mmt per year).

Roughly 7 mmt is just the added demand from households. Farmers, traders, rice millers, and even governments will also want to hold more stocks in these circumstances. As an example, the government of Malaysia announced that it was doubling the size of the national buffer stock held by BERNAS, even though it had to pay extremely high prices to do so. The Philippines increased its government-held stocks. Indonesia tripled its level of buffer stocks, from 1.0 mmt to 3.0 mmt.

To determine the impact on prices, short-run supply and demand parameters from the analytical model developed above can be inserted into the price determination mechanism: –0.1 for demand and 0.05 for supply. With a 25 percent increase in short-run demand on the world market (suddenly), the world price will have to rise by 167 percent to get a new equilibrium. That is what happened — *panic hoarding caused the rice price spike.*

Fortunately, a speculative run can be ended by 'pricking the bubble' and deflating expectations. Once the price starts to drop, the psychology reverses on hoarding behaviour by households, farmers, traders, and even governments. When the government of Japan announced in May, after considerable international urging, that it would sell 300,000 tons of its surplus 'WTO' rice stocks to the Philippines, prices in world rice markets started to fall immediately (Slayton and Timmer 2008). By late August, medium-quality rice for export from Vietnam was available for half what it sold for in late April, as dis-hoarding gained momentum.

The introduction of 'outside' stocks into the world rice market was what pricked the price bubble and ended the hoarding behaviour. What were these stocks 'worth?' They were very expensive for the Japanese government to store, and it was the effort by the Japanese Ministry of Finance to recoup their total investment cost during price negotiations with the Philippines that led to their ultimate failure. Alternative rice supplies were quickly available at a lower cost once the panic had subsided. From that perspective, the Japanese stocks were invaluable. They brought stability to the world rice market.

13.4   GRAIN RESERVES AND THE BEHAVIOUR OF POLICYMAKERS

Restricting the flow of commodities across international borders almost inevitably increases the volatility of prices for those commodities in the residual world market (Anderson 2012). Although WTO agreements have helped maintain relatively open markets on the import side, they have not been effective in preventing exporters from using trade restrictions to stabilise food prices domestically. The political economy of export restrictions seems pretty obvious. Most leaders understand they have a mandate to provide reasonably stable food prices to their citizens, and retaining more domestically produced food at home when prices are spiking in world markets is easy, visible, and politically popular.

History demonstrates that rice prices within many Asian countries *can* be kept reasonably stable with respect to world prices (Dawe and Timmer 2012). The problem is that there are often spillovers from the actions undertaken by countries to stabilise their domestic prices, and these spillovers increase price instability in world markets (Martin and Anderson 2012). A little-researched topic is how to *minimise* the impact of these spillovers, or *cope* with them on a country-by-country basis, rather than to follow the standard policy advice, which is to *avoid* the actions altogether, and thus avoid the spillovers in the first place. *The standard policy advice turns out to be politically impossible in times of turbulent markets.* Is there a better alternative, i.e. is there a way to keep borders more open to trade in basic food commodities, in both directions?

There are several components to the answer. First, we need a serious new research program on the benefits and costs of stabilising food prices *within domestic economies*, including a focus on implementation of policy, management of food logistics agencies, and instruments to control corruption in these agencies.[5] We would know a lot more about these topics if we had spent the same resources answering these questions as we have

---

5 A start on this research is in Bellemare, Barrett, and Just (2013), and Gouel (2013).

spent over the past three decades in estimating the gains from free trade in agriculture.

Second, we need to understand how to build political confidence in trade as a step towards more open trade policies. Recent confidence-building measures have helped renew trust in the world rice market, which has been more stable since 2009 than world wheat and maize markets—a very significant reversal of historical patterns of food price volatility. Severe damage to this trust was inflicted during the 2007–2008 food crisis, mostly because of the Indian ban on exports, the on-again, off-again ban on Vietnamese rice exports, and open talk in Thailand of withholding stocks from the market and creating an Organization of Rice Exporting Countries (OREC), to boost prices in the world market (Dawe and Timmer 2012; Dorosh and Rashid 2013). Still, there is plenty of blame to go around in explaining the political distrust of the world market for rice. Important importing countries, such as Indonesia and the Philippines, speak publically of their desire to end 'dependence' on supplies from the world market. Such rhetoric does not make them a market that exporting countries can trust.

This retreat into autarky comes at a very high price to economic efficiency and the welfare of poor consumers. It makes the world market even more unstable and less reliable. But by understanding the behavioural foundations of food security and its political economy, it is possible to re-build confidence and trust in international trade in general and in the world rice market in particular. These confidence-building measures will need to involve both exporting and importing countries, *acting in their own self-interest*. One possibility—already underway—is a country-by-country investment in greater rice reserves to cope with *shocks* to rice supplies, while gradually increasing the use of trade to *lower costs* of rice consumption. A higher level of stocks does not alter the requisite flow of rice from producers to consumers, but it does create a buffer against interruptions to that flow. Thus, larger stocks contribute directly to greater confidence in using the world rice market to lower the costs of food security in importing and exporting countries alike.

Third, we need an 'Asian Rice Forum' to meet regularly as a venue, especially for the largest countries, to discuss their policy approaches to the sector (and to express quietly any concerns about the behaviour of their trading partners). This might be an initiative for the ASEAN+6 group of countries, which includes all of the major rice players in Asia. A top agenda item for the first meeting of such a forum would be an *explicit* discussion, at the level of heads of state, of how to maintain and build greater trust in the world rice market. Trust can be both personal and institutional, and both are needed in this instance.

Because of the sheer size of their *domestic* rice economies, actions to increase production, reduce consumption, or alter the size of stocks held by public agencies in the largest Asian countries will also have a noticeable impact on the *international* rice economy. These countries certainly include China and India, probably Indonesia, and possibly the Philippines and Bangladesh.[6] Larger rice reserves in these countries are probably desirable for reasons of domestic food security, but they will also alter the perception of global observers about the adequacy of worldwide stocks. Fortunately, this process is already well underway. That is, *larger rice reserves in these countries – built up since 2008 – have had a positive spillover impact on the global rice economy by stabilising price expectations,* and thereby actual rice prices. The stability in global rice prices since 2008, relative to wheat and maize prices, is largely attributable to more attention in the large Asian countries to their own domestic food security, including holding larger rice stocks.

---

6   India, Thailand, and Vietnam, as the world's leading rice exporters, carry substantial stocks both seasonally and as part of their normal pipeline for regular deliveries to their customers. They are unlikely to need larger stocks for food security reasons.

References

Acemoglu, D & Robinson, J (2008), 'The role of institutions in growth and development', *Working Paper* no. 10, Washington DC: Commission for Growth and Development.

Acemoglu, D & Robinson, J (2012), *Why Nations Fail: The Origins of Power, Prosperity and Poverty*, New York: Random House.

Acemoglu, D, Johnson, S & Robinson, J (2001), 'The colonial origins of comparative development', *American Economic Review*, 91, pp. 1369–1401.

Acemoglu, D, Johnson, S & Robinson, J (2005), 'Institutions as the fundamental cause of long-run growth', in Aghion, P & Durlauf, S (eds), *Handbook of Economic Growth*, Amsterdam: North-Holland.

ADB (Asian Development Bank) (2012), *Asian Economic Integration Monitor*, Manila: Asian Development Bank.

ADB (Asian Development Bank) (2013), *Key Indicators for Asia and the Pacific 2013*, Manila.

Aghion, P, Burgess, R, Redding, SJ & Zilibotti, F (2008), 'The unequal effects of liberalization: evidence from dismantling the license raj in India', *American Economic Review*, 98(4), pp. 1397–1412.

Aitken, B, Harrison, A & Lipsey, RE (1996), 'Wages and foreign ownership: a comparative study of Mexico, Venezuela, and the United States', *Journal of Inter-national Economics*, 40(3-4), pp. 345–371.

Al-Samarrai, S & Cerdan-Infantes, P (2013), 'Where did all the money go? Financing basic education in Indonesia', in Jones, G & Suryadarma, D (eds) *Education in Indonesia*, Singapore: Institute for Southeast Asian Studies, pp. 109–138.

Alderman, H, Hoddinott, J & Kinsey, W (2006), 'Long term consequences of early childhood malnutrition', *Oxford Economic Papers*, 58(3), pp. 450–474.

Alfaro, L & Chari, A (2009), 'India transformed? Insights from the firm level 1988–2005', *NBER Working Paper* no. 15448, National Bureau of Economic Research.

Allford, J & Soejachmoen, MP (2013), 'Survey of recent developments', *Bulletin of Indonesian Economic Studies*, 49(3), pp. 267–288.

Almond, D & Currie, J (2011), 'Human capital development before age 5', in Ashenfelter, O & Card, D (eds), *Handbook of Labor Economics Volume 4b*, Amsterdam: North-Holland, pp. 1316–1486.

Almunia, M, Benetrix, A, Eichengreen, B, O'Rourke, KH & Rua, G (2010), 'From Great Depression to Great Credit Crisis: similarities, differences and lessons', *Economic Policy*, April, pp. 219–265.

Anderson, K (2012), 'Government trade restrictions and international price volatility', *Global Food Security*, 1(2), pp. 157–166.

Anderson, K (2013), *Which Winegrape Varieties are Grown Where? A Global Empirical Picture*, Adelaide: University of Adelaide Press. Freely available as an e-book at www.adelaide.edu.au/press/titles/winegrapes and as Excel files at www.adelaide.edu.au/wine-econ/databases.

Anderson, K & Nelgen, S (2011), *Global Wine Markets, 1961 to 2009: A Statistical Compendium*, Adelaide: University of Adelaide Press. Freely available as an e-book at www.adelaide.edu.au/press/titles/global-wine and as Excel files at www.adelaide.edu.au/wine-econ/databases.

Anderson, K & Smith, B (1981), 'Changing economic relations between Asian ADCs and resource-exporting developed countries', in Hong, W & Krause, L (eds), *Trade and Growth in the Advanced Developing Countries*, Seoul: Korea Development Institute Press.

Anderson, K & Strutt, A (2012), 'The changing geography of world trade: projections to 2030' *Journal of Asian Economics*, 23(4), pp. 303–323.

Anderson, K & Wittwer, G (2013), 'Modeling global wine markets to 2018: exchange rates, taste changes, and China's import growth' *Journal of Wine Economics*, 8(2), pp. 131–158.

ASEAN (Association of Southeast Asian Nations) (2010a), *ASEAN Statistical Yearbook 2010*, ASEAN Secretariat, Jakarta.

ASEAN (Association of Southeast Asian Nations) (2010b), *Roadmap for an ASEAN Community, 2009–2015*, ASEAN Secretariat, Jakarta.

Ashenfelter, O & Storchmann, K (2014), 'Wine and climate change', *AAWE Working Paper* no. 152, March. Available at www.wine-economics.org.

Asia–Pacific CoP-MfDR (2011), 'Community of practice on managing for development results', *Framework for Results-Based Public Sector Management and Country Cases*, Asian Development Bank. Available at http://cop-mfdr.adb.org.

Aswicahyono, H, Hill, H & Narjoko, D (2010), 'Industrialisation after a deep economic crisis: Indonesia', *Journal of Development Studies*, 46(2), pp. 1084–1108.

Aswicahyono, H, Hill, H & Narjoko, D (2011a), 'Indonesian industrialization: a latecomer adjusting to crises', *WIDER Working Paper* no. 2011/53.

Aswicahyono, H, Hill, H & Narjoko, D (2011b), 'Indonesian industrialization: jobless growth?', in Manning, C & Sumarto, S (eds) *Employment, Living Standards and Poverty in Contemporary Indonesia*, Singapore: Institute of Southeast Asian Studies, 113–33.

Aswicahyono, H, Narjoko, D & Hill, H (2008), 'Industrialization after a deep economic crisis: Indonesia', *Working Paper* no. 2008/18, Canberra: Australian National University, Arndt-Corden Division of Economics, College of Asia and the Pacific.

Athukorala, P (2009), 'The rise of China and East Asian export performance: is the crowding-out fear warranted?', *World Economy*, 32(2), pp. 234–266.

Athukorala, P & Devadason, ES (2012), 'The impact of foreign labour on host country wages: the experience of a Southern Host, Malaysia', *World Development*, 40(8), pp. 1497–1510.

Athukorala, P & Hill, H (2010), 'Asian trade; long-term patterns and key policy issues', *Asian–Pacific Economic Literature*, 24(2), pp. 52–82.

Athukorala, P & Wagle, S (2011), 'Foreign direct investment in Southeast Asia: is Malaysia falling behind?', *ASEAN Economic Bulletin*, 28(2), pp. 115–133.

Bai, J & Perron, P (1998), 'Estimating and testing linear models with multiple structural change', *Econometrica*, 66, pp. 47–78.

Baldwin, R (2004), 'The spoke trap: hub and spoke bilateralism in East Asia', *Working Paper 04-02*, Seoul: Korea Institute of Economic Policy.

Baldwin, R (2006a), 'Managing the noodle bowl: the fragility of East Asian regionalism', *Working Paper* no. 5561, London: Centre for Economic Policy Research.

Baldwin, R (2006b), 'Multilateralising regionalism: spaghetti bowls as building blocs on the path to global free trade', *World Economy*, pp. 1451–1518.

Balisacan, AM & Hill, H (eds) (2003), *The Philippine Economy: Development, Policies and Challenges*, Oxford University Press, New York, and Ateneo University Press, Manila.

Bank Indonesia (2010) *Report of a National Survey on Migrant Workers in Indonesia, 2009*, Directorate of Economic and Monetary Statistics, Jakarta: Bank Indonesia.

Barton, D, Chen, Y & Jin, A (2013), 'Mapping China's middle class', *McKinsey Quarterly*, June. Available at www.mckinsey.com/insights/consumer_and_retail/mapping_chinas_middle_class.

Behrman, G (2007), *The Most Noble Adventure*, New York: Free Press.

Bellemare, MF, Barrett, CB & Just, DR (2013), 'The welfare impacts of commodity price volatility: evidence from rural Ethiopia', *American Journal of Agricultural Economics*, 95(4), pp. 877–899.

Bello, W (2010), 'The China–ASEAN Free Trade Area: propaganda and reality'. Available at http://focusweb.org.

Bernard, AB & Jensen, JB (1997), 'Exporting, skill upgrading, and the wage gap', *Journal of International Economics*, 42(1–2), pp. 3–31.

Bernard, AB, Jensen, JB, Redding, SJ & Schott, PK (2007), 'Firms in international trade', *Journal of Economic Perspectives*, 21(3), pp. 105–130.

Bhagwati, J (1988), 'Export-promoting trade strategy: issues and evidence', *World Bank Research Observer*, 3(1), pp. 27–57.

Bhagwati, J (1991), *The World Trading System at Risk*, Princeton, NJ: Princeton University Press.

Bhagwati, J (1993), *India in Transition*, Oxford: Oxford University Press.

Bhagwati, J (1995), 'U.S. trade policy: the infatuation with free trade areas', *Discussion Paper Series* no. 726, Columbia University.

Bhagwati, J (2002), 'Introduction: the unilateral freeing of trade versus reciprocity', in Bhagwati, J (ed.), *Going Alone: The Case for Relaxed Reciprocity in Freeing Trade*, Cambridge, MA: MIT Press.

Bhagwati, J (2008), *Termites in the Trading System*, New York: Oxford University Press.

Blustein, P (2001), *The Chastening: Inside the Crisis that Rocked the Global Financial System and Humbled the IMF*, Public Affairs, New York.

Booth, A (1998), *Initial Conditions and Miraculous Growth*, London: SOAS, University of London.

Booth, A (2011), 'China's economic relations with Indonesia: threats and opportunities', *Journal of Current Southeast Asian Affairs*, 2/2011, pp. 141–160.

BPS (Badan Pusat Statistik), *The National Labour Force Survey* (Sakernas), 2002, 2007, and 2012.

BPS (Badan Pusat Statistik) (various years), *Statistik Industri* [*Industrial Statistics*], various volumes and underlying plant-level data, 1990–2011 issues, Jakarta: Badan Pusat Statistik.

Buckley, PJ & Casson, M (1992), *The Future of the Multinational Enterprise*, 2nd edition. London: Macmillan.

Cai, F (2010), *Mill Dilemma, Lewis Turning Point, and Social Protection*, Institute of Population and Labour Economics, Chinese Academy of Social Sciences, March.

Cali, M & Sen, K (2011), 'Do effective state business relations matter for economic growth? Evidence from Indian states', *World Development*, 39(9), pp. 1542–1557.

Card, D & Krueger, A (1994), 'Minimum wages and employment: a case study of the fast food industry in New Jersey and Pennsylvania', *American Economic Review*, 84(4), pp. 772–793.

Case, A & Paxson, C (2006), 'Stature and status: height, ability, and labor market outcomes', *Journal of Political Economy*, 116(3), pp. 499–532.

Case, A, Paxson, C & Islam, M (2009), 'Making sense of the labor market height premium: evidence from the British Household Panel Survey', *Economics Letters*, 102, pp. 174–176.

Casson, M (1987), *The Firm and the Market: Studies on the Multinational and the Scope of the Firm*, Cambridge, MA: MIT Press.

Caves, RE (2007), *Multinational Enterprise and Economic Analysis*, 3rd edition, London: Cambridge University Press.

CGD (Commission for Growth and Development) (2008), *The Growth Report: Strategies for Sustained Growth and Inclusive Development*, Washington DC: World Bank.

Chandran, BPS & Sudarsan, PK (2012), 'India–ASEAN Free Trade Agreement: implications for fisheries', *Economic and Political Weekly*, 47(16), 21 April.

Chapman, BJ & Harding, JR (1985), 'Sex differences in earnings: an analysis of Malaysian wage data', *Journal of Development Studies*, 21(3), pp. 362–376.

Cole, DC & Slade, BF (1998). 'Why has Indonesia's financial crisis been so bad?', *Bulletin of Indonesian Economic Studies*, 34(2), pp. 61–66.

Collins, EF (2007), *Indonesia Betrayed: How Development Fails*, University of Hawaii Press.

Corden, WM (1984), 'Booming sector and Dutch disease economics: survey and consolidation', *Oxford Economic Papers*, 36(3), pp. 359–380.

Coxhead, I (2007), 'A new resource curse? Impacts of China's boom on comparative advantage and resource dependence in Southeast Asia', *World Development*, 35(7), pp. 1009–1119.

Coxhead, I & Jayasuriya, S (2010), 'The rise of China and India: adjustment pressures and challenges for resource-rich Asian developing countries', in Athukorala, P (ed.), *The Rise of Asia: Trade and Investment in Global Perspective*, London: Routledge.

Coxhead, I (2014), 'Did Indonesia's boom leave its poor behind? Adverse labor market trends in the post-crisis era', unpublished paper, University of Wisconsin-Madison.

Coxhead, I & Li, M (2008), 'Prospects for skills-based exports in resource-rich developing economies: Indonesia in comparative perspective', *Bulletin of Indonesian Economic Studies*, 44(2), pp. 199–228.

Cross, R, Plantinga, AJ & Stavins, RN (2011), 'The value of terroir: hedonic estimation of vineyard sale prices', *Journal of Wine Economics*, 6(1), pp. 1–14.

Currie, J (2009), 'Healthy, wealthy and wise: socioeconomic status, poor health in childhood, and human capital development', *Journal of Economic Literature*, 47(1), pp. 87–122.

Dapice, D (2008), *Choosing Success: The Lessons of East and Southeast Asia and Vietnam's Future*, Harvard.

Das, SB (2012), 'Asia's Regional Comprehensive Economic Partnership', *East Asia Forum*, 27 August.

Dawe, D (ed.) (2010), *The Rice Crisis: Markets, Policies and Food Security*. London & Washington DC: Food and Agriculture Organization of the United Nations (FAO) & Earthscan.

Dawe, D (2012), 'Confronting food price volatility', editorial introduction to a special section in *Global Food Security*, 1(2), p. 126.

Dawe, D & Timmer, CP (2012), 'Why stable food prices are a good thing: lessons from stabilizing rice prices in Asia', *Global Food Security*, 1(2), pp. 127–133.

Dean, J, Fang, KC & Wang, Z (2009), 'Measuring vertical specialization: the case of China', *USITC Working Paper*.

DeLong, JB (2003), 'India since independence: an analytical growth narrative', in Rodrik, D (ed.), *In Search of Prosperity: Analytical Narratives on Economic Growth*, Princeton: Princeton University Press.

Di Gropello, E (2013), 'Role of the education and training sector in addressing skill mismatch in Indonesia', in Jones, G & Suryadarma, D (eds) *Education in Indonesia*, Singapore: Institute for Southeast Asian Studies, pp. 236–266.

Di Gropello, E, Kruse, A & Tandon, P (2011), *Skills for the Labor Market in Indonesia: Trends in Demand, Gaps and Supply*, Washington DC: World Bank.

Djiwandono, JS (2004), 'Liquidity support to banks during Indonesia's financial crisis', *Bulletin of Indonesian Economic Studies*, 40(1), pp. 59–75.

Djiwandono, JS (2005), *Bank Indonesia and the Crisis: An Insider's View*, Singapore: Institute of Southeast Asian Studies.

Dorosh, P & Rashid, S (2013), 'Trade subsidies, export bans and price stabilization: lessons of Bangladesh–India rice trade in the 2000s', *Food Policy* 41(C), pp. 103–111.

Dow Jones International News (1998), 'U.S. economist Krugman pans Indonesia currency board plans', 24 March.

Duncan, R & McLeod, RH (2007), 'The state and market in democratic Indonesia', in McLeod, RH & MacIntyre, A, *Indonesia: Democracy and the Promise of Good Governance*, Singapore: Institute of Southeast Asian Studies.

Dunning, JH (1993), *Multinational Enterprises and the Global Economy*, Wokingham, UK: Addison-Wesley Publishing Co.

Eichengreen, B & Tong, H (2006), 'Fear of China', *Journal of Asian Economics*, 17(2), pp. 226–240.

Eichengreen, B, Park, D & Shin, K (2013), 'Growth slowdowns redux: new evidence on the middle-income trap', *NBER Working Paper* no. 18673.

Fajgelbaum, P, Grossman, GM & Helpman, E (2011), 'Income distribution, product quality and international trade', *Journal of Political Economy*, 119(4), pp. 721–765.

Fane, G & McLeod, RH (2002), 'Banking collapse and restructuring in Indonesia, 1997–2001', *Cato Journal*, 22(2), pp. 277–295.

Feridhanusetyawan, T, Aswicahyono, H & Perdana, AA (2001), 'The male–female wage differentials in Indonesia', *Economics Working Paper Series* 059, Jakarta: Centre for Strategic and International Studies.

Fields, G & Wan, H, Jr (1989), 'Wage-setting institutions and economic growth', *World Development*, 17(9), pp. 1471–1483.

Findlay, CF, Farrell, R, Chen, C & Wang, D (2004), 'East Asia', in Anderson, K (ed.), *The World's Wine Markets: Globalization at Work*, Cheltenham UK: Edward Elgar.

Flick, K (ed.) (2011), *ASEAN–China Free Trade Area: One-Year Review*, Singapore: Rajaratnam School of International Studies, Nanyang Technological University.

Francis, S (2011), 'A sectoral impact analysis of the ASEAN–India Free Trade Agreement', *Economic and Political Weekly*, 46(2), 8 January.

Frécaut, O (2004), 'Indonesia's banking crisis: a new perspective on $50 billion of losses', *Bulletin of Indonesian Economic Studies*, 40(1), pp. 37–57.

Friberg, R, Paterson, RW & Richardson, AD (2011), 'Why is there a home bias: a case study of wine', *Journal of Wine Economics*, 6(1), pp. 37–66.

Galbraith, JK (1985), *The Anatomy of Power*, London: Corgi.

Gandhi, A & Walton, W (2012), 'Where do India's billionaires get their wealth?', *Economic and Political Weekly*, 47(40), pp. 1–15.

Garnaut, R & Song, L (2006) *The Turning Point in Chinese Economic Development*: Canberra: Asia-Pacific Press.

Gerguad, O & Ginsburg, V (2008), 'Natural endowments, production technologies and the quality of wines in Bordeaux: does terroir matter?', *Economic Journal*, 118(529), pp. F142–57. Reprinted in *Journal of Wine Economics*, 5(1), pp. 3–21, 2010.

Gilbert, CL (2012), 'International agreements to manage food price volatility', *Global Food Security*, 1(2), pp. 134–142.

Gill, I & Kharas, H (2007), *An East Asian Renaissance: Ideas for Economic Growth*, Washington DC: World Bank.

Giuliana, E, Morrison, A & Rabellotti, R (eds) (2011), *Innovation and Technological Catch-up: The Changing Geography of Wine Production*, Cheltenham UK: Edward Elgar.

Gladstones, J (1992), *Viticulture and Environment*, Adelaide: Winetitles.

Glewwe, P, Jacoby, H & King, EM (2001), 'Early childhood nutrition and academic achievement longitudinal analysis', *Journal of Public Economics*, 81(3), pp. 345–368.

Goldberg, P, Khandelwal, A, Pavnik, N & Topalova, P (2010) 'Multi-product and product turnover in the developing world: evidence from India', *Review of Economics and Statistics*, 92(4), pp. 1042–1049.

Gouel, C (2013), 'Rules versus discretion in food storage policies', *American Journal of Agricultural Economics*, 95(4), pp. 1029–1044.

Government of the Philippines with the World Bank and the Asian Development Bank (2003), *Philippines: Improving Government Performance: Discipline, Efficiency and Equity in Managing Public Resources, A Public Expenditure, Procurement and Financial Management Review*, Manila: Asian Development Bank.

Greenaway, D & Kneller, R (2007), 'Firm heterogeneity, exporting and foreign direct investment', *Economic Journal*, 117(517), pp. F134–F161.

Griliches, Z (1969), 'Capital-skill complementarity', *Review of Economics and Statistics*, 51(4), pp. 465–68.

Grindle, MS (2002), 'Good enough governance: poverty reduction and reform in developing countries', *Governance: An International Journal of Policy, Administration and Institutions*, 17(4), pp. 525–548.

Guerin, B (2002), 'Sony pullout plan rocks Indonesia', *Asia Times*, 7 December. Available at http://www.atimes.com/atimes/Southeast_Asia/DL07Ae01.html.

Haddad, M (2007), 'Trade integration in East Asia: the role of China and production networks', *World Bank Policy Working Paper* no. 4160, March.

Hadiz, V. (1997), *Workers and the State in New Order Indonesia*, London: Routledge.

Haltmaier, JT, Ahmed, S, Coulibaly, B, Knippenberg, R, Leduc, S, Marazzi, M & Wilson, BA (2007), 'The role of China in Asia: engine, conduit or steamroller?', *International Finance Discussion Paper* no. 904, September, Board of Governors of the Federal Reserve System.

Hamilton-Hart, N (2007), 'Government and private business: rents, representation and collective action', in McLeod, RH & MacIntyre, A, *Indonesia: Democracy and the Promise of Good Governance*, Singapore: Institute of Southeast Asian Studies.

Hanke, SH (1998), 'How to establish monetary stability in Asia', *Cato Journal*, 17(3), pp. 295–301.

Hanke, SH (2002), 'On dollarization and currency boards: error and deception', *Journal of Policy Reform*, 5(4), pp. 203–222.

Hanke, SH & Schuler, K (1994), *Currency Boards for Developing Countries: a Handbook*, San Francisco, International Center for Economic Growth.

Hanson, G (2010), 'Why isn't Mexico rich?' *NBER Working Paper* no.16470.

Hanson, G (2012), 'The rise of middle kingdoms: emerging economies in global trade', *Journal of Economic Perspectives*, 26(2), pp. 41–64.

Harrison, A, Martin, LA & Nataraj, S (2012), 'Learning versus stealing: how important are market-share reallocations to India's productivity growth', *World Bank Economic Review*, pp. 2012N228.

Hausmann, R, Pritchett, L & Rodrik, D (2005), 'Growth accelerations', *Journal of Economic Growth*, 10, pp. 303–329.

Hayami, Y & Ruttan, VW (1985), *Agricultural Development: An International Perspective*, Baltimore MD: Johns Hopkins University Press.

Heston, A, Summers, R & Aten, B (2012), *Penn World Tables Version 7.1*, Philadelphia: Center for International Comparisons of Production, Income and Prices at the University of Pennsylvania, July 2012.

Hill H, Yean, TS & Zin, R (2012), *Malaysia's Development Challenge: Graduating From the Middle*, London: Routledge.

Hill, H (1979), 'Choice of techniques in the Indonesian weaving industry', PhD thesis, Department of Economics, Research School of Pacific Studies, Australian National University.

Hill, H (1983), 'Choice of techniques in the Indonesian weaving industry', *Economic Development and Cultural Change*, 31(2), 337–353.

Hill, H (1994), 'Australia's Asia–Pacific connections', *Economics Division Working Paper* no. EA 94/2, Canberra: Research School of Pacific and Asian Studies, Australian National University.

Hill, H (1996), *The Indonesian Economy since 1966: Asia's Emerging Giant*, Cambridge: Cambridge University Press.

Hill, H (2000), *The Indonesian Economy*, 2nd edition, Cambridge: Cambridge University Press.

Hill, H & Menon, J (2008), 'Back to basics on Asian trade', *Far Eastern Economic Review*, 171(5), pp. 44–47.

Hill, H & Menon, J (2012), 'ASEAN economic integration: driven by markets, bureaucrats, or both?', in Kreinin, ME & Plummer, MG (eds), *The Oxford Handbook of International Commercial Policy*, Oxford: Oxford University Press, pp. 357–386.

Hill, H & Saldanha, JM (eds) (2001), *East Timor: Development Challenges for the World's New Nation*, Institute of Southeast Asian Studies, Singapore; Palgrave/MacMillan, London & New York; and Asia–Pacific Press, Canberra.

Hoddinott, J, Maluccio, J, Behrman, JR, Flores, R & Martorell, R (2008), 'Effect of a nutrition intervention during early childhood on economic productivity in Guatemalan adults', *The Lancet*, 371(9610), pp. 411–416.

Hofman, B, Gudwin, E & Thee, KW (2010), 'Managing the Indonesian economy: good policies, bad institutions', mimeo.

Holst, DR & Weiss, J (2004), 'ASEAN and China: export rivals or partners in regional growth?', *World Economy*, 27(8), pp. 1255–1274.

Holzmann, R & Vodopivec, M (2013), *Reforming Severance Pay: An International Perspective*, Washington DC: World Bank.

Houthakker, H (1987), 'Futures trading', in Eatwell, J, Milgate, M & Newman, P (eds), *The New Palgrave: A Dictionary of Economics*, vol. 2, London: Macmillan, pp. 447–449.

Hufbauer, G & Schott, JJ (2012), 'Will the World Trade Organization enjoy a bright future?', Policy Brief No. PB12–11, Washington DC: Peterson Institute for International Economics. Available at http://www.piie.com/publications/pb/pb12-11.pdf.

Hwan, SY (2011), 'Labour relations in Korean companies in Indonesia: focusing on the early period', *Kyoto Review of Southeast Asia*, 11. Available at http://kyotoreview.org/issue-11/labour-relations-in-korean-companies-in-indonesia-focusing-on-the-early-period/.

Ianchovichina, E, Suthiwart-Narueput, S & Zhao, M (2004), 'Regional impact of China's accession to the WTO', in Krumm, K & Kharas, H (eds), *East Asia Integrates: A Trade Policy Agenda for Shared Growth*, Washington DC: World Bank.

ILO (International Labour Organization) (2011), *Decent Work Country Profile: Indonesia*, Geneva: ILO.

ILO (International Labour Organization) (2013a), *Global Employment Trends 2013: Recovering from a Second Dip*, Geneva: ILO.

ILO (International Labour Organization) (2013b), *Measuring Informality: A Statistical Manual*, Geneva: ILO.

IMF (International Monetary Fund) (2013c), *Energy Subsidy Reform: Lessons and Implications*, Washington DC: IMF. Available at http://www.imf.org/external/np/pp/eng/2013/012813.pdf.

IMF (International Monetary Fund) (2014), *World Economic Outlook April 2014: Recovery Strengthens, Remains Uneven*, Washington DC: IMF. Available at http://www.imf.org/external/Pubs/ft/weo/2014/01/.

Irwin, S, Sanders, DR & Merrin, RP (2009), 'Devil or angel? The role of speculation in the recent commodity price boom (and bust)', *Journal of Agricultural and Applied Economics*, 41(2), pp. 377–391.

Ismail, R & Zin, RHM (2003), 'Earnings differentials determinants between skills in the Malaysian manufacturing sector', *Asian Economic Journal*, 17(4), pp. 325–340.

Japanese Ministry of Economy, Trade and Investment (2001), *Dai 29 Kai Wagakuni Kigyou no Gaikai Jigyou Katsudou* [*The 29th Survey of Overseas Business Activities of Japanese Companies*] (1998 data; in Japanese), Tokyo.

Jensen, RT & Miller, NH (2011), 'Do consumer price subsidies really improve nutrition?', *Review of Economics and Statistics*, 93(4), pp. 1205–1223.

Jerzmanowski, M (2006), 'Empirics of hills, plateaus, mountains and plains: a Markov-switching approach to growth', *Journal of Development Economics*, 81, pp. 357–385.

Jha, S & McCawley, P (2011), 'South–South economic linkages: an overview', *ADB Economics Working Paper Series* no. 270, August.

Johnson, C (1998), 'Survey of recent developments', *Bulletin of Indonesian Economic Studies*, 34(2), pp. 3–60.

Jones, B & Olken, B (2008), 'The anatomy of start-stop growth', *Review of Economics and Statistics*, 90(3), pp. 582–587.

Jones, G & Suryadarma, D (eds) (2013), *Education in Indonesia*, Singapore: Institute for Southeast Asian Studies.

Jones, RW & Kierzkowski, H (2004) 'Globalization and the consequences of international fragmentation', in Dornbusch, R, Calvo, G & Obstfeldt, M (eds), *Money, Factor Mobility and Trade: Essays in in Honor of Robert A. Mundell*, Cambridge, MA: MIT Press, pp. 365–381.

Kaplinsky, R & Messner,D (2008) 'Introduction: the Impact of Asian drivers on the developing world', *World Development*, 36(2), pp. 197–209.

Kar, D & Freitas, S (2012), *Illicit Financial Flows from China and the Role of Trade Misinvoicing*, Washington DC: Global Financial Integrity, Center for International Policy, October.

Kar, S, Pritchett, L, Raihan, S & Sen, K (2013a), *The Dynamics of Economic Growth: A Visual Handbook of Growth Rates, Regimes, Transitions and Volatility*, Effective States and Inclusive Development (ESID) Research Centre: University of Manchester. Available at http://www.effective-states.org/.

Kar, S, Pritchett, L, Raihan, S & Sen, K (2013b) 'Looking for a break: identifying transitions in growth regimes', *Journal of Macroeconomics*, 38, pp. 151–166.

Kathuria, V, Raj, RSN & Sen, K (2010), 'Organised versus unorganised manufacturing performance growth in the post-reform period', *Economic and Political Weekly*, 45(24), pp. 55–64.

Kaushal, N & Muchomba, F (2013), 'How consumer price subsidies affect nutrition', *NBER Working Paper* no. 19404, Cambridge MA, September.

Kawai, M & Wignaraja, G (2013), 'Addressing the challenges of Asian FTAs', *East Asia Forum*, 10 June.

Kerekes, M (2012), 'Growth miracles and failures in a Markov switching classification model of growth', *Journal of Development Economics*, 98(2), pp. 167–177.

Kessler, M & Borst, N (2013), 'Did China really lose $3.75 trillion in illicit financial flows?', *China Economic Watch*, 10 January, Washington DC: Peterson Institute for International Economics. Available at http://www.piie.com/blogs/china, accessed 12 June 2013.

Ketels, C, Cung, ND, Anh, NT & Hanh, DH (2010), *Vietnam Competitiveness Report, 2010*, Lee Kuan Yew School of Public Policy.

Kharas, H (2010), 'The emerging middle class in developing countries', *Working Paper* no. 285, OECD Development Centre, Paris, January.

King, MR (2001), 'Who triggered the Asian financial crisis?', *Review of International Political Economy*, 8(3), pp. 438–466.

Kohli, A (2012), *Poverty amid Plenty in the New India*, Cambridge: Cambridge University Press.

Koopman, R, Wang, Z & Wei, S-J (2012), 'How much of Chinese value-added is really made in China? Value-added when processing trade is pervasive', *Review of International Economics*, 19(64), pp. 609–625.

Krueger, AO (1977), *Growth, Distortions and Patterns of Trade Among Many Countries*, Princeton, NJ: International Finance Section.

Kubny, J & Voss, H (2010), *China's FDI in ASEAN: Trends and Impact on Host Countries*, Bonn: German Development Institute, and Leeds University Business School.

Lakshmanan, IAR (1998), 'For Indonesia, a big gamble: stability of nation at stake in plan to fix exchange rate of rupiah to another currency', *Boston Globe*, 12 February.

Lamy, P (2013), 'Putting geopolitics back at the trade table', speech at the IISS-Oberoi Discussion Forum, New Delhi, 29 January 2013. Available at http://www.wto.org/english/news_e/sppl_e/sppl264_e.htm.

Larsson, T (2013), 'The strong and the weak: ups and downs of state capacity in Southeast Asia', *Asian Politics and Policy*, 5(3), pp. 337–358.

Leamer, EE (1987), 'Paths of development in the three-factor, *n*-good general equilibrium model', *Journal of Political Economy*, 95(5), pp. 961–999.

Lee, J (2013), 'China's economic influence in Thailand: perception or reality?', *ISEAS Perspective* no. 44, 11 July.

Lee, J-W & Wie, D (2013), 'Technological change, skill demand, and wage inequality in Indonesia', *ADB Economics Working Paper Series* no. 340, Manila, March.

Lee, K-H & Nagaraj, S (1995), 'Sex differences in earnings: an analysis of Malaysian wage data', *Journal of Development Studies*, 31(3), pp. 467–480.

Lewin, B (2010), *Wine, Myths and Reality*, San Francisco: Wine Appreciation Guild.

Lim, D (1977), 'Do foreign companies pay higher wages than their local counterparts in Malaysian manufacturing?', *Journal of Development Economics*, 4(1), pp. 55–66.

Lin, JY (2013), 'Long live China's boom', Columbia University, New York, 16 August. Available at http://www8.gsb.columbia.edu/chazen/globalinsights/node/207/Long+Live+China%27s+Boom.

Lindblad, JT (1997), 'Survey of recent developments', *Bulletin of Indonesian Economic Studies*, 33(3), pp. 3–33.

Lipsey, RE & Sjöholm, F (2004a), 'Foreign direct investment, education, and wages in Indonesian manufacturing', *Journal of Development Economics*, 73(1), pp. 415–422.

Lipsey, RE & Sjöholm, F (2004b), 'FDI and wage spillovers in Indonesian manufacturing', *Review of World Economics*, 40(2), pp. 321–332.

Lipsey, RE & Sjöholm, F (2005), 'Host country impacts of inward FDI: why such different answers?', in Moran, TH, Graham, EM & Blomstrom, M (eds), *Does Foreign Direct Investment Promote Development?* Washington DC: Institute for International Economics, pp. 23–43.

Lipsey, RE & Sjöholm, F (2006), 'Foreign multinationals and wages in Indonesia', in Ramstetter, ED & Sjöholm, F (eds), *Multinationals in Indonesia and Thailand: Wages, Productivity and Exports*, Hampshire, UK: Palgrave-Macmillan, pp. 35–53.

Lipsey, RE & Sjoholm, F (2011), 'Foreign direct investment and growth in East Asia: lessons for Indonesia', *Bulletin of Indonesian Economic Studies*, 47(1), pp. 35–63.

Macan-Markar, M (2010), 'Asia: China–ASEAN Free Trade Area sparks cautious optimism', *Inter Press Service News Agency*, 19 January. Available at http://ipsnews.net.

MacLaren, L, Putra, AS & Rahman, EA (2011), 'How civil society organizations work politically to promote pro-poor policies in decentralized Indonesian cities', *Asia Foundation Occasional Paper* no. 6, June.

Malaysian Department of Statistics (2002), *Census of Manufacturing Industries 2001* [2000 data], Putrajaya.

Malaysian Department of Statistics (2011), *Annual National Accounts, Gross Domestic Product (GDP) 2000–2010*, Putrajaya.

Malaysian Department of Statistics (various years), *Annual Survey of Manufacturing Industries*, 2002–2005 issues [2001–2004 data], Kuala Lumpur.

Manning, C (1999), 'Labour markets in the ASEAN-4 and the NIEs', *Asia-Pacific Economic Journal*, 13(1), pp. 50–68.

Manning, C (2006), 'Potential winners and losers from labour regulation in the formal sector: the case of Indonesia', in Brassard, C & Acharya, S (eds), *Labour Market Regulation and Deregulation in Asia: Experiences in Recent Decades*, New Delhi: Academic Foundation, pp. 11–37.

Manning, C (2013), 'A robust wage campaign in 2013', *Jakarta Post*, 4 June.

Manning, C & Aswicahyono, H (2012), *Trade and Employment in Services: The Case of Indonesia*, Jakarta and Geneva: Trade and Employment Programme, ILO.

Markusen, JR (2002), *Multinational Firms and the Theory of International Trade.* Cambridge, MA: MIT Press.

Markusen, JR (2013), 'Putting per-capita income back into trade theory', *Journal of International Economics*, 90(2), pp. 255–265.

Martin, W & Anderson, K (2012), 'Export restrictions and price insulation during commodity price booms', *American Journal of Agricultural Economics*, 94(2), pp. 422–427.

McGovern, P (2003), *Ancient Wine: The Search for the Origins of Viticulture*, Princeton NJ: Princeton University Press.

McGovern, P (2009), *Uncorking the Past: The Quest for Wine, Beer, and Other Alcoholic Beverages*, Berkeley CA: University of California Press.

McLeod, RH (1993), 'Analysis and management of Indonesian money supply growth', *Bulletin of Indonesian Economic Studies*, 29(2), pp. 97–128.

McLeod, RH (1998a), 'Indonesia', in McLeod, RH & Garnaut, R (eds), *East Asia in Crisis: From Being a Miracle to Needing One?* London and New York: Routledge, pp. 31–48.

McLeod, RH (1998b), 'From crisis to cataclysm? The mismanagement of Indonesia's economic ailments', *World Economy* 21(7), pp. 913–930.

McLeod, RH (2000), 'Soeharto's Indonesia: a better class of corruption', *Agenda*, 7(2), pp. 99–112.

Medalla, E (2011), 'Taking stock of the ROOs in the ASEAN+1 FTAs: toward deepening East Asian integration', *Discussion Paper Series* no. 2011-36, Manila: Philippine Institute of Development Studies.

Mehta, PB & Walton, M (2014), 'India's political settlement and development path', mimeo.

Meier, GM (2005), *Biography of a Subject: An Evolution of Development Economics*, New York: Oxford University Press.

Menon, J (2012), 'Supporting the growth or spread of international production networks in Asia: how can trade policy help?', *ADB Working Papers in Regional Economic Integration* no. 112, Manila: Asian Development Bank.

Menon, J (2013a), 'The challenge facing Asia's Regional Comprehensive Economic Partnership', *East Asia Forum*, 23 June.

Menon, J (2013b), 'Preferential and non-preferential approaches to trade liberalisation in East Asia: what differences do utilisation rates and reciprocity make?', *ADB Working Paper Series on Regional Economic Integration* no. 109, Manila: Asian Development Bank.

Menon, J (2014a), 'A way out of preferential deals', presentation to the OECD Global Forum on Trade 2014, 11–12 February, OECD, Paris. Available at http://www.oecd.org/tad/events/OECD-gft-2014-way-out-preferential-deals-menon-presentation.pdf.

Menon, J (2014b), 'TPPing Over?', *VoxEU*, 1 July. Available at http://www.voxeu.org/article/tipping-over-tpp.

Menon, J (2014c), 'From spaghetti bowl to jigsaw puzzle? Fixing the mess in regional and global trade', *Asia and the Pacific Policy Studies*, forthcoming.

Menon, J & Melendez, AC (2011), 'Trade and investment in the Greater Mekong Subregion: remaining challenges and the unfinished policy agenda', *ADB Working Paper Series on Regional Economic Integration* no. 78, Manila: Asian Development Bank.

Milanovic, B (2006), 'Inequality and determinants of earnings in Malaysia', *Asian Economic Journal*, 20(2), pp. 191–216.

Mincer, J (1974), *Schooling, Experience, and Earnings*, New York: NBER.

Mody, A, Nath, A & Walton, M (2011), 'Sources of corporate profits in India: business dynamism or advantages of entrenchment?', in Bery, S, Bosworth, B & Panagariya, A (eds), *The India Policy Forum 2010–2011*, Washington DC: Brookings Institute.

Movshuk, O & Matsuoka-Movshuk, A (2006), 'Multinationals and wages in Thai manufacturing', in Ramstetter, ED & Sjöholm, F (eds), *Multinationals in Indonesia and Thailand: Wages, Productivity and Exports*. Hampshire, UK: Palgrave-Macmillan, pp. 54–81.

Mustopadidjaja, AR et al. (2012), *Bappenas dalam Sejarah Perencanaan Pembangunan Indonesia 1945–2025* [Bappenas in the History of Development Planning in Indonesia 1945–2025], Jakarta: LP3ES.

Myint, H (1972), *Southeast Asia's Economy in The 1970s*, Middlesex, UK: Penguin.

Myrdal, G (1968), *Asian Drama: An Inquiry into the Poverty of Nations*, New York: Pantheon.

Nagaraj, R (2013), 'India's dream run, 2003-2008: understanding the boom and its aftermath', *Economic and Political Weekly*, 48(20), pp. 10–18.

Nasution, A (1998), 'The meltdown of the Indonesian economy in 1997–1998: causes and responses', *Seoul Journal of Economics*, 11(4), pp. 447–482.

National Bureau of Statistics of China (2010), *China Statistical Yearbook 2010*, no. 29, Beijing: China Statistics Press.

Nayak, A (2011), 'Does variety fit the quality bill? Factor-endowments driven differences in trade, export margins, prices and production techniques', mimeo, Purdue University, West Lafayette IN, May. Available at www.auburn.edu\~azn0018.

Nehru, V (2013), 'Manufacturing in India and Indonesia: performance and policies', *Bulletin of Indonesian Economic Studies*, 49(1), pp. 35–60.

Nellor, D (2013) 'Overview', *Memo for AIPEG*, November 2013.

Newhouse, D & Suryadarma, D (2011), 'The value of vocational education: high school type and labor market outcomes in Indonesia', *Bulletin of Indonesian Economic Studies*, 25(2), pp. 296–322.

Nguyen, KT, (2014), 'Economic reforms, manufacturing employment and wages in Vietnam', unpublished dissertation, Australian National University, Canberra.

Nitisastro, W (2010), *Pengalaman Pembangunan Indonesia: Kumpulan Tulisan dan Uraian Widjojo Nitisastro* [The Experience of Development in Indonesia: A Collection of the Writings of Widjojo Nitisastro], Jakarta: Penerbit Buku Kompas [Kompas Book Publishing].

North, DN, Wallis, JJ & Weingast, BR (2009), *Violence and Social Orders*, Cambridge: Cambridge University Press.

Nurridzki, N & Rahardja, S (2009), *The Remaining Barriers for the Liberalization of Trade in Services in Indonesia* (Air Transport, Logistics and Health Care Services), Report prepared for the World Bank, Jakarta.

OECD & WTO (Organization for Economic Cooperation and Development & World Trade Organization) (2013), *Measuring Trade in Value Added: An OECD-WTO Joint Initiative*. Available at http://www.oecd.org/sti/ind/measuringtradeinvalue-addedanoecd-wtojointinitiative.htm.

Olmstead, AL & Rhode, PW (2007), 'Biological globalization: the other grain invasion', in Hatton, TJ, O'Rourke, KH & Taylor, AM (eds), *The New Comparative Economic History: Essays in Honor of Jeffrey G. Williamson*, Cambridge MA: MIT Press.

Ozawa, T (2009), *The Rise of Asia: The 'Flying-Geese' Theory of Tandem Growth and Regional Agglomeration*, London: Edward Elgar.

Pal, P & Dasgupta, M (2008), 'Does a free trade agreement with ASEAN make sense?', *Economic and Political Weekly*, 15 November, pp. 8–12.

Pal, P & Dasgupta, M (2009), 'The ASEAN–India Free Trade Agreement: an assessment', *Economic and Political Weekly*, 44(38), 19 September.

Pangestu, M (2013) 'The multilateral trading system and WTO: challenges and priorities', in Hoekman, B & Mavroidis, PC (eds), *Race for the WTO Director-General Job: Seven Candidates Speak*, London: Centre for Economic Policy Research, pp. 63–76.

Pangestu, M & Nellor, D (2014) 'Grouping must shape a new world trade regime', *East Asia Forum Quarterly*, 6(2), p. 9.

Papua New Guinea Government (2011). *National Informal Economic Policy (2011–2015)*, Department for Community Development, Boroko, National Capital District.

Park, D-H & Shin, K (2010), 'Can trade with the People's Republic of China be an engine of growth for developing Asia?', *Asian Development Review*, 27(1), pp. 160–81.

Perdana, AA & Maxwell, J (2005), 'Poverty targeting in Indonesia', in Weiss, J (ed.), *Poverty Targeting in Asia*, Cheltenham, UK: Edward Elgar for ADB Institute.

Peterson, W (1979), 'International farm prices and the social cost of cheap food', *American Journal of Agricultural Economics*, 61(1), pp. 12–21.

Pham, TTT (2013), 'Does exporting spur firm productivity? Evidence from Vietnam', unpublished paper.

Pham, TTT & Riedel, J (2012), 'On the conduct of monetary policy in Vietnam', *Asia Pacific Economic Literature*, 26(1), pp. 35–45.

Phan, DN (2009), *A Report on Vietnam's Labor Market*, Central Institute for Economic Management (Hanoi) and Danida.

Phan, D & Coxhead, I (2013), 'Long-run costs of piecemeal reform: wage inequality and returns to education in Vietnam', *Journal of Comparative Economics*, published online April 2013.

Phan, D & Coxhead, I (2014), 'Human capital development in Southeast Asia', in Coxhead, I (ed.), *Routledge Handbook of Southeast Asian Economics*, in press.

Pirmana, V (2006), 'Earnings differential between male–female in Indonesia: evidence from Sakernas data', *Working Paper in Economics and Development Studies* 2006-08, Bandung: Padjadjaran University.

Pritchett, L (2000), 'Understanding patterns of economic growth: searching for hills among plateaus, mountains and plains', *World Bank Economic Review*, 14(2), pp. 221–250.

Pritchett, L (2011), 'How good are good transitions for growth and poverty? Indonesia since Suharto, for instance?', in Manning, C & Sumarto, S (eds), *Employment, Living Standards and Poverty in Contemporary Indonesia*, Singapore: Institute of Southeast Asian Studies, pp. 23–44.

Pritchett, L & Werker, E (2013), 'Developing the guts of GUT (Grand Unified Theory): elite commitment and inclusive growth', *ESID Working Paper* no. 16/12. Available at www.effective-states.org.

Pritchett, L, Sen, K, Kar, S & Raihan, S (2013), 'Trillions gained and lost: estimating the magnitude of growth episodes', *ESID Working Paper* no. 26. Available at www.effective-states.org.

Psacharopoulos, P & Patrinos, HA (2004), 'Returns to investment in education: a further update', *Education Economics* 12(2), pp. 111–134.

Purnastuti, L, Miller, P & Salim, R (2011), 'Economic returns to schooling in a less developed country: evidence for Indonesia', *Proceedings: International Conference on Applied Economics 2011*.

Purnastuti, L, Miller, PW & Salim, R (2013), 'Declining rates of return to education, evidence for Indonesia', *Bulletin of Indonesian Economic Studies*, 49(2), pp. 213–236.

Rajan, RS (2008) 'Will the big tiger leave any crumbs for the little dragons? China vs. Southeast Asia', in Rajan, RS & Rongala, S (eds), *Asia in the Global Economy: Finance, Trade and Investment*, Singapore: World Scientific.

Ramstetter, ED (1998), 'Measuring the size of foreign multinationals in the Asia-Pacific region and local firms in Asian manufacturing over time', in Thompson, G (ed.), *Economic Dynamism in the Asia Pacific: The Growth of Integration and Competitiveness*, London: Routledge, pp. 185–212.

Ramstetter, ED (2004), 'Labor productivity, wages, nationality, and foreign ownership shares in Thai manufacturing, 1996–2000', *Journal of Asian Economics*, 14(6), 861–884.

Ramstetter, ED (2012a), 'Do multinationals pay high wages in Malaysian manufacturing?', *Working Paper* 2012-05, Kitakyushu: International Centre for the Study of East Asian Development.

Ramstetter, ED (2012b), 'Foreign multinationals in East Asia's large developing economies', *Working Paper* 2012-06, Kitakyushu: International Centre for the Study of East Asian Development.

Ramstetter, ED (2013), 'Wage differentials between foreign multinationals and local plants and worker quality in Malaysian manufacturing', *Working Paper* 2013-22, Kitakyushu: International Centre for the Study of East Asian Development.

Ramstetter, ED (2014), 'Exporting, education, and wage differentials between foreign multinationals and local plants in Indonesian and Malaysian manufacturing', *Working Paper* 2014-03, Kitakyushu: International Centre for the Study of East Asian Development.

Ramstetter, ED & Narjoko, D (2012), 'Ownership and energy efficiency in Indonesia's manufacturing plants', *Working Paper* 2012-14, Kitakyushu: International Centre for the Study of East Asian Development.

Ramstetter, ED & Narjoko, D (2013), 'Wage differentials between foreign multinationals and local plants and worker education in Indonesian manufacturing', *Working Paper* 2013-22, Kitakyushu: International Centre for the Study of East Asian Development.

Ramstetter, ED & Phan, MN (2007), 'Employee compensation, ownership, and producer concentration in Vietnam's manufacturing industries', *Working Paper* 2012-07, Kitakyushu: International Centre for the Study of East Asian Development.

Ravenhill, J (2006), 'Is China an economic threat to Southeast Asia?', *Asian Survey*, 46(5), pp. 653–674.

Ravenhill, J (2010), 'The "new East Asian regionalism": a political domino effect', *Review of International Political Economy*, 17(2), pp. 178–208.

Riedel, J (1988), 'Economic development in East Asia: doing what comes naturally?', in Hughes, H (ed.), *Achieving Industrialization in East Asia*, Cambridge University Press, pp. 1–38.

Riedel, J (1991), 'Strategy wars: the state of debate on trade and industrialization in developing countries', in Koekkoek, KA & Mennes, LBM (eds), *Inter-national Trade and Global Development: Essays in Honor of Jagdish Bhagwati*, London: Routledge, pp. 130–150.

Riedel, J (1993), 'Vietnam: on the trail of the tigers', *World Economy*, 16(4), 401–422.

Riedel, J (2010), The global economic crisis and its long-term implications for Vietnam', *UNDP Working Paper*, September.

Riedel, J & Pham, TTT (2010), 'An assessment of globalization in Vietnam under the BTA and WTO', *STAR-Vietnam Report*.

Roberts, MJ & Schlenker, W (2013), 'Identifying supply and demand elasticities of agricultural commodities', *American Economic Review*, 103(6), pp. 2265–2295.

Robison, R (1986), *Indonesia: The Rise of Capital*, London: Allen and Unwin.

Robison, R & Hadiz, V (2004), *Reorganising Power in Indonesia: The Politics of Oligarchy in an Age of Markets*, London: Routledge Curzon.

Rodrik, D (2005), 'Growth strategies', in Aghion, P & Durlauf, S (eds), *Handbook of Economic Growth*, Amsterdam: Elsevier.

Rodrik, D (2013), 'The past, present and future of economic growth', Global Citizen Foundation, *Working Paper* no. 1. Available at http://www.gcf.ch/?page_id=5758, accessed 29 November 2013.

Rosser, A (2002), *The Politics of Economic Liberalisation in Indonesia*, Richmond: Curzon.

Rugman, AM (1980), 'Internalization as a general theory of foreign direct investment: a re-appraisal of the literature,' *Weltwirtschaftliches Archiv*, 116(2), pp. 365–379.

Rugman, AM (1985), 'Internalization is still a general theory of foreign direct investment', *Weltwirtschaftliches Archiv*, 121(3), pp. 570–575.

Sadli, M (1998), 'The Indonesian crisis', *ASEAN Economic Bulletin*, 15(3) pp. 272–280.

Salidjanova, N (2011), 'Going out: an overview of China's outward foreign direct investment', *USCC Staff Research Report*, Washington DC: U.S.–China Economic and Security Review Commission.

Sanger, DE (1999), 'Longtime IMF director resigns in midterm', *New York Times*, 10 November.

Schafgans, MMA (2000), 'Gender wage differences in Malaysia', *Journal of Development Economics*, 63(2), pp. 351–378.

Schiavo-Campo, S & Sundaram, P (2000), *To Serve and to Preserve: Improving Public Administration in a Competitive World*, Manila: Asian Development Bank.

Schuler, K (1998), '*Sistem dewan mata uang*', *Media Indonesia*, 7, 8, 10, 11, 12 and 13 February [translated from 'Stabilizing the Indonesian rupiah through a currency board' by Armida Alisjahbana]. Both versions available at https://web.archive.org/web/20010516230912/http://www.dollarization.org/.

Schuler-Zhou, Y & Schuller, M (2009), 'The internationalization of Chinese companies', *China Management Studies*, 3(1), pp. 25–42.

Scissors, D (2011), 'China's investment overseas in 2010', *Heritage Foundation Web Memo*, no. 3133, 3 February.

Scissors, D (2012), *China Global Investment Tracker, 2012*, Washington: Heritage Foundation. Available at www.heritage.org/research/reports/2012/01/china, accessed 10 October 2012.

SEADI (2012) *Improving the Application of the Decent Standard of Living (KHL) for Minimum Wage Adjustments*, Policy Brief 4, Bappenas, Jakarta, April.

SEADI (2013) 'Productivity, wages and employment: findings of a field survey in Bandung', Labour Productivity Policy Brief 4, Bappenas, Jakarta, January.

Sen, K (2007), 'Why did the elephant start to trot? India's growth acceleration re-examined', *Economic and Political Weekly*, 43, pp. 37–49.

Sen, K (2013), 'The political dynamics of economic growth', *World Development*, 47, pp. 71–86.

Sen, K, Kar, S & Sahoo, J (2014), 'Boom and bust? A political economy reading of India's growth experience, 1993–2013', mimeo.

Shah Commission (2012a), 'Interim report on illegal mining of iron ore and manganese', Interim Report. Available at http://mines.nic.in.

Shah Commission (2012b), 'Final report on illegal mining of iron ore and manganese, Interim Report. Available at http://mines.nic.in.

Silventoinen, K (2003), 'Determinants of variation in adult body height', *Journal of Biosocial Sciences*, 35(2), pp. 263-285.

Singal, V (1999), 'Floating currencies, capital controls, or currency boards: what's the best remedy for the currency crises?', *Journal of Applied Corporate Finance*, 11(4), pp. 49-56.

Sjöholm, F (2003), 'Which Indonesian firms export? The importance of foreign networks', *Papers in Regional Science*, 82, pp. 333-350.

Sjöholm, F & Lipsey, RE (2006), 'Foreign firms and Indonesian manufacturing wages: an analysis with panel data', *Economic Development and Cultural Change*, 55(1), pp. 201-221.

Slater, D (2010), *Ordering Power: Contentious Politics and Authoritarian Leviathans in Southeast Asia*, Cambridge: Cambridge University Press.

Slayton, T. (2009), 'Rice crisis forensics: how Asian governments carelessly set the world rice market on fire', *Working Paper* no. 163, Center for Global Development, Washington DC.

Slayton, T & Timmer, CP (2008), 'Japan, China and Thailand can solve the rice crisis – but US leadership is needed', *CGD Notes*, Washington DC: Center for Global Development, May.

Sohn, K (2013), 'Monetary and nonmonetary returns to education in Indonesia', *Developing Economies*, 51(1), pp. 34-59.

Solomon, J & Linebaugh, K (1998), 'Indonesia entertains US economist's currency board plan', *Dow Jones International News*, 3 February.

Spence, M (2011), *The Next Convergence: The Future of Economic Growth in a Multi-speed World*, Crawley, West Australia: UWA Publishing.

Stigler, GJ & Becker, GS (1977), 'De gustibus non est disputandum', *American Economic Review*, 67(2), pp. 76-90.

Strauss, J, Witoelar, F, Sikoki, B & Wattie, AM (2009), 'The fourth wave of the Indonesia Family Life Survey: overview and field report, volume 1', *RAND Labor and Population Working Paper* WR-675/1-NIA/NICHD, Santa Monica, CA: RAND.

Streeten, P (1996), 'Governance', in Quibria, MG & Dowling, JM, *Current Issues in Economic Development: An Asian Perspective*, Hong Kong: Oxford University Press.

Suharti (2013), 'Trends in education in Indonesia', in Jones, G & Suryadarma, D (eds) *Education in Indonesia*, Singapore: Institute for Southeast Asian Studies, pp. 15-52.

Suryadarma, D & Jones, GW (2013), 'Meeting the education challenge', in Suryadarma, D & Jones, GW (eds), *Education in Indonesia*, Singapore: Institute of Southeast Asian Studies, pp. 1-14.

Tadesse, G, Algiera, B, Kalkuhl, M & von Braun, J (2013), 'Drivers and triggers of international food price spikes and volatility', *Food Policy*. Available at http://dx.doi.org/10.1016/j.foodpol.2013.08.014.

Takii, S & Ramstetter, ED (2005), 'Multinational presence and labour productivity differentials in Indonesian manufacturing 1975-2001', *Bulletin of Indonesian Economic Studies*, 41(2), pp. 221-242.

The Asian Wall Street Journal (1998), 'A case for a currency board', 11 February.

Thee, KW (2009), 'Neolib, neoliberal, apa itu?' [Neolib, neoliberal, what is it?], *Kompas*, 26 May 2009.

Thee, KW (2011), 'Indonesia: blessed by strong economic growth and the curse of resources', *East Asia Forum*, 11 January.

Timmer, CP (2009a), 'Management of rice reserve stocks in Asia: analytical issues and country experiences', paper presented to the experts' meeting on 'Institutions and Policies to Manage Global Market Risks and Price Spikes in Basic Food Commodities' by the FAO Trade and Markets Division, October 26–27, Food and Agriculture Organization of the United Nations (FAO), Rome.

Timmer, CP (2009b), 'Rice price formation in the short run and the long run: the role of market structure in explaining volatility', *Working Paper* 172, Washington DC: Center for Global Development, May.

Timmer, CP (2012), 'Behavioral dimensions of food security', *Proceedings of the National Academy of Sciences (PNAS)*, 109(31), pp. 12315–12320.

Tjandraningsih, I, Herawati, R & Suhadmadi (2010), *Praktek Kerja Kontrak dan Outsourcing Buruh di Sektor Industri Metal*, Bandung: Yayasan Akatiga 2010.

Tongzon, JL (2005), 'ASEAN–China Free Trade Area: a bane or boon for ASEAN countries', *World Economy*, 28(2), pp. 191–210.

Torchia, C (1998), 'U.S. economist has ear of Suharto', *USA Today*, 20 February.

Toyo Keizai (various years), *Kaigai Shinshutsu Kigyou Souran: Kaisha Betsu Hen* [*A Comprehensive Survey of Firms Overseas: Compiled by Company*], 1997 and 2007 issues, Tokyo: Toyo Keizai.

UNCTAD (United Nations Conference on Trade and Development) (2013), *World Investment Report 2012*, Geneva: United Nations Conference on Trade and Development.

van der Eng, P (2009), 'Capital formation and capital stock in Indonesia, 1950–2008', *Bulletin of Indonesian Economic Studies*, 45(3), pp. 345–371.

Venables, AJ (2004), 'Small, remote and poor', *World Trade Review*, 3(3), pp. 453–457.

Vézina, PL (2010), 'Race-to-the-bottom tariff cutting', *IHEID Working Paper* 12, Geneva: IHEID.

Warr, P, (2012). 'A nation caught in the middle-income trap', *East Asia Forum Quarterly*, 3(4), pp. 4–6.

Weerakoon, D (2008), 'India's role in SAARC: integration and the way ahead', paper presented to the ADB-ICREAR workshop on South Asian Integration, New Delhi, March.

Weiss, J (2005), 'Experiences with poverty targeting in Asia: an overview', in Weiss, J (ed.), *Poverty Targeting in Asia*, Cheltenham, UK: Edward Elgar for ADB Institute.

Weymar, FH (1968), *The Dynamics of the World Cocoa Market*. Cambridge, MA: Massachusetts Institute of Technology Press.

Wickizer, VD & Bennett, MK (1941), *The Rice Economy of Monsoon Asia*. Stanford, CA: Food Research Institute, Stanford University. Published in cooperation with the International Secretariat, Institute of Pacific Relations.

Wihardja, MM (2013) 'Indonesia living dangerously as it neglects economic reform', *East Asia Forum*, 2 October.

Williams, A (1995), *Flying Winemakers: The New World of Wine*, Adelaide: Winetitles.

Williams, JC & Wright, BD (1991), *Storage and Commodity Markets*. Cambridge: Cambridge University Press.

Wilson, T & Skinner, AS (1976), *The Market and the State: Essays in Honour of Adam Smith*, Oxford, UK: Clarendon Press.

Wittwer, G, Berger, N & Anderson, K (2003), 'A model of the world's wine markets', *Economic Modelling*, 20(3), pp. 487–506.

Wong, J & Chan, S (2003), 'China–ASEAN Free Trade Agreement', *Asian Survey*, 43(3), pp. 507–526.

Woo, WT (2009), 'Getting Malaysia out of the middle-income trap', unpublished paper, University of California, Davis, 13 August.

Working, H (1949), 'The theory of the price of storage', *American Economic Review*, 31(December), pp. 1254–1262.

World Bank (1993), *The East Asian Miracle: Economic Growth and Public Policy*, New York: Oxford University Press.

World Bank (1997), *World Development Report 1997: The State in a Changing World*. New York: Oxford University Press.

World Bank (2002), *World Development Report 2002: Building Institutions for Markets*, New York: Oxford University Press.

World Bank (2005), *Global Economic Prospects 2005: Trade, Regionalism, and Development*, Washington DC: World Bank.

World Bank (2006), *Revitalizing the Rural Economy: An Assessment of the Investment Climate Faced by Non-Farm Enterprises at the District Level*, Jakarta: World Bank.

World Bank (2007), *Doing Business 2007*.

World Bank (2010a), *East Asian and Pacific Economic Update 2010*.

World Bank (2010b), *Indonesia Jobs Report: Towards Better Jobs and Social Security for All*, Washington DC.

World Bank (2011a), 'Current challenges, future potential', *Indonesian Economic Quarterly*, Jakarta, June.

World Bank (2011b), *Revitalizing Public Training Centres in Indonesia: Challenges and the Way Forward*, Human Development Department, Washington DC, April.

World Bank (2013a), *East Asia and the Pacific Economic Update 2013*. Available at   http://data.worldbank.org/sites/default/files/east_asia_economic_ update_figures_and_tables.pdf.

World Bank (2013b), *Global Economic Prospects*, vol. 6, January 2013. Washington DC: World Bank.

World Bank (2013c), *World Development Report 2013: Jobs*, Washington DC.

World Bank (2014) 'Hard choices', *Indonesian Economic Quarterly*, Jakarta, July.

World Economic Forum (2013) *World Competitiveness Index, 2012–13*, Geneva.

WTO (World Trade Organization) (2011), *World Trade Report 2011*. Geneva: WTO.

WTO & IDE/JETRO (World Trade Organization and Institute of Developing Economies) (2011), *Trade Patterns and Global Value Chains in East Asia: From Trade in Goods to Trade in Tasks*, Geneva: WTO Secretariat.

Wu, HX (2014), 'Re-estimating Chinese growth: how fast has China's economy really grown?', *Special Briefing Paper*, China Center for Economics and Business, New York: The Conference Board Inc.

Yang, Y (2006), 'China's integration into the world economy: implications for developing countries', *Asian-Pacific Economic Literature*, 20(1), pp. 40–56.

Yusuf, AA (2013), 'The evolution of inequality in Indonesia, 1990-2012', *Working Papers in Economics and Development Studies* no. 2013114, Department of Economics, Padjadjaran University.

Index

www.ingramcontent.com/pod-product-compliance
Lightning Source LLC
Chambersburg PA
CBHW050224270326
41914CB00003BA/560